# A Shining City

## THE LEGACY OF RONALD REAGAN

# RONALD REAGAN

SIMON & SCHUSTER

SIMON & SCHUSTER
Rockefeller Center
1230 Avenue of the Americas
New York, NY 10020

*Simon & Schuster* and colophon are trademarks of Simon & Schuster Inc.

Designed by Jeanette Olender
Manufactured in the United States of America

1   3   5   7   9   10   8   6   4   2

Library of Congress Cataloging-in-Publication Data
Reagan, Ronald.
A shining city : the legacy of Ronald Reagan / Ronald Reagan; [D. Erik Felten, editor]
p.      cm.
1. Reagan, Ronald.   2. Presidents—United States—Biography.   I. Felten, D. Erik.   II. Title.
E877.R44   1998   973.927'092—DC21   97-36576   CIP
ISBN 0-684-84678-0

Photographs have been provided courtesy of the Ronald Reagan Presidential Library, White House staff photographers, and the Office of Ronald Reagan. Supplemental photographs have been provided by ABC Inc. (p. 37), Newsweek Inc. (p. 59), and Mike Guastella (pp. 199 and 250).

Excerpts from "Burnt Norton," "East Coker" and "The Dry Salvages" in *Four Quartets,* copyright 1943 by T. S. Eliot and renewed 1971 by Esme Valerie Eliot, reprinted by permission of Harcourt Brace & Company.

"Thank You, Ronald Reagan" by William J. Bennett is reprinted with permission from the September 1995 *Reader's Digest.* Copyright © 1995 by The Reader's Digest Association, Inc.

*All royalties from the sale of this book will benefit The Ronald Reagan Presidential Foundation, 40 Presidential Drive, Simi Valley, California 93065. (805) 522-8444.*

*The Ronald Reagan Presidential Library is located in Simi Valley, California. The Reagan Library complex is a place where scholars and the general public can immerse themselves in the documentary record and significant events of President Reagan's life and career.*

*The Reagan Library & Museum was built with funds raised privately by The Ronald Reagan Presidential Foundation. This foundation continues to support library programs through the Ronald Reagan Center for Public Affairs. These activities include scholarly and popular conferences, high-profile speakers, a rich menu of temporary museum exhibits spanning the whole range of American history, and the annual Ronald Reagan Lecture. Each year the Ronald Reagan Freedom Award is presented to a figure of international significance who has advanced President Reagan's vision of individual freedom and global understanding.*

# Acknowledgments

BY D. ERIK FELTEN

Since many projects undertaken are never finished, it is especially rewarding when a noble project conceived is seen through to completion. Such is how I feel toward the publishing of this work.

As with any endeavor of merit, the list of thank-yous is long. I would first like to thank the "Ladies of the 34th Floor"—the personal staff to President Reagan. Joanne Drake, Eileen Foliente, Peggy Grande, Bernadette Schurz, Kay Paietta and Libbie Brady are, quite simply, the most dedicated and talented team I have ever had the privilege to encounter. The nation should know how well the fortieth President is served by his loyal staff. The readers of this work should know the book in their hands would not have been possible without them. Eileen especially contributed more energy and enthusiasm to this project than I could have hoped. And Joanne made sure no obstacle slowed its progress.

Further appreciation goes to Cathy Busch,

Johanna Afshani, Steve Christensen, Mike Guastella and Steve Branch, who each contributed essential talents to this project.

Continuing on, I owe a great debt to Mrs. Reagan, Fred Ryan and the entire Board of Trustees of the Ronald Reagan Presidential Foundation for encouraging this work from inception. Mrs. Reagan's foreword is one of the most eloquent overviews of their life's journey I have ever read. Bob Barnett and Jackie Davies at Williams & Connolly are responsible for bringing the entire project to print. Both Bob and Jackie were complete professionals and lent much wisdom in the arduous process of finding our publisher and "making the deal." Bill Rosen, Sharon Gibbons and the team at Simon & Schuster did a magnificent job of transforming our initial text into the final product.

I also wish to thank my partner at Pacific Group, LLC and Pacific Capital Fund, Mark Lehman, for tending the fort and allowing me time to work on this endeavor. Now that it is finished, I believe I can vouch the time was well invested.

I am extremely appreciative for the tributes that were submitted. Every person who was invited to participate faced hectic schedules and other pressing demands. The fact that they each responded within such a short time is a testament to the respect each feels for President and Mrs. Reagan. I am especially pleased that this transcends political lines, and I consider it a personal honor to have had Senator Sam Nunn submit a tribute. As a college intern to Senator Nunn, I was the standout Republican in a Democrat's office and an unabashed Reaganite to the core. It made for lively debate and a lot of learning, and I have always been grateful for the good Senator's respect and encouragement of a young mind to hold fast to his convictions. It was a fantastic training ground.

I would feel remiss if I did not also mention the thankfulness I feel toward Jackie Pullinger-To and the St. Stephen's Society in Hong Kong. While I was in the deepest part of completing this project I was in Hong Kong for a business dinner and happened upon this most unique group. I was privileged to spend a day with this private ministry at work with the island's many poor and needy. This timely experience reminded me anew of President Reagan's passion for self-initiative and the great importance of helping your neighbor. At the time of this special island's transition to Chinese control, it seemed especially poignant. It still does.

Lastly, I want to formally thank President Reagan. It has been the privilege of a lifetime to have known the President these last few years and to have been entrusted with this project. I know I am biased, but whenever I am asked my reflections on the President, I never hesitate to respond, "He is one of the greatest individuals our country has ever produced." I'll leave each reader to decide the politics for him- or herself, but the President as a person is simply the best. I am reminded each day of his humility, steadfast adherence to principle and genuine love for people. These remain, I believe, his genius and the centerpiece to his leadership. Sometimes nice guys do indeed finish first—some even get to fly around in Air Force One.

# Contents

# CONTENTS

# CONTENTS

# CONTENTS

# *Foreword*

BY NANCY REAGAN

Over thirty years ago Ronnie came to national attention with his famous speech for Barry Goldwater in 1964, "A Time for Choosing." At the time we were living in Pacific Palisades, enjoying our family and the cool ocean breeze that would roll through our home in the evenings. Neither he nor I had any interest in either state or national politics, and never could we have imagined what the next thirty years would hold.

I believe that it is important to know that Ronnie never sought higher office on his own, but rather as an answer to the party's call for unity and someone to lead. No one thought he had much of a chance at the time to beat the incumbent Governor, Pat Brown, but then many people have gone bankrupt betting against Ronnie from that time since. I will always remember those early days, for they provided a life we never envisioned having. The last three decades have been interesting, challenging, utterly fascinating and sometimes very frightening. There were times when it seemed the sun forgot to shine. But now those days have dimmed in comparison to the accomplishments that continue to glow so brightly.

It is because of these accomplishments that this post-Presidential book was undertaken. At a time when our nation needs to be reminded of our nonpartisan greatness and the glorious mission which is still before each one of us, I can think of no better commentator for this than my roommate. Ronnie, more than any one person I know, truly lives the American dream. And more than any other one person, he wants to share that dream with every citizen in a country he loves so dearly.

His dream is a simple dream and still very obtainable. It is the vision of a shining city that Ronnie saw as "a tall, proud city, built on rocks stronger than oceans, windswept, God-blessed, and teeming with people of all kinds living in harmony and peace; a city with free ports that hummed with commerce and creativity. And if there had to be city walls, the walls had doors and the doors were open to anyone with the will and the heart to get here." That's how he saw it, and still sees it.

Ronnie and I are no longer as young as we were then, so the house we hope to yet see built is no longer one for our generation, but for those after us. The undertaking of this effort, then, is for you—America—not just Republicans or Democrats. In an age when politics has become so petty, it is our prayer that Ronnie's words will light a new fire in each of you for a renewed vision of America's greatest potential—the heritage of a united people pressing toward her best days, which are still to come. May God always bless America.

*President and Mrs.*
*Reagan leading*
*naval troops in*
*the Pledge of*
*Allegiance aboard*
*the U.S.S.* Missouri,
*July 4, 1986.*

# Introduction

BY D. ERIK FELTEN

The impetus for this book was the Republican Convention held in San Diego the second week of August 1996. There I was struck by the degree to which the spirit of Ronald Reagan continues to permeate convention halls where the party faithful gather.

Even more amazing, though, is that eight years after he left the Presidency, and beyond two separate administrations which have since occupied the Oval Office, people of all political stripes still savor and reminisce about the genuine leadership and contagious optimism President Reagan brought to our nation.

At a time when politics has become so trivial and sound-bite driven, the message is many times being lost in the madness. This is unfortunate. It is my hope that through this collection of post-Presidential speeches, the purity of President Reagan's words might shine anew on the deep heritage we share as citizens of this unique, great land.

You will also find in this collection many tributes from other great leaders and writers of our time, reflecting on the impact that President Reagan has had on our nation and the world. These tributes bring to mind very quickly many of the words and phrases one thinks of when describing the President— humble, God-fearing, optimistic and a truly great communicator holding simple but fast convictions. I believe the words I would use are "quintessentially American." Ronald Reagan represents for me all the great things our nation can encompass.

If nothing else, it is the collective hope of the team behind this project that this book will serve as a gentle whisper in a very loud world, where each one of us has a mission, a destiny and a duty. A great President is one who fosters this and gives citizens the tools by which to contribute their finest efforts. President Reagan is such a man and our nation is greater for his time at the helm.

13

# A Shining City

$\mathcal{R}$onald Reagan will go down in history as one of the greatest Presidents that America has ever had. Historians will undoubtedly focus on his enormous political impact, both domestically and internationally. But his emphasis on moral and spiritual values was one of his greatest contributions. Mr. Reagan made Americans feel good about themselves, no matter what the problems were. More than that, he pointed them to the moral and spiritual foundations which have made this nation great—foundations derived from the Biblical Judeo-Christian heritage.

*President Reagan presents the Reverend Billy Graham with the Presidential Medal of Freedom, February 23, 1983.*

Standing by his side on all occasions has been one of the most beautiful and talented first ladies America has ever had. It was Nancy's mother who introduced me to Ronald Reagan while he was still an actor. I sensed immediately not only his warm and engaging personality, but his perceptive mind and strong qualities of leadership.

I consider Ronald Reagan one of the best friends I have. I thank God for our relationship across the years and pray for God's special grace upon the Reagans in the future.

THE REVEREND BILLY GRAHAM

MY FELLOW AMERICANS:

This is the thirty-fourth time I'll speak to you from the Oval Office and the last. We've been together eight years now, and soon it'll be time for me to go. But before I do, I wanted to share some thoughts, some of which I've been saving for a long time.

It's been the honor of my life to be your President. So many of you have written the past few weeks to say thanks, but I could say as much to you. Nancy and I are grateful for the opportunity you gave us to serve.

One of the things about the Presidency is that you're always somewhat apart. You spend a lot of time going by too fast in a car someone else is driving, and seeing the people through tinted glass—the parents holding up a child, and the wave you saw too late and couldn't return. And so many times I wanted to stop and reach out from behind the glass, and connect. Well, maybe I can do a little of that tonight.

People ask how I feel about leaving. And the fact is, "parting is such sweet sorrow." The sweet part is California and the ranch and freedom. The sorrow—the goodbyes, of course, and leaving this beautiful place.

You know, down the hall and up the stairs from this office is the part of the White House where the President and his family live. There are a few favorite windows I have up there that I like to stand and look out of early in the morning. The view is over the grounds here to the Washington Monument, and then the Mall and the Jefferson Memorial. But on mornings when the humidity is low, you can see past the Jefferson to the river, the Potomac, and the Virginia shore. Someone said that's the view Lincoln had when he saw the smoke rising from the Battle of Bull Run. I see more prosaic things: the grass on the banks, the morning traffic as people make their way to work, now and then a sailboat on the river.

I've been thinking a bit at that window. I've been reflecting on what the past eight years have meant and mean. And the image that comes to mind like a refrain is a nautical one—a small story about a big ship, and a refugee, and a sailor. It was back in the early eighties, at the height of the boat people. And the sailor was hard at work on the carrier *Midway,* which was patrolling the South China Sea. The sailor, like most American servicemen, was young, smart and fiercely observant. The crew spied on the horizon a leaky little boat. And crammed inside were refugees from Indochina hoping to get to America. The *Midway* sent a small launch to bring them to ship and safety. As the refugees made their way through the choppy seas, one spied the sailor on deck, and stood up and called out to him. He yelled, "Hello, American sailor. Hello, freedom man."

A small moment with a big meaning, a moment the sailor, who wrote it in a letter, couldn't get out of his mind. And when I saw it, neither could I. Because that's what it was to be an American in the 1980s. We stood again for freedom. I know we always have, but in the past few years the world again—and in a way, we ourselves—rediscovered it.

It's been quite a journey this decade, and we held together through some stormy seas. And at the end, together, we are reaching our destination.

The fact is, from Grenada to the Washington and Moscow summits, from the recession of '81 to '82, to the expansion that began in late '82 and continues to this day, we've made a difference. The way I see it, there were two great triumphs, two things that I'm proudest of. One is the economic recovery, in which the people of America created—and filled—19

million new jobs. The other is the recovery of our morale. America is respected again in the world and looked to for leadership.

Something that happened to me a few years ago reflects some of this. It was back in 1981, and I was attending my first big economic summit, which was held that year in Canada. The meeting place rotates among the member countries. The opening meeting was a formal dinner for the heads of government of the seven industrialized nations. Now, I sat there like the new kid in school and listened, and it was all François this and Helmut that. They dropped titles and spoke to one another on a first-name basis. Well, at one point I sort of leaned in and said, "My name's Ron." Well, in that same year we began the actions we felt would ignite an economic comeback—cut taxes and regulation, started to cut spending. And soon the recovery began.

Two years later another economic summit with pretty much the same cast. At the big opening meeting we all got together, and all of a sudden, just for a moment, I saw that everyone was just sitting there looking at me. And then one of them broke the silence. "Tell us about the American miracle," he said.

Well, back in 1980, when I was running for President, it was all so different. Some pundits said our programs would result in catastrophe. Our views on foreign affairs would cause war. Our plans for the economy would cause inflation to soar and bring about economic collapse. I even remember one highly respected economist saying, back in 1982, that "The engines of economic growth have shut down here, and they're likely to stay that way for years to come." Well, he and the other opinion leaders were wrong. The fact is, what they called radical was really right. What they called dangerous was just desperately needed.

And in all of that time I won a nickname, the Great Communicator. But I never thought it was my style or the words I used that made a difference: It was the content. I wasn't a great communicator, but I communicated great things, and they didn't spring full bloom from my brow, they came from the heart of a great nation—from our experience, our wisdom and our belief in the principles that have guided us for two centuries. They called it the Reagan revolution. Well, I'll accept that, but for me it always seemed more like the great rediscovery, a rediscovery of our values and our common sense.

Common sense told us that when you put a big tax on something, the people will produce less of it. So, we cut the people's tax rates, and the people produced more than ever before. The economy bloomed like a plant that had been cut back and could now grow quicker and stronger. Our economic program brought about the longest peacetime expansion in our history: real family income up, the poverty rate down, entrepreneurship booming, and an explosion in research and new technology. We're exporting more than ever because American industry became more competitive, and at the same time we summoned the national will to knock down protectionist walls abroad instead of erecting them at home.

Common sense also told us that to preserve the peace, we'd have to become strong again after years of weakness and confusion. So, we rebuilt our defenses, and this New Year we toasted the new peacefulness around the globe. Not only have the superpowers actually begun to reduce their stockpiles of nuclear weapons— and hope for even more progress is bright— but the regional conflicts that rack the globe are also beginning to cease. The Persian Gulf is no longer a war zone. The Soviets are leaving Afghanistan. The Vietnamese are preparing to pull out of Cambodia, and an American-mediated accord will soon send 50,000 Cuban troops home from Angola.

The lesson of all this was, of course, that because we're a great nation, our challenges seem complex. It will always be this way. But as long as we remember our first principles and believe in ourselves, the future will always be ours. And something else we learned: Once you begin a great movement, there's no telling where it will end. We meant to change a nation, and instead, we changed a world.

Countries across the globe are turning to free markets and free speech and turning away from the ideologies of the past. For them, the great rediscovery of the 1980s has been that, lo and behold, the moral way of government is the practical way of government. Democracy, the profoundly good, is also the profoundly productive.

When you've got to the point when you can celebrate the anniversaries of your thirty-ninth birthday you can sit back sometimes, review your life and see it flowing before you. For me there was a fork in the river, and it was right in the middle of my life. I never meant to go into politics. It wasn't my intention when I was young. But I was raised to believe you had to pay your way for the blessings bestowed on you. I was happy with my career in the entertainment world, but I ultimately went into politics because I wanted to protect something precious.

Ours was the first revolution in the history of mankind that truly reversed the course of government, and with three little words: "We, the People." "We, the People," tell the government what to do; it doesn't tell us. "We, the People," are the driver; the government is the car. And we decide where it should go, and by what route, and how fast. Almost all the world's constitutions are documents in which governments tell the people what their privileges are. Our Constitution is a document in which "We, the People," tell the government what it is allowed to do. "We, the People," are free. This belief has been the underlying basis of everything I've tried to do these past eight years.

But back in the 1960s, when I began, it seemed to me that we'd begun reversing the order of things—that through more and more rules and regulations and confiscatory taxes, the government was taking more of our money, more of our options and more of our freedom. I went into politics in part to put up my hand and say, "Stop." I was a citizen-politician, and it seemed the right thing for a citizen to do.

I think we have stopped a lot of what needed stopping. And I hope we have once again reminded people that man is not free unless government is limited. There's a clear cause and effect here that is as neat and predictable as a law of physics: as government expands, liberty contracts.

Nothing is less free than pure communism—and yet we have, the past few years, forged a satisfying new closeness with the Soviet Union. I've been asked if this isn't a gamble, and my answer is no because we're basing our actions not on words but deeds. The détente of the 1970s was based not on actions but promises. They'd promise to treat their own people and the people of the world better. But the gulag was still the gulag, and the state was still expansionist, and they still waged proxy wars in Africa, Asia and Latin America.

Well, this time, so far, it's different. President Gorbachev has brought about some internal democratic reforms and begun the withdrawal from Afghanistan. He has also freed prisoners whose names I've given him every time we've met.

But life has a way of reminding you of big things through small incidents. Once, during the heady days of the Moscow summit, Nancy and I decided to break off from the entourage one afternoon to visit the shops on Arbat Street—that's a little street just off Moscow's main shopping area. Even though our visit was a surprise, every Russian there immediately recognized us and called out our names and reached for our hands. We were just about swept away by the warmth. You could almost feel the possibilities in all that joy. But within seconds a KGB detail pushed their way toward us and began pushing and shoving the people in the crowd. It was an interesting moment. It reminded me that while the man on the street in the Soviet Union yearns for peace, the government is Communist. And those who run it are Communists, and that means we and they view such issues as freedom and human rights very differently.

We must keep up our guard, but we must also continue to work together to lessen and eliminate tension and mistrust. My view is that President Gorbachev is different from previous Soviet leaders. I think he knows some of the things wrong with his society and is trying to fix them. We wish him well. And we'll continue to work to make sure that the Soviet Union that eventually emerges from this process is a less threatening one. What it all boils down to is this: I want the new closeness to continue. And it will, as long as we make it clear that we will continue to act in a certain way as long as they continue to act in a helpful manner. If and when they don't, at first pull your punches. If they persist, pull the plug. It's still trust but verify. It's still play, but cut the cards. It's still watch closely. And don't be afraid to see what you see.

I've been asked if I have any regrets. Well, I do. The deficit is one. I've been talking a great deal about that lately, but tonight isn't for arguments, and I'm going to hold my tongue. But an observation: I've had my share of victories in the Congress, but what few people noticed is that I never won anything you didn't win for me. They never saw my troops, they never saw Reagan's regiments, the American people. You won every battle with every call you made and letter you wrote demanding action. Well, action is still needed. If we're to finish the job, Reagan's regiments will have to become the Bush brigades. Soon he'll be the chief, and he'll need you every bit as much as I did.

Finally, there is a great tradition of warnings in Presidential farewells, and I've got one that's been on my mind for some time. But oddly enough it starts with one of the things I'm proudest of in the past eight years: the resurgence of national pride that I called the new patriotism. This national feeling is good, but it won't count for much, and it won't last, unless it's grounded in thoughtfulness and knowledge.

An informed patriotism is what we want. And are we doing a good enough job teaching our children what America is and what she represents in the long history of the world? Those of us who are over thirty-five or so years of age grew up in a different America. We were taught, very directly, what it means to be an American. And we absorbed, almost in the air, a love of country and an appreciation of its institutions. If you didn't get these things from your family you got them from the neighborhood, from the father down the street who fought in Korea or the family who lost someone at Anzio. Or you could get a sense of patriotism from school. And if all else failed you could get a sense of patriotism from the popular culture. The movies celebrated democratic values and implicitly reinforced the idea that

America was special. TV was like that, too, through the mid-sixties.

But now, we're about to enter the nineties, and some things have changed. Younger parents aren't sure that an unambivalent appreciation of America is the right thing to teach modern children. And as for those who create the popular culture, well-grounded patriotism is no longer the style. Our spirit is back, but we haven't reinstitutionalized it. We've got to do a better job of getting across that America is freedom—freedom of speech, freedom of religion, freedom of enterprise. And freedom is special and rare. It's fragile; it needs protection.

So, we've got to teach history based not on what's in fashion but what's important—why the Pilgrims came here, who Jimmy Doolittle was and what those 30 seconds over Tokyo meant. You know, four years ago, on the fortieth anniversary of D-Day, I read a letter from a young woman writing to her late father, who'd fought on Omaha Beach. Her name was Lisa Zanatta Henn, and she said, "We will always remember, we will never forget, what the boys of Normandy did." Well, let's help her keep her word. If we forget what we did, we won't know who we are. I'm warning of an eradication of the American memory that could result, ultimately, in an erosion of the American spirit. Let's start with some basics: more attention to American history and a greater emphasis on civic ritual.

And let me offer lesson number one about America: All great change in America begins at the dinner table. So, tomorrow night in the kitchen I hope the talking begins. And children, if your parents haven't been teaching you what it means to be an American, let 'em know and nail 'em on it. That would be a very American thing to do.

And that's about all I have to say tonight, except for one thing. The past few days when I've been at that window upstairs, I've thought a bit of the "shining city upon a hill." The phrase comes from John Winthrop, who wrote it to describe the America he imagined. What he imagined was important because he was an early Pilgrim, an early freedom man. He journeyed here on what today we'd call a little wooden boat; and like the other Pilgrims, he was looking for a home that would be free.

I've spoken of the shining city all my political life, but I don't know if I ever quite communicated what I saw when I said it. But in my mind it was a tall, proud city built on rocks stronger than oceans, windswept, God-blessed, and teeming with people of all kinds living in harmony and peace; a city with free ports that hummed with commerce and creativity. And if there had to be city walls, the walls had doors and the doors were open to anyone with the will and the heart to get here. That's how I saw it, and see it still.

And how stands the city on this winter night? More prosperous, more secure and happier than it was eight years ago. But more than that: After two hundred years, two centuries, she still stands strong and true on the granite ridge, and her glow has held steady no matter what storm. And she's still a beacon, still a magnet for all who must have freedom, for all the pilgrims from all the lost places who are hurtling through the darkness toward home.

We've done our part. And as I walk off into the city streets, a final word to the men and women of the Reagan revolution, the men and women across America who for eight years did the work that brought America back. My friends: We did it. We weren't just marking time. We made a difference. We made the city stronger, we made the city freer, and we left her in good hands. All in all, not bad, not bad at all.

$\mathcal{A}$mericans will look back upon Ronald Reagan's Presidency as a period of great achievement, not only domestically but also internationally, for it was his administration that was the turning point when the end of the era of the Cold War became inevitable.

It was a seminal time for the United States and for the world, when old alliances were crumbling and a new world order was emerging, opening the way for the spread of democracy on the one hand, or fragmentation and chaos on the other. Few Presidents in recent time have been called upon to navigate such difficult shoals with so few dependable charts.

But Ronald Reagan developed a foreign policy of extraordinary consistency and relevance to the core issues of the period. He had an uncanny talent for uniting the American people because he possessed an extraordinary intuitive rapport with the wellsprings of American motivation and an unshakable faith in the greatness of our country. President Reagan demonstrated that having a sense of direction and the strength of one's convictions are the key ingredients of leadership—along with a healthy dose of humor and common sense.

*President Reagan and Henry Kissinger sharing a laugh, June 10, 1981.*

These latter qualities can be illustrated by one of my favorite anecdotes about Ronald Reagan, which took place while he was Governor of California. As National Security Advisor, I would brief him from time to time on the key foreign policy issues of the day. It was during the Middle East war of 1973, when the small Israeli Air Force was suffering crippling losses. I told him that we would be announcing that the United States would replace the downed Israeli planes, but I was uncertain as to how to limit the Arab reaction. "Why don't you just announce that you will replace all the aircraft the Arabs claim to have shot down?" he replied, knowing that these claims were wildly inflated. I wish I had had him on my staff when I became Secretary of State!

Ronald Reagan's achievements were many, but the most important was the lasting legacy he left to the United States, a legacy of confidence in ourselves and vision for the future of a strong and just America.

HENRY A. KISSINGER
*Secretary of State, 1973–1977*

*I*T'S BEEN MY responsibility, my duty and very much my honor to serve as Commander in Chief of this nation's Armed Forces these past eight years. That is the most sacred, most important task of the Presidency. Since our nation's founding, the primary obligation of the national government has been the common defense of these United States. But as I have sought to perform this sacred task as best I could, I have done so with the knowledge that my role in this day-to-day-to-day effort, from sunrise to sunrise, every moment of every hour of every day of every year, is a glancing one compared to yours.

Yes, today America is at peace, today her defenses are strong, and she stands proud and tall in the sight of the world. And the credit, the gratitude of a nation comfortable and at peace, properly goes not to me but rather to all of you, for you have, of your own free and true goodwill, chosen to spend all or part of your lives in service to your country and your countrymen.

We live in an age of great prosperity and ease, a time when many people your age are getting themselves established in the world in circumstances of comfort that would astonish your ancestors. You have chosen a different path, a path of service to country and to others rather than to self. You have made yourselves a shining example of how men and women can find within themselves qualities of self-sacrifice, bravery, camaraderie and true courage. These are many of the noblest virtues to which humankind can aspire. They are martial virtues. You have made the comfortable lives of your fellow Americans possible by taking on these responsibilities by choice. And over the past eight years the luster has been restored to the reputation of our fighting forces after a time during which it was shamefully fashionable to deride and even condemn service such as yours. Those days will never come again.

But it's not just your fellow Americans who owe you a debt. No, I believe many more do, for I believe that military service in the Armed

Forces of the United States is a profound form of service to all humankind. You stand engaged in an effort to keep America safe at home, to protect our allies and interests abroad, to keep the seas and the skies free of threat. Just as America stands as an example to the world of the inestimable benefits of freedom and democracy, so too an America with the capacity to project her power for the purpose of protecting and expanding freedom and democracy abroad benefits the suffering people of the world.

Some might consider those words somewhat controversial, but to them I just say this: Just ask the freedom-loving people of Grenada whether American military power is a good thing or not. Because we remained strong, because we acted when we believed we had to, in the past eight years not one inch of ground on this earth fell under Communist control. We cannot name the tens of millions who have been saved from that fate, so we cannot ask them. Rather ask those unfortunate enough to have lived under communism. Ask them whether America should be strong. Ask them whether America should stand tall. Ask them. You don't have to. You know the answer.

*W*hen I think about President Reagan these days a number of images arise and come together. I was thinking the other day of how he seems like a man of another time, a true gentleman, a man whose personal integrity and sincerity and ingenuousness were never really questioned. We knew he was good. We knew he was worthy of our respect—which was good, because we all respected him. And by "we" here I mean the vast majority of the American people.

It has changed now, and the vast majority of us don't feel that way about our President. We may like him or dislike him, support him or not, but—respect for his personal goodness? For his decency and inherent sincerity?

I miss admiring the President. There was something refreshing about it, after Watergate and Vietnam and all the things that made us start not liking our Presidents. It was like a cool glass of water.

*President Reagan shaking hands with speechwriter Peggy Noonan in the Oval Office, December 20, 1988.*

And lately, for reasons I don't completely understand, I keep thinking of how children reacted to Reagan. Once, sitting at my desk in the Executive Office Building, I got a bunch of copies of that week's letters from citizens to the President. I read them with curiosity—what were the people telling him? It was during the '84 campaign, and most of the letters were encouraging in one way or another, but the one I really remember was from a little girl, I think aged nine or ten. The President had just had his first, disastrous, debate with Walter Mondale. The little girl was trying to inspirit him. She told Reagan, "My parents say

Mondale may beat you in the next debate but I told them, 'Next time Ronnie's going to blow that guy's doors off.'"

From a kid. She was completely comfortable calling him Ronnie and talking the way kids talk. He must have thrown back his head laughing—you could feel the little girl's fervor. She got a nice, handwritten reply.

Another child, this one a boy, a teenager, in China. Reagan had gone there in '84 and made a series of striking speeches about democracy, about what kind of country America is. The government gerontocracy watched coolly, appraisingly. But the young people listened to him, and fell in love. Ben Elliott, who headed the President's speechwriting shop came back and told me that this young Chinese boy had listened to Reagan at one of his stops and then said to someone, a friend, or Ben, "He is a great Yankee man!" We called the President Yankeeman in speechwriting for a while after that.

Oh, a last image. Ben's secretary, Donna, was young, in her early twenties, humorous and high-spirited. When the President's helicopter used to take him back to the White House after a trip, our office would shake with the noise as Marine One landed on the White House lawn just a few hundred yards from our offices. We'd hear the sound and Donna would yell out with a singsong voice, like a housewife in an old movie, "Daddy's home."

Looking back, that's how we felt when he was President. Daddy was home.

PEGGY NOONAN

*T*HANK ALL OF YOU very much. As you know, Dr. Zumberg told you two weeks ago I went into retirement. I'm glad that's over. I just didn't like retirement—took all the fun out of Saturdays. But for two weeks I tried adjusting to private life and growing old gracefully without being a nuisance to anyone. But that's not my style, so here I am, saddled up and ready to ride again.

You know, it's wonderful—I got all sorts of offers on where to appear first. The Disney people called and kindly asked if I'd do one of their commercials. They wanted to put the camera on my face and then the announcer's voice would say, "Mr. President, you just completed two successful terms in office. What are you going to do now?" And they wanted me to say, "I'm going to Disneyland." And I told them, "No, I'm going to USC." And what a great coming-out party this is.

I'll tell you why I wanted to come here first. I'm so proud of this country's young people. I have absolutely no doubt about what you can accomplish for this nation. I like the fact you get things done and the fact that you're impatient. This morning I thought I'd talk about some things *I* still want to get done and some things that I've become impatient about after eight years in Washington. And I no longer speak to you as President; I speak to you from a position that's even more important to the health of this democracy: as a private citizen.

I believe the citizens of this nation must be vigilant and protective of their powers or those powers would be ceded to Washington. I've said this before, but one of my biggest disappointments as President was that I wasn't able to balance the budget. After all, I'd made a pledge to the American people that I wasn't able to fulfill, at least yet. But I haven't forgotten my pledge. And today I start stumping to help future Presidents—Republican or Democrat—get the tools they need to bring the budget under control. And those tools: the line-item veto and the constitutional amendment calling for a balanced budget.

The first President who ever did that was Thomas Jefferson, and when that constitution was ratified he said it has one glaring omission: it does not have a clause preventing the government from borrowing. Well, I'm not even going to call upon the Congress to pass these measures. I know they'd pass because the American people would demand it.

All I'm asking is that Congress is allowed a vote. I don't think that's too much for the people to expect from their elected representatives. This is a democracy and let's vote for those two ways to bring the deficit under control. Now let's go on record with a fair up-and-down vote on the line-item veto and the balanced budget amendment. How long can the Congress continue to evade its democratic duty to consider the people's business? How long can the will of the people be denied? I'm going to make sure the answer is, "Not long."

I've just learned one of the great things about being an ex-President is that I can now say what I want. And I'll tell you what a basic problem is with the budget and I'll tell you the biggest lesson that I've learned as President. The Congress has wrapped the budget process in kryptonite—even Superman himself couldn't get to it. And part of the reason for the Budget Act of 1974—the Congress never lets up on trying to reduce the powers of the Presidency.

In a recent article one legal commentator wrote that, in his words, the 1974 act "was crafted by Congress to rob the President of his ability to limit spending while making it possible for a fragmented collection of Congress-

men to spend and at the same time evade responsibility for doing so."

You know recently we've heard so many lines that I've seen in print, my name coupled with the President's budget deficit. You know something? The President of the United States can't spend a dime. Only the Congress can spend money. And really the big deficit started coming immediately after that act was passed and it kept right on rolling ever since. The Congress won't do anything major about the budget deficit and they don't want anybody else to either. The way the Congress loves to spend money reminds me of a T-shirt I saw. It said on the front of it, "How can I be without money? I still have checks."

Now there are two things you constantly hear. One is that the tax cuts that we started back in 1981 caused the deficit. You hear that a lot because that's what they'd like you to think, but don't you believe it.

The federal revenues, since we reduced the tax rates, have increased by $375 billion—since the 1981 tax cut. The problem is that Congressional spending grew even faster. When they say, but all that increase went to defense, that's what they'd like you to think. And again don't you believe it. Revenues increased $375 billion but spending increased in the same period $450 billion. And less than a third of that went to defense. And now, here we are facing fiscal year 1990. The Office of Management and Budget estimates the government will take in $83.8 billion in new tax revenues. Almost $84 billion more tax dollars in one year—$84 billion we never had before and still there's going to be a huge budget deficit. As the *Wall Street Journal* said, the voters are smart enough to realize that $84 billion more a year ought to be enough for anyone's federal priorities. So let me go back to what I've said countless times. We don't have a budget deficit because we, our people, aren't taxed enough. We have a deficit because the Congress spends too much.

I have to interject here a little something that I learned back during the war. I was a cavalry officer, but I found myself flying a desk in the Air Force. We were directly under Air Corps Intelligence. Well, it was a big matter of records and where to put them. And we knew there was a warehouse full of filing cabinets and the filing cabinets were full of government papers that had no historical value and had no bearing on anything that was going on. So through the channels we sent a request all the way up to the top asking permission to destroy those obsolete records so we could use the filing cabinets for the papers that were now of importance to the war. And back down from on top, being endorsed at every step of the way, came the permission: "Permission granted provided copies are made of each record destroyed." That was a lesson in government that I didn't forget.

You know, I heard a TV correspondent on the news one day say that "Ronald Reagan states we need a balanced budget and yet he has never submitted one to Congress." Well, that's absolutely true. I may be old but I'm not stupid. The budgets I sent up to the Hill that had even a modest cutback in them were declared dead on arrival by the Congress.

Trying to wipe out the deficit in a single budget has been an exercise in futility. It's taken more than half a century to build up that total deficit now, and granted, you can't do away with it in one term, but what I always had in mind is we can set our course on an annual reduction down to the point that we can fix a date for reaching a balanced budget. The Congress of the United States is not psychologically prepared for a balanced budget and they won't be until there's an amendment requiring one.

Another absolutely essential things is a line-item veto. Forty-three Governors already have it. I had it as Governor of California. I used it 943 times and was never overridden once. With this the President can go through the budget, vetoing out the pork and the fat. You see, people have these gimmicks and they stick them in a great voluminous budget hoping they'd be overlooked when the whole thing is passed. Well, if you can go through and pick those out, then they have to override your veto. They know they don't have the nerve if those things are exposed to the people. The people would recognize how foolish and ridiculous these spending items were. Well, you know, if a President could eliminate those items the Congress has no right forcing on the American people to pay for them—things like trucks the Pentagon didn't want, anthracite coal that it didn't need, or money to finance cranberry research or the commercialization of wildflowers—well, there are so many people in this country who need the government's help and deserve it. We should use the taxpayer money for programs that are important and needed and not programs that are political payoffs for some Congressmen or Senators.

Why won't the leadership of Congress schedule a vote on the line-item veto? Well, they're afraid it might pass, but it's the people's right to have this matter considered—their right to have their elected representatives debate this public issue. What you see is with so many other things in Washington—the budget deficit is not just about money, it's about political power. I wish the Congress and so many others in Washington would learn that power belongs to the people and not to them.

There's another abuse of power that distorts the democratic process, one that's pure dynamite because it deals with political greed. It's called gerrymandering—the practice of rigging boundaries on Congressional districts. This is the greatest single blot on the integrity of our nation's electoral system. It'll be a big issue in the 1990s and I intend to be in the thick of it. What happens is that after each federal census—the next one will be in 1990—state legislatures must redraw the lines of Congressional districts to reflect the population shifts that have taken place. Fair enough. Unfortunately, many times these new districts aren't drawn in a politically neutral way; they don't resemble anything that's honest or natural. The party in power, which dominates the legislature, they do the redistricting. They cram as many of the opposing party's members or voters as they can in as few districts as possible. Now, naturally, that makes those districts sure opposition seats. But they're fewer than the

seats that the other side will have. These districts are outnumbered, and so one party will always be in the minority as long as the other party is doing the redistricting.

This always reminds me of a story about a fellow who decided to remake himself, to undergo a complete rejuvenation. He took up jogging, stopped drinking, lost some weight, married a younger woman, got a hair transplant and a new wardrobe—the veritable picture of youth. And the first time he was out on the street, he was hit by a truck. When he got upstairs, he asked the Almighty why he was called to Heaven just when he was beginning to enjoy himself. The Almighty took a closer look and said, "Oh, I'm sorry. I didn't recognize you."

Well, neither can one recognize a gerrymandered district as anything resembling a political unit. They're the greatest symbols of political chicanery. One district even became known as a fishhook because of its dimensions and the way it was laid out. A California Congressman, for the 1980 redistricting, drew up the plan that the California legislature approved and he, laughingly, said that he believed his redistricting had been a contribution to modern art.

Well, for years, gerrymandering was used in this country to prevent the election of black Congressmen. Now it's used by both Democratic and Republican state parties to guarantee a continued edge where one or the other is in power.

In the 1988 Congressional elections 98 percent of all incumbents seeking re-election were re-elected. The House of Representatives has become virtually a permanent chamber with less turnover than the Supreme Soviet. Only one of California's forty-five districts has changed parties since the last gerrymander here in 1982.

No Congressional district should be safe because of the way it's drawn. It should be safe because the Congressman represents the interests of the people in that district.

Our system of redistricting needs what the Soviets call perestroika, "restructuring." It's a conflict of interest for state legislatures to feather their own political nests. I believe the states should each set up a bipartisan citizens' commission that would draw the district lines based on the principle of why they should be redrawn. Some states already have this, but all states should. So I'm putting the state legislatures on notice to keep it fair, or they may find the Gipper on the statehouse steps calling attention to their shenanigans.

Now, briefly, let me touch one other area where the people's democratic rights are being thwarted—the Twenty-second Amendment of the Constitution. That is the amendment that prevents the President from serving more than two terms. Now I couldn't say anything about that while I was still there—sounds a little like personal interest there—but no, since I'm already out to pasture, this amendment doesn't affect me, and I believe this preemption of the people's right to vote for whomever they want should be repealed.

Now I have to say the Republicans own the fault on this one. After Franklin Roosevelt was

elected four times they decided not to ever let that happen again, particularly to a Democrat. But I've learned what Franklin Delano Roosevelt already knew: two times isn't necessarily enough to get all that you want done done. I can't help but think of a little boy whose father came home from work with work from his office every night. The kid asked him one night why. Well, he said, he had so much to do he couldn't get it all done in a workday. And the little boy said, well, maybe he belonged in a slower group.

Well, I don't know, maybe I belonged in a slower group because I still had things to do when I left. The first term we turned the economy around. The second term we opened a new relationship with the Soviets and possibly turned around the Cold War. And if I had had a third term I would have gone into full combat on the budget, even if it meant shutting down the government. But my basic point on the Twenty-second Amendment is this: If the American people want to elect a President more times than twice, why shouldn't you be able to? The Twenty-second Amendment is politically motivated and should be repealed.

There are so many battles ahead for you and me as private citizens and they're important not just because the outcome is critical but because it's important simply to care enough to be in the fray. So I have a request to make of you today.

In his memoirs of imprisonment in the Soviet Union, Natan Sharansky tells how he was taken during a break in his trial to a special holding cell. Think of the hopelessness of one who, despite his bravery and deep conviction, knows that years in the gulag are ahead for him and his once normal life is soon to be only a memory. And then in a dark moment in that cell, his eyes rested on graffiti scratched in a stone in the wall by an earlier prisoner, a prisoner of conscience. It simply said, "Be strong and courageous."

What better prescription for dark days or sure formula for happy ones. I can't think of a better principle to guide our actions as individuals or as a nation.

So my friends, for yourselves, for your country: Be strong. Be courageous.

Thank you for inviting me here today and God bless you all.

*I* remember President Reagan with the utmost respect but also with great warmth and affection. I remember in particular among the many interviews we did together visiting President and Mrs. Reagan at their ranch in California. I rode with the President in his old beat-up Jeep. I sat beside him as he drove, with a big shaggy dog in the back seat. I remember laughing and saying, "I know you want to economize, Mr. President, but this is the scroungiest Jeep I have ever seen." It seems to me we ran the pictures of him in that Jeep again and again.

*President Reagan with Barbara Walters in an interview at Rancho del Cielo in 1981. (© 1997 ABC Inc.)*

The interview was done not too long after the assassination attack on the President, but he seemed fit and hardy, chopping logs for us while Mrs. Reagan watched with concern.

In the years since President and Mrs. Reagan left the White House, I have had occasion to see Mrs. Reagan many times. I am always impressed by her warmth and sensitivity. She protected her husband in the White House, and she protects him still. I consider it an honor to know them both.

BARBARA WALTERS

*I* interviewed Reagan for CNN's *Larry King Live* shortly after he left the Presidency. I was—and continue to be—a great fan of his essence. He is a man of simple principles that he fully believes in.

I remember asking him what it was like to be shot. He answered in engrossing detail:

Well, I'll tell you what it was like. I didn't know I'd been shot. I heard a noise, and we came out of the hotel and headed for the limousine. And I heard some noise and I thought it was firecrackers.

And the next thing I knew, one of the Secret Service agents behind me just seized me here by the waist and plunged me headfirst into the limo. I landed on the seat and the seat divider was down, and then he dived in on top of me, which is part of their procedure to make sure that I'm covered.

*President Reagan appearing on CNN's* Larry King Live, *January 11, 1990.*

Well, as it turned out later, the shot that got me careened off the side of the limousine and hit me while I was diving into the car. It hit me back here, under the arm, and then hit a rib, and that's what caused an extreme pain, and then it tumbled—it turned and went tumbling down within an inch of my heart.

But when I got in the car, I hadn't felt anything. And he landed on top of me, and then the pain, which now I know came from the bullet hitting that rib—that terrific pain—and I said, "Jerry, get off, I think you've just broken a rib of mine." And he got off very quickly. And just then I coughed, and I had a handful of bright red frothy blood.

So I said that evidently the broken rib had pierced the lung. Well, he simply turned and said, "George Washington Hospital," and we were on our way.

I used up my handkerchief and then I used up his, but when I got to the emergency entrance I got out of the car and walked in, and a nurse met me, and I told her I was having a little trouble breathing, and what I thought it was. And the next thing I knew, my knees began to turn to rubber and I wound up on a gurney. And I was wearing a suit like this, the first time I'd ever worn it—it was brand-new—and they were taking scissors and cutting it off of me.

What a moment in history. It remains, for me, one of the most riveting and poignant experiences I've had behind the mike. There's no doubt that future historians will find this man, his Presidency and his global impact to be a highlight of this century.

LARRY KING
*CNN*

*D*URING MY YEARS as President of the United States, I had the honor of presenting American Cancer Society courage awards to some truly outstanding Americans, including Ann Jillian and Jill Ireland, whose courage and strength are inspiration to us all.

I have always been impressed and humbled by the American Cancer Society because of your numbers—2.5 million volunteers across the country, making you the largest volunteer health organization in the country—and because of your enthusiasm and positive spirit that breeds hope and gives strength to those who need it.

Over the years I've seen many examples of people helping people. But the American Cancer Society is one of the best examples of the selfless American spirit that sets us apart from all others.

Volunteerism is rooted in the world's religions and cultures, and just as those religions and cultures have found haven in America, so has the spirit of neighborly compassion that

Emerson envisioned when he wrote, "The only gift is a portion of thyself."

Throughout our history Americans have reached out in service to others, near and far, and thereby strengthened their communities, our country and the entire world. From the smallest act of kindness to the dedication of a lifetime, volunteers respond in times of joy and tragedy alike. From the smallest child to the most venerable senior citizen, more than half of all Americans give of their time and energy in private sector initiatives—for each other.

Volunteerism's essence is the willingness to share blessings and the courage to pursue an ideal. Volunteerism's currency is love, and volunteers measure their riches in terms of what they freely give their countrymen and the people of the world.

When I saw that there was nothing that the American Cancer Society couldn't do if they set out to accomplish something, I was envious. The United States government could not afford to pay for all the great work that the volunteers do. The government could never do it as efficiently, nor with as much humanity and devotion.

It was that great American spirit that got the American Cancer Society started over seventy-six years ago when a small group of people saw a problem—cancer—and got together to find a solution.

Back then most physicians and nearly all patients believed that cancer was an incurable disease. At a time when everyone feared cancer, those first volunteers talked about it and taught others. Because of their efforts, cancer no longer has the stigma it once had.

Through the years the American Cancer Society has earned a reputation as the most well-known and respected health organization in the country.

Your volunteers have worked hard and saved many lives. You teach smokers how to quit. You show people how to eat healthier. You help people learn how to protect themselves from cancer and how to practice early detection. You are the largest private supporter of cancer research in the country.

Volunteers have been behind the development of most of the society's effective service programs. I learned that some got started because a certain group of people identified a need. Sometimes it was one individual—a perfect example of people helping people in need.

Last year over 650,000 cancer patients were helped by American Cancer Society volunteers. Your services are the reason why cancer patients don't have to remain alone with their crushing fears. You help them to express their feelings and offer them comfort in knowing that dignity is always possible.

I heard about Charles Leeds, a local resident who has spent ten hours each week for eight years driving cancer patients to treatments and coordinating other drivers.

Then there was Kris Ehler, a teenager so young, so full of life and compassion for others, whose desperate search for a lifesaving bone-marrow donor united the community. The Lord blessed him with strength and courage to meet this difficult challenge. The response from the community to his plea for help was overwhelming. Countless people donated money and raised funds to cover the cost of blood testing for potential donors. But sadly, Kris left this earth, and today he is in a better place, safe in the arms of God.

It's during those rough times when a helping hand is extended and people show they care. That helps you get through the critical times, helps you cope.

There's a terrible fear that comes when you're told that you have cancer, a fear that is the same whether you are eight or eighty. But that fear was not the end for you but a challenge. And that's where that courage begins. You accept the challenge to fight cancer any way you can. And for many of you here today, your battle with cancer has become more than a personal battle. That is because you've all made conscious decisions to help others who have cancer. Many of you are active volunteers for the American Cancer Society. Some are officers in their units or divisions. Some have written books and worked on instructive videotapes. You've all used your experiences with cancer to help others come to terms with cancer in their lives.

Nancy and I faced that same decision ourselves. We made a conscious decision that it was important to go public with the fact that—in both her case and mine—good medical supervision, early detection and prompt treatment were the keys to victory over cancer. People need to know that cancer isn't something to run and hide from. Cancer is a fact that must be faced and dealt with.

Knowing that the American Cancer Society was there for us if we needed it was a great comfort and source of strength.

We've come a long way and made great progress. Today nearly half of the people diagnosed with cancer will survive. In fact, there are over 6 million Americans alive today who have a history of cancer.

We're halfway there, but as you know, the fight isn't over. I urge you to continue your fight with diligence, I salute you for all your efforts, and I join you because, in many senses, I too am an American Cancer Society volunteer. I believe in your cause, am committed to your mission of eliminating cancer and have been personally touched by the disease.

I'm happy to share with others the lifesaving messages of the American Cancer Society.

Thank you for inviting me here today and God bless you.

$\mathcal{R}$onald Reagan brought to the White House that sense of dignity without which true leadership is diminished. Along with it came a man of convictions. One knew what our President believed even when one disagreed. That perception tended to provide public confidence in the execution of his duties. His deep commitment to democracy, his rock-solid opposition to the Soviet system permitted him to negotiate even while he publicly spoke of the evil empire. And above all, President Reagan had great personal charm in his dealings with other human beings, whether in high or low estate. He greeted each one warmly with a smile and a handshake. That is charm. That is Ronald Reagan.

RICHARD HELMS

W<small>E ARE GATHERED</small> here today to receive part of history. And we do so not on behalf of any one Presidency or any one state, or even any one nation. We do so on behalf of the 191 brave people who lost their lives trying to escape this wall and on behalf of the millions of brave citizens who brought this wall down.

For more than twenty-eight years the Berlin Wall stood as an unnatural, ugly, unwelcome, but undeniable symbol of the oppression of communism. It stood as a grim reminder of what happens when dictators strip the people of their freedom. It stood as a testimony to the failure of totalitarianism. It stood in stark contrast to open societies where governments get their power from the consent of the governed. It divided families. It kept friends apart. It shattered dreams and crushed hopes. It made us angry.

And yet, it stood as a challenge. It seemed, for a time at least, to be impenetrable. It seemed to some that we had gotten used to life with the Berlin Wall. But had we really? Had we really given up hope that somehow—one day—it would come down? No, we hadn't.

The yearning for freedom that burned brightly in the hearts of the German people, and indeed freedom-loving people everywhere, was not dimmed. Even as the wall was built and family and friends hugged each other for what they feared might be the last time, we knew the wall would not—could not—stay up forever.

We knew it wouldn't be easy, and we knew it wouldn't be without a struggle, but we knew that one day the wall would come down. And come down it did. With tears and shouts of joy, the wall came tumbling down and I don't think there is anyone here or anywhere who will ever forget the pictures of the celebrations at the Brandenburg Gate. That night all freedom-loving people of the world were Berliners. Finally, after so much pain and suffering, freedom had come, as we always knew it would. Families and friends were reunited. A whole new world, once denied to the people of East Germany, was welcoming them with open arms. The people had won.

The wall came down because man's yearning for freedom can be satisfied in only one way—freedom. It came down because man has a right to worship as he wishes. He has a right to read the books he chooses. He has a right to pursue the career he desires. He has a right to be informed by a free press. He has a right to be safe and secure in his home. He has a right to reap the fruits of his labors—these rights cannot be kept from man by brick and mortar.

Life, liberty and the pursuit of happiness are man's inalienable rights and no one—no matter how many sharpshooters they have in watchtowers—can deny man these rights. And yet, sadly, we sometimes take these rights for granted. Imagine what life would be like if the government assigned you your job at the end of high school.

Imagine what life would be like if you could not observe Passover or Easter. Imagine what life would be like if you could read only one newspaper published by the government. Imagine what life would be like if you could never leave. This is what life was like for those on the other side of the wall.

Some have been surprised by the speed and drama of recent events in Eastern Europe and Nicaragua. But when you come to think of it, should we ever really be surprised when man chooses freedom?

Later this spring I plan to travel back to Berlin to hear firsthand the accounts of those whose heroism brought us to this happy moment today. It's been almost three years since I stood at the Brandenburg Gate and called for the wall to come down. It wasn't merely a polite suggestion. I was angry because as I looked over the wall into East Germany, I could see the people being kept away—their government didn't want them to hear what we were saying. But I think that they knew what we were saying and they wanted a better life. And it took a little time, but they organized and they struggled and they didn't give up. And now, here we are, in the greatest free country on earth, with a piece of that wall for all to see—and remember.

It is fitting that this symbol of man's continuing struggle for freedom rest here, in this beautiful expanse. Soon—as you can see—there will be a Presidential Library here. It will not be a monument to any one man or party. It will, instead, be a place where mothers and fathers can bring their children to learn about an important—indeed a pivotal—time in American and world history. The story that will be told here is the story of a determined movement dedicated to the greatness of America and faith in its bedrock traditions, in the essential goodness of its people, in the essential soundness of its institutions and yes, faith in our very essence as a nation.

Freedom is the very essence of our nation. To be sure, ours is not a perfect nation. But even with our troubles, we remain the beacon of hope for oppressed peoples everywhere—even people who lived behind walls.

We accept this piece of the Berlin Wall with

justifiable joy at recent events in Eastern Europe and with great hope for the future. And we accept it with somber remembrances of the past and the resolution that what happened must never happen again. Never again must families and friends be separated in this way. Never again must people be walled in against their will and denied their rights as human beings. Never again must fear rule.

Let our children and grandchildren come here and see this wall and reflect on what it meant to history. Let them understand that only vigilance and strength will deter tyranny. Let them join with us in a solemn pledge to never give up the fight for freedom—a fight which, though it may never end, is the most ennobling known to man.

Thank you and God bless you.

*R*onald Reagan is a man of great personal integrity. He has a warm, gentle manner that instantaneously makes him a charismatic figure to all with whom he comes in contact. His strong, unwavering adherence to principle is an unusual coupling with his disarming smile.

All of us felt that Ronald Reagan was a "man of destiny." Subsequent historical world events have proven that prophecy to be true. Despite his great achievements he has always remained essentially a humble man of the people and of the soil. He loved his ranch, his horses, chopping wood and building fences by hand.

*President Reagan greeting the Director of the United States Information Agency, Charles Wick, in the Oval Office, December 22, 1986.*

A born leader, he was recognized by his peers for his leadership qualities of vision, personal integrity, courage and decision making. His peers elected him for many terms as president of the Screen Actors Guild. Then came the two-term Governorship of California followed by eight years as President of the United States.

Reagan's instincts and decisions have been manifested in critical areas. When he was warned that we had only twenty-four hours to blunt the coming Soviet invasion of Grenada in this hemisphere, unhesitatingly he took immediate action. That country escaped the Soviet clutches.

Reagan had the courage to call the Soviet Union an evil empire. He was touched by history to destroy this scourge of mankind. At Reykjavík, he rejected Gorbachev's offer to cut by 50 percent their missile arsenal if Reagan would abandon the Strategic Defense Initiative ("Star Wars"). The summit came to an abrupt end. The calling of Gorbachev's bluff by Reagan was vindicated with the subsequent implosion of the "evil Soviet empire." Reagan knew that Gorbachev, with his deteriorating, fragile economy, could not afford to compete with the massive costs to match our Strategic Defense Initiative.

In the context of mutual goodwill, with a smile on his face, Reagan said to Gorbachev, *"Doveryai, no proveryai,"* which is "Trust, but verify."

People who disagreed with him on various issues felt that the most important characteristic in their voting for him was that they could trust him with their welfare and safety.

Probably Ronald Reagan's greatest asset in his chronology of achievements has been the inspirational support of the love of his life, his teammate, Nancy.

CHARLES Z. WICK

*Director of the United States Information Agency, 1981–1989*

*I*T IS A GENUINE pleasure for me to be once again in Miami with you, "Free Cubans"! As the winds of freedom sweep through the world, it is particularly fitting that we gather here today to celebrate freedom's expansion and to consider the state of freedom in Cuba.

It is especially in southern Florida where one can get a true sense of what could have been Cuba's future and what will be Cuba's future once it is free.

The economic vitality, entrepreneurial skills and love of freedom of the Cuban American community stand as a glowing example of your past, present and future.

You came to America fleeing the tragic Communist tyranny that betrayed your hopes for a democratic Cuba. You took full advantage of all the blessings and opportunities the United States can offer. You have contributed much in return and still have much to offer.

Yet, you have retained your marvelous culture, your commitment to family, God and es-pecially your homeland, Cuba. You have never forgotten Cuba and will not cease your efforts until Cuba is once again free!

The principled work of the Cuban American National Foundation to promote a free and democratic Cuba has distinguished the Cuban American community. This commitment to a democratic outcome in Cuba has led to important initiatives that were spearheaded by the talented men and women of the foundation with the overwhelming support of the Cuban American community.

When I came to the Presidency, with help and support from all of you, for which I remain grateful, the task at hand was enormous. Freedom had lost ground all over the world, and Cuba was a difficult problem.

But Cuban Americans had some ideas about what to do about Castro, and it was a pleasure for me, as President, to work closely with your leaders to develop these ideas. At the most fundamental level, these ideas addressed an area that U.S. policy had neglected for decades: the condition of the lives of the Cuban people.

By turning policy attention to the Cuban people, you have made an important contribution to U.S. policy for Cuba and helped the lives of those you never forgot, cannot forget, will not forget: the mothers, fathers, brothers, sisters, grandparents, families and the countrymen you left behind in Cuba.

By its skillful persuasion in Washington, the foundation was the most instrumental force behind the creation of Radio Martí. What a delightful experience it was for me and the officials of my administration to work with you and get it on the air. And I want to add a special word here about a truly great public servant, Charles Wick. Charlie served as director of the United States Information Agency during the eight years we were in Washington. He was, and still is, a dedicated, tireless believer that the communications revolution will be the greatest force for the advancement of human freedom the world has ever seen. But that was only the beginning. With imagination and determination, during the last years of my administration, your leaders worked to develop the concept of TV Martí. And today it is a reality.

This is an authentic breakthrough in U.S. information programs because it is television that holds such promise and potential: the power of pictures, the visual images of freedom that are sweeping the world.

TV Martí will provide uncensored visual images to the people of Cuba for the first time in thirty-one years. The oppressed people of Cuba can now hear and see the truth.

They will see Cuban Americans who have distinguished themselves and become important members of American society and culture. They will see your new Congresswoman, Ileana Ros-Lehtinen. They will see José Canseco hitting home runs; the queen of salsa, Celia Cruz, and Gloria Estefan, who so aptly combines her Cuban American heritage in her music; and they will see Cuban American movie stars like Andy Garcia.

They will see distinguished diplomats like José Sorzano and Otto Reich, who served so ably in my administration. They will see the important contributions Cuban Americans have made in all fields—medicine, law, business, art, music, academia and literature. And they will see you, and how you live in freedom and prosperity.

They will see the Berlin Wall coming down, the last speech of Romania's dictator, the Soviet citizens massing by the thousands in front of the Kremlin in support of broader democracy in the Soviet Union. They will see how the long struggle of Poland's Solidarity Movement led to their now leading the government of that country. And they will see free elections: in Nicaragua, Chile and Hungary.

In retrospect, the information policies for Cuba that were developed in the 1980s, and continue today with President Bush's strong support, showed enormous wisdom and foresight.

We hear continuous testimony from recently liberated peoples about how fundamentally important reliable information was in their struggle for freedom. And so we can understand why Fidel Castro is so hysterical in his denunciations of TV Martí. What is he afraid of? He is afraid of the truth.

Here with me on the dais is that great hero of the Cuban spirit, Armando Valladares. His life's work to bring international attention to Castro's gulag began as a political prisoner of conscience in that gulag.

His efforts to inform the world about the truth about Castro's tyranny were explosively pushed forward with the publication of his prison memoirs, *Against All Hope.* His description of the hell in Castro's prisons meant that the world could no longer ignore the horrors that Castro had been perpetrating for thirty-one years against the Cuban people.

It was my honor to appoint Armando Valladares to represent the United States as our ambassador before the United Nations Human Rights Commission. He has served brilliantly there, and this year the United Nations voted to scrutinize human rights violations in Cuba.

Joining with the Western nations in that vote were representatives of recently liberated peoples: Panama, Hungary, Poland, Czechoslovakia and Bulgaria. This is the truth that Castro fears.

I hope it won't be too much longer before the Soviet Union joins the Eastern Europeans in redefining its relationship with Cuba. Maintaining their economic umbilical cord to Castro, the world's most vehement critic of Soviet-style reforms, is anachronistic behavior in today's world.

Castro maintains himself in power because he uses force and violence against the Cuban people. Their only sin is the sin of all who resist the slavery and misery of life under communism.

We are just beginning to understand that life in these countries was even worse than we could have imagined in our most terrible nightmares. As witness after witness from these newly democratizing countries step forward, we have been learning of the depravity that characterized the lives of ordinary citizens.

It is interesting to reflect how much of the world has changed. Only a decade ago, when I became President, to be anti-Communist was considered in a very negative way. But today we can stand in solid solidarity with the most visible anti-Communist people on the face of the earth: the people of Nicaragua, Hungary, Poland, Czechoslovakia, Romania, East Germany, Bulgaria.

And it is only a matter of time before the Cuban people will join them as well.

In 1980, how was Castro perceived? Cuba was, incredibly, portrayed as an alternative model of development for the Third World. Castro was seen as a romantic, revolutionary leader who had created a socialist Caribbean paradise in Cuba.

In 1980, Fidel Castro went to Nicaragua to celebrate the triumph of the first anniversary of the Sandinista's stolen revolution. Returning to Cuba, he was unable to contain his euphoria, saying in a speech, *"Somos tres!"* We are now three—meaning that Cuba had been joined by Grenada and Nicaragua.

Today, Mr. Castro, *"tú eres uno,"* you are the only one left. Isolated, rejected, beleaguered, the anachronistic fossil Marxist lurches from one bad day to the next, alone, solo.

The nations and peoples of Latin America have totally rejected the so-called Cuban model, choosing instead the systems that produce freedom and prosperity: democracy and capitalism. And within the Communist world, Castro keeps company with those who refuse to submit to the will of their peoples.

For thirty-one years Fidel Castro has been responsible for staggering levels of human suffering. He has promoted subversion and terrorism in almost every country in Latin America. Thousands have suffered by his hand, the progress of freedom stunted by his intervention.

And inside Cuba an armed camp exists. Cuba is one of the most militarized countries on the face of the earth today, and her citizens live in fear and terror, not in a paradise at all. We all know what the true fruits of Castro's years in power are: economic deprivation, repression, militarization and spiritual weariness.

Today in Cuba there are shortages of flour for bread, eggs whose price have doubled. Soap, cooking oil and milk are scarce. Adequate housing is in short supply. And Cuban officials are saying, "We'll eat grass," if necessary, before anything in Cuba will change.

It is precisely in this pessimistic, gloomy, rigid Stalinist vision of the future where Fidel Castro's downfall is located.

For thirty-one years Castro has been telling the Cuban people that his version of how life should be lived will produce the good life for them all. But they have always known better.

Today he tells them that more sacrifice, more deprivation and more submission is required. But the Cuban people know better.

With TV Martí they will *see* another vision of the future, an alternative to what Castro is telling them. They will see the changes in today's world and understand that change is possible for them, too.

And they will understand how vulnerable and isolated Castro is, that he is a liability to them. They will understand better that Castro's refusal to change is the biggest obstacle to improvements in their lives. And they will seek change.

The call for free elections in Cuba is growing with an irresistible momentum. From Caracas, Brazil, Costa Rica, Chile, Poland, Mexico and America, the call grows for Castro to submit himself and his rule to the only process that can provide legitimacy for those who seek to lead: free and fair democratic elections.

We read so frequently of the myths Castro propagates around the world as he scrambles to react to change. We read that Cuba is different than all the other countries on the face of the earth that were Communist.

Why? Because, they say, Castro is charismatic. Or that Castro came to power on the back of a popular revolution, and was not installed in power by Soviet tanks as in Eastern Europe. And that makes Cuba different, they say.

Well, after thirty-one years it ought to be put to the test. Fidel Castro should submit himself to the only test that will prove whether or not any of this is true: free, democratic elections. Don't the Cuban people have the right to finally have their voices heard?

The elections in Nicaragua are a case in point. Most of the world was amazed that Violeta Chamorro and her coalition, UNO, carried the day in Nicaragua. All the polls showed that Daniel Ortega of the Sandinista Front would win.

But in police states, people do not speak freely or openly about their hopes, wishes and desires for the future. In the sanctity of the secret polling booth, however, the voice of freedom triumphs.

The struggle for freedom in Nicaragua occupied a good deal of time and attention during my years as President. It is a tribute to the brave, committed patriots of the Nicaraguan democratic resistance that the conditions which would permit free and democratic elections to be held in that country were finally produced.

The Nicaraguan people can now begin to reconstruct their lives and their country with dignity and commitment. And Daniel Ortega can now join the ranks of other discredited leaders.

As the popular Miami bumper sticker says: "FIRST MANUEL, THEN DANIEL, NOW FIDEL!"

Don't the people of Cuba deserve the right to express themselves about whether or not Cuba should continue its involvement in the international affairs of countries like El Sal-vador and Guatemala? Don't the people of Cuba deserve the right to express themselves about the transfer of economic resources to military purposes?

Don't the people of Cuba have the right to express themselves about their right to worship? Their right to a free press? Their right to gather in peaceful assembly? To study what they want? To work where they want? To travel where they want? To live in peace? To live in freedom?

They do, and they will have that right, just as all the people in the world have those rights.

"There is no medicine, no spoons, no eggs, candy, buses, taxis, money, work, clothes, shoes, flour for bread, telephones, there is noth-ing," writes the Cuban teenager to her Cuban American uncle. "Now I will tell you what exists in abundance in this first socialist country in the Americas. There is," she lists, "hunger, need, fear, much unemployment, red tape, desire to leave the island, desire to get rid of this government, desire for so many things. . . ."

The poignant narrative of this young Cuban girl speaks volumes about the truth, the truth Castro fears.

Test yourself in a vote, Mr. Castro. Let the voices of the Cuban people be heard.

Because what is really happening in today's world is that the relationship between those who seek to rule and citizens is being based on the consent of the governed—that old and sacred principle of freedom. The word "revolution" is back in the West, where it always belonged.

Revolution means democracy in today's world, not the enslavement of peoples to the corrupt and degrading horrors of totalitarianism.

So we gather here today to celebrate the triumph of Western ideals and values. And to express our prayers and hopes for the day that the *real* revolution, the democratic revolution, comes to Cuba.

And that day will be soon. Together, we will continue our work to expand the frontiers of freedom in Cuba. And you will have an important contribution to make to a democratic Cuba.

Because when it is all said and done, it is clear that freedom is a condition of the spirit. And the spirits of Cubans, whether in Miami or Havana, are strong. The state of freedom in the hearts and spirits of Cubans is strong and vigorous.

I look forward to the day that this gathering can be held in a free Cuba and I know that day will come, and soon.

Thank you and God bless you.

*T*he Cold War was a unique experience in American history. Although we never directly fought our antagonist, the Soviet Union, we were faced for the first time in our history with an antagonistic opponent who was both ideologically committed to the overthrow of our system and physically equipped to destroy us.

*President and Mrs. Reagan with Jim Billington aboard Air Force One, May 29, 1988.*

President Ronald Reagan was the single most important political figure in the world in ending the Cold War without either major loss of human life or serious concessions. It was an astonishing accomplishment, and the essential ingredients were so disarmingly simple that they are often still overlooked by convoluted academic and journalistic commentators. As someone who has studied Russia and was among those accompanying President and Mrs. Reagan to the Moscow summit in May/June 1988, I had the privilege of observing some of the special magic involved in his strategy.

The first part of the strategy was to make it absolutely clear at the beginning of his administration that tokenism in arms reduction and photo-op summit solutions to serious substantive problems would no longer do. By pressing ahead, despite an intimidating chorus of negative criticism, with significant military restrengthening, by introducing the wild card of strategic defense, by going beyond normal diplomatic language at times and by proving that an American President could be re-elected without having had a summit meeting, President Reagan raised the ante to a level that the strained Soviet system could not meet. At the same time his support of human rights encouraged the forces of moral reconstruction which were challenging from within the legitimacy of the Soviet kind of rule.

The second part of his strategy, which has not perhaps been appreciated as much as the first, was his ability to be an altogether gracious winner. He eased the transition away from communism in a way that did not humiliate but, in fact, honored an opponent who was moving things in the right direction. More dramatic even than the friendly relationship he developed with Gorbachev was his instinctive reaching out, particularly during his own visit to Russia, to the Russian people. He presented the values of freedom and democracy not just as American exports but with universal appeal that could draw on the deep religious and cultural traditions of Russia just as they drew on such traditions in America.

In the deadly world of high diplomacy, trying to diffuse the potentially most dangerous conflict in history, President Reagan brought into play both inner serenity and an outgoing ability to spread contagious pleasure through a shared story.

JAMES H. BILLINGTON
*Librarian of Congress*

*I* AM GRATEFUL to the International Medical Corps for presenting me with the first Ambassadors' Humanitarian Award. For me, it holds great significance, representing our country's ideals of human freedom and service to humanity.

The world owes a debt to the brave Afghan freedom fighters who resisted the ten-year Soviet occupation of their land. The withdrawal of Soviet troops in February 1989 was an example of how a courageous people could defeat oppression. The peoples of Eastern Europe took courage from this example. The new-found freedoms of Eastern Europe may not have happened if the Afghans had not successfully defied the Soviet troops.

We also owe a great debt to the men and women of the International Medical Corps who, since 1984, have been sharing their medical skills with the Afghan victims of Soviet aggression. Under the leadership of Dr. Robert Simon, the IMC Afghan Project represents assistance of the highest order: the kind that helps people help themselves.

The Soviet invasion of Afghanistan in 1979 brought about the total destruction of the health-care system. During the early years of the war most clinics and hospitals were destroyed. Many doctors were executed, imprisoned or driven into exile. Without foreign medical aid, Afghanistan would have had no effective medical care.

The International Medical Corps, a group of American volunteer doctors and nurses, responded to the destruction of the Afghan health system by providing medical assistance inside Afghanistan's most devastated regions.

Dr. Simon was the first American physician to enter Afghanistan after the country was invaded by the Soviet Union. He established a hidden medical station in one of the country's most remote areas. Today the International Medical Corps has fifty clinics and hospitals inside Afghanistan where more than 50,000 patients, civilian victims of the long war, are treated each month.

Realizing that the most effective health-care system would be one run by the Afghans, the International Medical Corps opened a clinic on the Pakistan border to train Afghans in the basics of public health, medicine and surgery. These Afghan medics then return to their war-torn country to work in one of the IMC medical-surgical units.

The IMC training program is one of the highest regarded of its kind. It has brought about the existence of scores of trained Afghan medics who know the country, its people and its language, and are able to bring their skills to bear throughout the ravaged nation.

Countless lives have been saved, the lives of mujahideen, of civilians and perhaps most important, of children.

But the medical tragedy in Afghanistan is one of immense proportions. The continuing fighting, the millions of hidden land mines that blow off limbs and mutilate, the spread of infectious diseases, all of these make the work of the International Medical Corps more important than ever.

The tragedy is not over. The brave people of Afghanistan, and the 6 million Afghan refugees who are waiting to go home again, need our help in rebuilding their health-care system.

The men and women of the International Medical Corps, the volunteer doctors and nurses who willingly share their knowledge and give of their valuable time, many of whom are present here tonight, have strengthened my conviction that working side by side with shared hopes and goals, we can fulfill our country's aspiration of promising freedom and help for the Afghan people.

By their actions, the men and women of the International Medical Corps have spread a message of goodwill and cooperation throughout the world that serves as an inspiration to all Americans.

The men, women and children of Afghanistan are still dying. There are still too few doctors left in the country to cope with the medical emergency facing this proud people. I hope the proceeds from this event will provide the much desperately needed medical assistance and other humanitarian aid to the civilian victims of Afghanistan. And I sincerely hope that we will not forget the Afghan people. They never gave up. Let us not give up on them.

Nancy joins me this evening in expressing our heartfelt appreciation for this humanitarian award. The world truly needs more organizations like the International Medical Corps.

Thank you and God bless you.

*D*uring a thirty-year decline in the public's trust of government, polls have measured a marked increase in trust only during the Presidency of the man who thirty years ago denounced the overbearing nature of the far distant capital.

The most cheerful of Presidents was the product of the first and most consequential protest movement of the decade of protests: the conservative insurgency in the Republican Party. The oldest President ever elected, Reagan had a sure sense of modernity.

A political actor, Reagan did not deal in unreality. Rather, he created realities that mattered—perceptions, emotions, affiliations. Reagan was diligent about making vivid the values that produce cohesion and dynamism in a continental nation. That is a central task to the problem of governance.

Reagan understood the economy of leadership—the husbanding of the perishable hold any President has on the attention of this complacent, inattentive nation. He knew the importance of happiness in a nation where the pursuit of it was affirmed at the instant independence was arrested. Reagan's greatest gift to his country has been his soaring sense of possibilities.

*President Reagan and George Will in the Oval Office, January 22, 1981. (Newsweek— Larry Downing. © 1981 Newsweek Inc. All rights reserved. Reprinted with permission)*

GEORGE F. WILL
*Syndicated Columnist*

*I* KNOW I HAVE to tell you that even though I had two terms as President, I was not able to accomplish everything that I had hoped for. Some things I got done—some things I didn't. And I thought I'd talk to you today about one of the things I'd still like to get done.

One of the things that I'm out on the mashed potato circuit talking about is an abuse of power that distorts the democratic process, one that is pure dynamite because it deals with political greed. It's called gerrymandering—the practice of rigging boundaries of Congressional districts. This is the greatest single blot on the integrity of our nation's electoral system, and it is a travesty of democracy.

State legislatures must redraw the lines of Congressional districts to reflect population shifts. Fair enough. Unfortunately, many times the new districts aren't drawn in a politically neutral way; they don't resemble anything that's honest or natural.

In communities throughout California, neighbors living across the street from each other are in different Congressional districts for no rhyme or reason except the interest of that legislator to stay in office.

They combined part of Fresno, in our Central Valley, with Carmel on the coast. They ran a corridor to put the minority citizens of Pasadena in the same district with Bakersfield. They cut up Irvine and combined it with Newport Beach and connected them with the Mexican border at Calexico.

For years gerrymandering was used to prevent the election of black Congressmen. Now it's used by both the Democratic and Republican state parties to guarantee a continued edge where one or the other is in power.

In the 1988 Congressional elections 98 percent of all incumbents seeking re-election won. The House of Representatives has become virtually a permanent chamber with less turnover than the Supreme Soviet. Only one of California's forty-five districts has changed parties since the last gerrymander here in 1982.

I don't think any Congressional district should be safe because of the way it's drawn. It should be safe because the Congressman represents the interests of the people.

Our system of redistricting needs what the Soviets call perestroika, or "restructuring." It's a conflict of interest now for the state legislatures to feather their own political nests.

I believe states should set up a bipartisan blue-ribbon reapportionment citizen commission to draw district lines. Some states already have these. I believe all states should.

For the last year and a half, a remarkable group of citizens have been working to devise just such a commission. This group, started by San Mateo County supervisor Tom Huening, has worked with the League of Women Voters of California; the late great tax crusader Paul Gann; A. Alan Post, who was the legislative independent analyst when I was Governor, and literally a score of other interested people to put on the ballot just such an independent bipartisan redistricting commission. Over 970,000 Californians have already signed this initiative, called Proposition 119.

This independent commission will be composed of five Republicans, five Democrats and two Independents—no politicians—truly a citizens' commission.

With just over three weeks until election day, Proposition 119 is ahead in the polls—but we all know polls change very quickly.

Speaker Willie Brown has vowed to spend millions of dollars to defeat Proposition 119.

Seven years ago Speaker Brown ran the most shameless campaign against Governor Deukmejian's efforts to end gerrymandering. I believe we lost that election because we did not have the money to respond to the commercials paid for by Speaker Brown.

The Yes on Proposition 119 Committee must have the funds to counter another set of deceitful ads. This year we must not let that happen. By turning out today, you have shown your commitment on this vital issue.

Now I ask you to go one step further. Talk to friends, neighbors and business associates. Encourage them to join you in contributing financially to Proposition 119. Explain to them how it will end the division of cities and counties; how districts will be competitive so that the most qualified man or woman wins, not just because of potential party deals. And you can tell them that the future of our American dream depends on ending gerrymandering and restoring fair elections to all Americans.

So I'm putting the state legislatures on notice to keep it fair, or they may find the Gipper on the steps of their state capitols calling attention to their shenanigans.

Thank you and God bless you.

$\mathcal{R}$onald Reagan was one of those rare political figures who consistently defied the stereotypes placed on him by others without ever changing his principles or outlook.

Although he was called an extremist by his critics to the very day he entered the White House, his personality rebutted this assertion. He was stubborn in his basic beliefs, but always willing to listen to contrary points of view. He was as gracious in victory as in defeat, and he instinctively grasped large historical developments, not least of which was the inner collapse of the Soviet empire.

Most of all, Ronald Reagan was a politician who never fit the image of the profession. He came to politics relatively late in life and succeeded immediately because of the power of his voice and the strength of his ideas. Although he received a level of adulation from his supporters unmatched in recent political history, he never believed his own press clippings or lost his ability to laugh at himself whenever the occasion arose.

During my tenure in the U.S. Senate, I agreed with Ronald Reagan on some key issues and disagreed on others. But I always held him, and do today, in the highest regard as a man who exemplifies three of our proudest national traits: decency, courage and conviction.

*President Reagan sharing an anecdote with Senator Sam Nunn in the White House, November 20, 1987.*

SAM NUNN
*Democratic Senator from Georgia, 1972–1997*

As you know, I have always been a strong supporter of the democratic form of government—one which is elected by the people, for the people. I understand you all know of my history as a critic of communism. I am, therefore, thrilled that you now have the opportunity to exercise your democratic right to vote for the individuals who will represent you in your next government.

This is a momentous time for you, and I want you to know that the free world supports the steps you have taken toward a truly democratic government. We all care about Bulgaria and the future which is facing you. Many countries will have international observers in Bulgaria, watching the process on election day and ensuring that the process guarantees a secret ballot, and reporting to the rest of the world about this historic event. The international press will be there to cover this exciting time in history.

I urge each of you to take this opportunity to stand up for the democratic values you hold. It is a cherished right, which some who have always had it take for granted. But you who have not been able to vote a secret ballot for years, and many of you who are younger and who have never known the excitement of the democratic process, now is your time.

We in the United States are very excited about the opportunity you have and want you to know that you are not alone. The winds of change have swept through Europe, Central America and Asia. Nicaragua, East Germany and Hungary have in the last months elected a democratic government. Just this weekend the Burmese people elected a new government even though the leaders of the democratic movement have been imprisoned and held in house arrest. History is with you as you take this giant step.

I wish you well on June 10th. I am sorry that I cannot tell you in person how excited I am that Bulgaria is shortly going to experience such an unprecedented event. My congratulations to the Bulgarian people for your hard work and dedication to democracy, and I hope that on June 10th you will each cast a secret ballot for the candidate of your choice and start on the road to a completely democratic society.

"History is a ribbon always unfurling," Ronald Reagan told us in his second inaugural address; "history is a journey. And as we continue on our journey, we think of those who traveled before us . . . and we see and hear again the echoes of our past." Those words came back to me with special force on a brilliant California afternoon in November 1991. On that day I had the privilege of joining President and Mrs. Reagan, along with Presidents Nixon, Carter and Bush, in dedicating the nation's newest Presidential Library and Museum.

The view from the Reagan Library, spectacular as it is, can hardly compare to the life and legacy celebrated inside the building. There visitors are themselves taken on an extraordinary journey—from a world bristling with nuclear weapons to one in which the Cold War is relegated to the history books. The same journey shows the reversal of centralized power in Washington that has marked much of this century, and a corresponding new trend to return dollars and decisions to grassroots Americans.

Ronald Reagan's journey began in Tampico, Illinois, at the dawn of the American century. Its effects will be felt long after his contemporaries have passed from the scene. But on that brilliant autumn afternoon atop a California mountain, my thoughts were less directed at posterity than at the very special person who was America's fortieth President.

Ronald Reagan has always had a genius for bringing people together, and that day was no exception. As I looked around me, I realized that each of the Presidents who had come to pay our friend tribute had, at one time or another, run against him for the nation's highest office. Something else struck me as well—that we were honoring a prophet as much as a President. For long before he entered the White House, Ronald Reagan had anticipated history's journey in ways both unconventional and uncompromising.

In the great defining struggle of the twentieth century, he well understood both the moral and economic bankruptcy of the Communist state. In an age of relativism, he held absolute beliefs of good and evil. Understanding human liberty to be a gift from

*President and Mrs. Reagan and President and Mrs. Ford in the Oval Office, March 3, 1981.*

God, not government, he never hesitated to stand up and speak out against those who would put the soul itself in bondage. Like a modern-day Joshua, he blew his trumpet and the walls that once divided humanity were leveled.

And so his fellow members of the Presidential trade union assembled in Simi Valley to salute the vision as well as the visionary.

In Ron Reagan we recognized qualities of strength and character and faith that were—and are—every bit as awe-inspiring as the rugged mountains or the crystal-blue Pacific as seen from the library terrace. Every President makes headlines. It goes with the job. But only a few make history of the kind that affects who we are and how we see ourselves. Ronald Reagan was such a leader. In reviving American confidence, he restored our faith in the Presidency itself.

The enormity of his achievements at home and aboard becomes more apparent with every passing year. And as our recognition of this grows, so does our gratitude. I count it a privilege to have shared, even a little, in Ronald Reagan's American journey.

GERALD R. FORD
*Thirty-eighth President of the United States, 1974–1977*

Y OU KNOW, before I ever lived in California, I grew up in a small town in Illinois. Before I ever stepped in front of a movie camera or a lineup of reporters, I worked at a radio station in Des Moines, Iowa. And I learned long ago that in order to find the *heart* of America you need only visit the *heartland* of America.

I have a hunch that's what Ike had in mind when he said, "The proudest thing I can claim is that I am from Abilene." Abilene for him was not just a place on the map, however hallowed in memory. Ike's Abilene was a state of mind and a set of values first learned in this simple white frame house. Here David and Ida Eisenhower raised six boys. They took root in the rich black earth of Dickinson County; they grew to embody the American dream.

When he returned after the war to lay the cornerstone of a museum bearing his family's name, Eisenhower remembered Abilene as a leveling ground where bank accounts counted for little and bloodlines for even less.

"I have found out in later years we were very poor," he said, "but the glory of America is that we didn't know it then. All that we knew was that our parents—of great courage—could say to us: Opportunity is all about you. Reach out and take it."

Here on Southeast Fourth Street, Ike and his brothers learned to believe in hard work and high standards, in strong families and close-knit communities. His neighbors were never ashamed to kneel in prayer to their Maker. Nor were they ever embarrassed to feel a lump in the throat when Old Glory passed by. No one in Abilene ever burned a flag. No one in Abilene would tolerate it.

For Dwight Eisenhower, this house was both classroom and launching pad. There is a story that when he was ten years old and denied the right to accompany two older brothers in Halloween mischief, Ike pounded his fists bloody against an old apple tree in the backyard. His father, a traditionalist in such matters, took a hickory switch to the boy and sent him straight to his room.

After a while the door opened to reveal Ike's mother. She sat in a rocking chair for a long time, saying nothing. Then she began to paraphrase the Bible, talking of the need to master one's temper. "He that conquereth his own soul is greater than he who taketh the city," she said.

As a great soldier Ida Eisenhower's son would take many cities. As a great statesman he would take bold steps toward a freer, more peaceful world. As a great patriot he took pains to remind the American people that they were more than the sum of their possessions.

"The things that make us proud to be Americans are . . . not the jewels we wear, or the furs we buy, the houses we live in, the standard of living, even, that we have," he once said. "All of these things are wonderful to the aesthetic and to the physical senses. But let us never forget that the deep things that are American are of the soul and the spirit."

How did Ike come by such a philosophy? Look around you. Look to the endless wheat fields that stretch a man's vision even as they open his mind. Look to your own state's motto: "To the stars through difficulties." In this house Ida Eisenhower taught her sons to look up at the stars.

From here Ike went on to West Point. Through difficulties that would have overwhelmed lesser men, he forged the greatest fighting machine in all history. He hurled it with devastating effect against the heavily fortified beaches of fortress Europe. And when the guns at last fell silent in the spring of 1945, the man from Abilene had rescued civilization itself from a long starless night of the soul.

In common with millions of his countrymen, Dwight Eisenhower fought not for territory but for justice, not for plunder but for righteousness. He fought for America's faith in the extraordinary qualities that lie within seemingly ordinary people. He fought to extend to other people in other lands the freedom that every American takes for his birthright.

But with freedom goes responsibility. And so Ike warned against the perils of complacency and self-indulgence. "A people that values its privileges above its principles soon loses both," he declared. You don't have to remind the newly freed people of Eastern Europe of that. They know how hard it is to live without them. The same can be said on any street corner in Managua, any hut in the jungles of Panama, any church newly opened to the faithful in Moscow.

Whenever the winds of change enable men and women to throw off the shackles of oppression and reject those who would put the soul itself into bondage, there you will find millions who still like Ike. Lest we forget: Those winds were first born on the Kansas prairie. They swept across the desert of North Africa in an operation called Torch. They propelled the historic armada of June 1944 that liberated Europe. They gave rise to NATO and they ended the war in Korea.

After inauguration day 1953 they brushed the cobwebs out of Washington, D.C. They inspired Atoms for Peace and People to People. They broke down resistance when nine black children sought admission to Central High School in Little Rock, Arkansas. And they launched America into space.

Thirty years before the Berlin Wall crumbled, Ike told his countrymen that they were part of an irreversible tide in human affairs. "Take courage," he said, "from the sure knowledge that the current of history flows toward freedom . . . in the long run, dictators and despotism must give way."

President Eisenhower did not live to see such changes. But he knew they were coming, for he had set them in motion. He understood that man can no sooner be deprived of freedom than of the very air he breathes. All this and more—his legacy to us—was Abilene's legacy to him.

Ike's greatest work may have been done on distant battlefields and in the marble hallways of official Washington. But his greatest debt was to Abilene. That is why he chose this site for a library to house the records of his life and a museum to educate future generations about the price of freedom. And that is why he chose to make his final homecoming in an $80 regu-

lation Army casket, to lie in a plain stone chapel on the edge of the Kansas prairie.

I have just come from the place of meditation, where Ike and his beloved Mamie keep watch over the infant son whose loss was, in President Eisenhower's own words, "the greatest disaster of my life." In that simple setting, as unpretentious as Ike himself, they are a family once more. Neither time nor distance nor the judgment of history can ever separate them, or diminish the loving bond that unites husband and wife, parent and child.

Standing there, reading the prayer he composed on the morning of his inauguration and reflecting on the lifetime of service that really began in this house, I found myself recalling the words spoken by Ike on the last day of his life. "I have always loved my wife," he said. "I have always loved my children. I have always loved my grandchildren. And I have always loved my country."

Today, a generation after he left us, Ike's love is returned by countless admirers the world over. Yet for him to be truly at peace, we must make this world a more peaceful place. We must run the course that leads to freedom and opportunity in every corner of the globe. We must be prepared to overcome difficulties. And we must never lose sight of the stars.

Thank you very much and God bless you.

*I*t is indeed a pleasure to add my few words of praise to the encomium that is due Ronald Reagan from the hearts of the American people. During his Presidency the country found its soul again and began to believe in itself, and its divine heritage, because he did.

From his hospital bed, following the assassination attempt, when his own life hung in the balance, he thought to pardon two FBI agents who had been venomously targeted for persecution.

For all his great accomplishments—the restoration of the nation's military power and pride, the concomitant collapse of the Soviet Union and a decade of unprecedented prosperity at home—he remained always a simple man of simple virtues, whose equal has not been seen since Lincoln.

EFREM ZIMBALIST, JR.

*Actor*

*J*EAN, MEMBERS OF the Smith family and friends:

For more than two decades Nancy's and my life was enriched—yes, blessed—by the friendship of William French Smith.

Today we gather to mourn the loss of this very special man. But as much, we gather to honor the memory of someone who we are all better for knowing.

It was the mid-sixties when I first met Bill. I was immediately impressed by his intelligence, his grace and his wisdom. When he spoke, he made sense, and when he spoke, I listened. He had a gift for clear, reasoned thinking and I came to rely on his advice more and more. I always knew I could count on Bill for wise counsel and he never let me down.

And he never let his country down. Even though it meant leaving family and friends behind, Bill and Jean Smith came to Washington in 1981 so that he could serve as our nation's attorney general. As you've been told, he was a magnificent head of the Justice Department. Always honest, always fair, always careful and always motivated by an abiding desire to do what was right, Bill Smith served his country with the greatest dedication and distinction. And from a personal standpoint, I must tell you it was a source of the greatest comfort for me to have a friend from home at the cabinet table.

And what a friend Bill was. Generous, warm, kind and loyal, Bill was the best you could ever hope to find. I am filled with so many fond memories today of our happy times together. How I will miss those in the days ahead.

Bill's loyalty was evident until the very moment he left us. You see, at my request he served as chairman of the Board of Trustees of the Ronald Reagan Presidential Foundation. And when that library opens next year, I will think of Bill and be grateful to God for making Bill part of my life.

It is difficult to think of Bill being gone. But rather than be consumed by sadness today, Nancy and I are comforted by knowing that our dear friend Bill is in a better place. He has gone through the door that God promised us, where there is no pain or sorrow and where one day we shall all be together again.

God bless you, William French Smith. Rest in peace, old friend.

FROM THE REMARKS OF WINSTON S. CHURCHILL, MP,
*at the opening of an exhibition of his grandfather's paintings at the
Ronald Reagan Presidential Library.*

$\mathcal{M}$r. President,

You have made reference to Sir Winston Churchill's Iron Curtain speech at Fulton, Missouri, in 1946, but more than any other single person, it was *you* who brought about the collapse of the Iron Curtain and the demise of the "evil empire."

Historians will ponder the intriguing fact that in 1979 electorates on both sides of the Atlantic simultaneously smelled a rat. They sensed that if things were allowed to drift on through the 1980s as they had so disastrously in the 1970s, with the West in full retreat in the face of Soviet expansionism in Africa, Asia and Latin America, the free world would be heading for catastrophe.

Accordingly, the U.S. and British electorates placed you and Margaret Thatcher in office—and what a formidable partnership you forged! You inspired NATO with a new resolve. You strengthened the defenses of the West. You made clear that the bugle would no more sound "retreat!"

When you unveiled your Strategic Defense Initiative, it was mockingly dubbed "Star Wars" and dismissed by all too many in both our countries as pure Hollywood hype. Fortunately, there were a few people who believed it would work.

I believe that when the history of this cataclysmic period comes to be written, it will be seen that it was SDI—more than any other factor—that broke the Soviet camel's back by convincing the incumbents of the Kremlin that they could no longer afford to compete militarily with the United States, as their economy could no longer bear the burden.

All mankind owes you a debt of gratitude for bringing the Cold War to an end, for putting the arms race in reverse and for promoting reconciliation between East and West, so that today we all live in a safer world.

WINSTON S. CHURCHILL III
*Member of Parliament*

*President Reagan and Winston Churchill III at the unveiling of a portrait of Winston Churchill at the Ronald Reagan Presidential Library, December 18, 1992.*

CAN HARDLY visit this magnificent setting, so rich in memory and symbolism, without recalling the comment Sir Winston Churchill made when he was congratulated on the size of an audience gathered to hear him speak. Any other politician would have been flattered. Not Churchill. It was no great achievement to draw a crowd, he said. Twice as many would have turned out for a public hanging.

Maybe so, but I am deeply grateful to each of you for your warm welcome. What an honor it is for me to come to Fulton, indelibly stamped with the name and eloquence of Churchill. What a privilege to be on hand to help dedicate Edwina Sandys's sculpture celebrating the triumph of her grandfather's principles. And what a source of pride to receive an honorary degree from this distinguished college, whose illustrious past is equaled only by its future promise.

Today we rejoice in the demise of the Berlin Wall that was permanently breached just one year ago.

We remember brave men and women on both sides of the Iron Curtain who devoted their lives—and sometimes sacrificed them—so that we might inhabit a world without barriers. And we recall with the intensity born of shared struggles the greatest Briton of them all, a child of parliamentary democracy who boasted of an American mother and who therefore claimed to be an English-speaking union all by himself.

Who standing here beside this magnificent twelfth-century church that commemorated Sir Winston's 1946 visit can ever forget the indomitable figure with the bullfrog expression and the upthrust V for victory?

As the greatest communicator of our time, Sir Winston enlisted the English language itself in the battle against Hitler and his hateful doctrines. When the Nazi might prevailed from Warsaw to the Channel Islands and from

Egypt to the Arctic Ocean, at a time when the whole cause of human liberty stood trembling and imperiled, he breathed defiance in phrases that will ring down through centuries to come.

And when guns at last fell silent in the spring of 1945, no man on earth had done more to preserve civilization during the hour of its greatest trial.

Near the end of World War II but before the election that everyone knew must follow V-E Day, *The Times* of London prepared an editorial suggesting that Prime Minister Churchill run as a nonpartisan figure, above the fray of parliamentary politics, and that he gracefully retire soon after to rest on his laurels and bask in the glow of yesterday's triumph.

The editor informed Sir Winston of both points he intended to make. Churchill had a ready reply. As for the first suggestion, "Mr. Editor," he said, "I fight for my corner." And as for the second, "Mr. Editor, I leave when the pub closes."

For a while in the summer of 1945 it looked as if perhaps the pub *had* closed.

We all know that democracy can be a fickle employer. But that does little to ease the pain. It's hard to be philosophical on the day after an election slips through your fingers. Clementine Churchill, trying to think of anything to say that might console her husband, looked at the returns and concluded that it might well be a blessing in disguise.

The Old Lion turned to his wife and said, "At the moment it seems quite effectively disguised."

"I have no regrets," Churchill told visitors

in the aftermath of his defeat. "I leave my name to history." But Winston Churchill rarely did the easy thing.

He could not rest so long as tyranny threatened any part of the globe. So when Harry Truman invited him to speak at Westminster College in the spring of 1946, Churchill leapt at the chance. He hoped that by traveling to the heartland of America he might reach the heart of America. He would do so in an address whose timeless eloquence would be matched by its indisputable logic. Churchill addressed a nation at the pinnacle of world power, but a nation unaccustomed to wielding such authority and historically reluctant to intrude in the affairs of Europe.

In the exhausted aftermath of World War II, few were prepared to listen to warnings of fresh danger. But Churchill was undaunted. Once before his had been a voice crying out in the wilderness against the suicidal dogmas of appeasement. Once before he had sounded an alarm against those deluded souls who thought they could go on feeding the crocodile with bits and pieces of other countries and somehow avoid his jaws themselves. His warnings had been ignored by a world more in love with temporary ease than long-term security. Yet time had proven him tragically correct.

His Fulton speech was a fireball in the night, a Paul Revere warning that tyranny was once more on the march.

"From Stettin in the Baltic to Trieste in the Adriatic, an iron curtain has descended across the Continent," he said.

Churchill titled his speech "The Sinews of

Peace." But the reaction it provoked was anything but peaceful. Newspaper editors on both sides of the Atlantic rushed to brand its author a warmonger. Labour MPs asked Prime Minister Attlee to formally repudiate his predecessor's remarks. From Moscow came a blast of rhetoric labeling Stalin's former wartime ally "false and hypocritical" and claiming that having lost an election in his homeland he had decided to try his luck in the United States. Harry Truman knew better. The people of Missouri were highly pleased by Churchill's visit, and had enjoyed what their distinguished visitor had to say.

And for those trapped behind the Iron Curtain, spied on and lied to by their corrupt governments, denied their freedoms, their bread, even their faith in a power greater than that of the state—for them Churchill was no warmonger and the Western alliance no enemy. For the victims of Communist oppression, the Iron Curtain was made all too real in a concrete wall surrounded by barbed wire and attack dogs and guards with orders to shoot on sight anyone trying to escape the so-called workers' paradise of East Germany.

Today we come full circle from those anxious times. Ours is a more peaceful planet because of men like Churchill and Truman and countless others who shared their dream of a world where no one wields a sword and no one drags a chain. This is their monument. Here, on a grassy slope between the Church of St. Mary the Virgin and Champ Auditorium, a man and woman break through the wall and symbolically demolish whatever remaining barriers stand in the way of international peace and the brotherhood of nations.

Out of one man's speech was born a new Western resolve—not warlike, not bellicose, not expansionist, but firm and principled in resisting those who would devour territory and put the soul itself into bondage. The road to a free Europe that began there in Fulton led to the Truman Doctrine and the Marshall Plan, to NATO and the Berlin airlift, through nine American Presidencies and more than four decades of military preparedness.

By the time I came to the White House, a new challenge had arisen. Moscow had decided to deploy intermediate-range nuclear missiles like the SS-20 that would threaten every city in Western Europe. It never launched those missiles, but fired plenty of trial balloons into the air, and it rained propaganda on the United States and the Federal Republic of Germany in an effort to prevent the modernization of NATO's forces on West German soil.

But the government in Bonn was not deterred. Neither was the rest of Western Europe deceived. At the same time we in the United States announced our own intention to develop SDI, the Strategic Defense Initiative, to hasten the day when the nuclear nightmare was ended forever and our children's dreams were no longer marred by the specter of instant annihilation.

Of course, not everyone agreed with such a course. For years, it had been suggested by some opinion makers that all would be well in the world if only the United States lowered its profile. Some of them would not only have us lower our profile—they would also lower our flag. I disagreed. I thought that the 1980s were a time to stop apologizing for America's legitimate national interests and start asserting them.

I was by no means alone. Principled leaders like Helmut Kohl and Margaret Thatcher reinforced our message that the West would not be blackmailed and that the only rational course was to return to the bargaining table in Geneva and work out real and lasting arms reductions fair to both sides.

A new Soviet leader appeared on the scene, untainted by the past, unwilling to be shackled by crumbling orthodoxies. With the rise of Mikhail Gorbachev came the end of numbing oppression. Glasnost introduced openness to the world's most closed society. Perestroika held out the promise of a better life, achieved through democratic institutions and a market economy. And real arms control came to pass, as an entire class of weapons was eliminated for the first time in the atomic age.

Within months the Soviet empire began to melt like a snowbank in May. One country after another overthrew the privileged cliques that had bled their economies and curbed their freedoms. Last month Germany itself was reunited in the shadow of the Brandenburg Gate and under the democratic umbrella of NATO. I know something about that neighborhood. Back in June 1987, I stood in the free city of West Berlin and asked Mr. Gorbachev to tear down the wall.

Was he listening? Whether he was or not, neither he nor the rulers of Eastern Europe could ignore the much louder chants of demonstrators in the streets of Leipzig and Dresden and dozens of other German cities.

In the churches and the schools, in the factories and on the farms, a once silent people found their voice and with it a battering ram to knock down walls, real and imagined.

Because of them, the political map of Europe has been rewritten. The future has been redefined, even as the veil has been lifted on a cruel and bloody past. Just last week thousands of Soviet citizens, many of them clutching photographs of relatives who died in Stalin's labor camps, marched to the Moscow headquarters of the KGB to unveil a monument to the victims of Stalinist repression. An aging woman named Alla Krichevskaya held up a photograph of a young man in an old-fashioned high collar. She wept softly.

"This is my father," she said. "I never knew him. He was sent to Solovetsky [labor camp] in 1932, a few months before I was born, and they shot him in 1937."

In dedicating this memorial, may we pause and reflect on the heroism and the sacrifice of Alla's father and so many, many others like him. Fifty years after Winston Churchill rallied his people in the Battle of Britain, the world is a very different place. Soviet Russia is coming out of the dark to join the family of nations. Central and Eastern Europe struggle to create both freedom and prosperity through market economies. How pleased Sir Winston would be!

Let me conclude with a special word to the

students of Westminster College, the empire builders of the twenty-first century. Before you leave this place, do not forget why you came. You came to Westminster to explore the diversity of ideas and experience what we call civilization. Here you discover that so long as books are kept open, then minds can never be closed. Here you develop a sense of self, along with the realization that self alone is never enough for a truly satisfying life, for while we make a living by what we get, we make a living by what we give.

Tragically, many walls still remain to endanger our families and our communities.

In Fulton, Missouri, as in London, Berlin or Los Angeles, the future is what you make it.

Certainly it was unreasonable for a sixty-five-year-old parliamentarian, his counsel rejected until the emergency was at hand, to believe that he could defy the world's most lethal fighting force and crush Hitler in his Berlin lair.

It was unreasonable to suggest that an ancient church, all but destroyed by enemy bombs, could be reconstructed five thousand miles away as a permanent tribute to the man of the century. It was unreasonable to hope that oppressed men and women behind the Iron Curtain could one day break through to the sunlight of freedom—and that the Soviet Politburo itself would yield to people in the streets.

All this was unreasonable, but it all came true. My fondest wish is that each of you will be similarly unreasonable in pursuing Churchill's objectives—justice, opportunity and an end to walls wherever they divide the human race.

Shortly before he died, Sir Winston received a letter from his daughter Mary. "In addition to all the feelings a daughter has for a loving, generous father," she wrote, "I owe you what every Englishman, woman and child does—liberty itself." We owe him nothing less.

In dedicating this magnificent sculpture, may we dedicate ourselves to hastening the day when all God's children live in a world without walls. That would be the greatest empire of all.

Thank you and God bless you all.

*I*t is interesting that most discussions and debates over the legacies of past Presidents are conducted among historians, while Reagan's legacy remains current, controversial and relevant. The arguments made both for and against the Reagan Presidency are current because Reagan hewed to a few simple yet powerful ideas on which it is still impossible to be neutral. Inevitably, nearly every discussion of Reagan becomes either a passionate defense or attack of his principles in today's terms.

Whereas most politicians tend to deal in transient policy issues, Ronald Reagan was always mindful of the more significant principles which reign over policy decisions. We have witnessed Presidents, past and present, who shift policy with every whim of public opinion. Reagan chose to adhere to his deeply held beliefs. His leadership style was based on the understanding that policies, in and of themselves, can be compromised, but principles are either obeyed or abandoned.

Whether the issue was foreign policy or tax policy, Ronald Reagan held to his faith in the principle that a free system is the only system in which excellence, goodness, prosperity and ingenuity can thrive. He constantly appealed to the power of free people, free markets, free enterprise and free trade—as opposed to the power of government—as the best means of addressing our challenges. "We believe," he said, "that no power of government is as formidable a force for good as the creativity and entrepreneurial drive of the American people."

Armed with his indomitable faith in the promise of freedom, President Ronald Reagan combated the Keynesian and socialist dogmas which had contributed to building an age of austerity. As a result he ushered in a new American decade of growth and prosperity—a prosperity which opened up opportunities, and therefore freedoms, for all Americans. And he also made it possible for millions of people abroad to have a taste of freedom for the first time in their lives.

Such a victorious result is testament to the truth of the principles to which President Reagan so faithfully adhered, and it is a tribute to the force that an idea can have when it is advocated with deep-rooted conviction and advanced with indefatigable optimism.

I cannot help but reflect upon the remarkable list of victories of freedom which Ronald Reagan achieved for Americans and for the world. For those of us at home, President Reagan achieved relief from the restraining effects of crippling inflation and from highly burdensome tax rates. For the world, he orchestrated the downfall of one of its most heavily entrenched and utterly oppressive regimes. However, the extraordinary victories and the immediate accomplishments of President Reagan do not begin to account for the contribution he made to the people of our nation and to people who seek freedom and opportunity everywhere. Rather, his enduring legacy and its relevance for the twenty-first century is his lasting impact on our world.

JACK KEMP
*Co-Director, Empower America*

YOU KNOW I have a special association with both USC and Notre Dame. It was the Trojans who welcomed me back to California when my term on "the Eastern Front" ended and USC hosted a birthday party for me last year. And I will always be grateful to Coach Smith for allowing me to interrupt his team's Rose Bowl practice last year.

And being a fighting Irishman, I recall with special fondness when Coach Holtz brought his team to the Rose Garden at the White House just before I left. And, of course, there was a certain movie about a certain college player in which I played a certain football player.

I was a teenager when the USC–Notre Dame football series began and I have followed it with great interest ever since, not just because it is the longest-running series between two teams, but because it represents one of the greatest traditions in America.

Now I know I am taking a chance here in the presence of so many great football players and coaches in suggesting I know anything about the game, but I did play for eight years—four in high school and four in college—and I enjoyed every minute of it. In my day we played offense and defense, and I'm sure it will come as no surprise to any of you that I was a right guard. I always wished I had been a better player and been good enough for the NFL. That way I could have ended up influential and famous. Instead, I went into the picture business, wound up as Governor of California, was later sent to Washington, where I had to live in public housing and now here I am, out of work!

Seriously, as some of you may know, my studies in college came second to football to me. Eureka was in a conference called the Little 19 and was unquestionably the smallest school in that conference. Some of our opponents had ten times our enrollment. There were no such things as athletic scholarships.

The school saved all the campus jobs it could for needy students. I didn't find that unpleasant—one of my jobs was washing dishes in the girls' dormitory.

The coach, Ralph McKinzie, was a graduate of Eureka and had played football there. The school used to display the front page of a Peoria newspaper on the bulletin board. It read "MCKINZIE BEATS BRADLEY U. 52 TO 0." He had made every one of the fifty-two points himself. I'm ashamed to say I got off on a wrong foot and thought he didn't like me. Coming from a high school several times bigger than Eureka, I guess I thought I should automatically make the varsity. But he knew what he was doing. In my second year I made varsity at right guard, and I've come to realize he was a great and good influence on me. He still lives in Eureka, is in his nineties and up till a few years ago was helping coach Eureka's wide receivers.

In those dark Depression days we had a number of fellows who had gotten out of high school in the Roaring Twenties. They had gone to work, but when the crash came and the jobs were gone many decided to try college. In my last year I was the only one of the top first eleven who had come directly from high school to college. The tackle beside me was twenty-eight years old.

One night during a chalk talk in one of the classrooms, Coach Mac somehow brought up the subject of prayer. I would never have told my teammates—those older guys—that I prayed before every kickoff. But as the conversation went on, I learned that every man in the room started the game with a prayer. Now I never asked for victory. I didn't think I had a right to ask the Lord to take sides. I prayed there would be no injuries, that I'd do my best and there would be no regrets when the game was over. Well, to my surprise, that was the gist of every prayer by each one of my teammates. It was quite an eye-opener to me.

By now you must have gathered that I love football. It is the only sport in which men engage in bodily attack on each other. It's a kind of nonlethal war. You charge and fling yourself through the air to take down an opposing player before he can do the same to you. There is no other sport quite like it. It is total physical contact without hatred or death.

You know, I have always been struck by something about college sports—really sports in general—that I would like to share with you as a parting thought. And that is when the men and women competitors put on their uniforms and walk onto the playing field, socioeconomic stations disappear. It doesn't matter what color your skin is, it doesn't matter whether you are a Christian or a Jew, it doesn't matter whether you are rich or poor, it doesn't matter what side of the tracks you come from. It just matters that you are out there doing your best. And that same equality is not restricted to the playing field. No, in the stands, too, the only thing that matters is the term you are rooting for. A corporate president can be seated next to the janitor who cleans the office at night. Cheering together for the home team, high-fiving each other when they score and booing loudly at a bad call—for those few precious moments, it doesn't matter who wears pinstripes and who wears overalls. Which makes me wonder, why should it matter at all?

I've often wondered if there isn't a way that somehow we could capture that spirit of togetherness, and yes, brotherhood, and have it be the guiding light of our lives after the games, too. Wouldn't that be something?

I've gone on too long here now. I just get carried away when it comes to football.

In closing, I know some of you are wondering if I'm going to say that line from that certain movie. But I know better than to take sides. So I've come up with what I hope will be a good compromise. As you may know, tomorrow I will flip the coin to officially start the game. So if you'll permit a little modification: Will you tell your teams to go out there and "win one for the flipper"?

Thank you and God bless you.

*I*t falls to few to have the chance to turn the tide of history. It falls to fewer still to take that opportunity and, in so doing, to help bring liberty to millions who had hitherto known only oppression.

In 1981, when President Reagan delivered his first inaugural address, the West still had to confront the threat of a Soviet Union confident of its military might, in Afghanistan and beyond. Within a year of his passing the torch to President Bush the Berlin Wall was to be torn down and the Soviet empire dissolved.

In the interim, the United States had found renewed confidence, strength and authority as the leader of the free world. The cause of liberty was one in which the United States and the United Kingdom found a common belief and which united them in joint endeavor. The relationship between our two countries was forged anew, and flourished anew, as we stood shoulder to shoulder then—as we have since—in the defense of freedom.

And at the center of all this was the strength, determination and vision of one man. An inspiration for millions in the free world and far beyond then, now and in the future. A very remarkable man: Ronald Reagan.

JOHN MAJOR
*Prime Minister of Great Britain, 1990–1997*

85

*I*T IS AN HONOR to be invited to address you here today at the climax of your Michaelmas term program and the 175th anniversary year of the Cambridge Union Society.

Time, as we all know, is relative. I continue to be awed by the sweep of human activity when I think about that which has occurred thus far in my own lifetime.

When I was born, in 1911, television and radio were still in the future and so were countless lifesaving medicines regularly used today. Then, if one were to travel in an automobile, the highest speed would have been about 20 miles an hour. Now, on the Concorde, we cross oceans at twice the speed of sound. Then, the idea of space travel was the stuff of Jules Verne adventure stories and we scanned the heavens from earthbound telescopes on hilltops. Now, we routinely send manned missions into space. Humans have stood on the moon, and we photograph the surface of distant planets by means of satellites guided by

that ubiquitous and quintessential twentieth-century invention, the computer.

Humankind has changed much in these seven decades, yet twice in that time we were unable to change the fact that countries still go to war to settle disputes. The two World Wars of this century did, however, bring profound change to society. Some of it came quickly, some slowly. Some of it was beneficial and some of it brought misery.

Time being relative, as I stand here I realize I am something of a youngster compared with the Cambridge Union, founded, as it was, the year the Duke of Wellington's armies defeated Napoleon at Waterloo. Yet, that founding date itself seems like the day before yesterday when compared to the age of Cambridge as an educational center. If the oldest stones in Cambridge could speak they would tell us they had witnessed—from the thirteenth century onward—the gradual but inexorable growth of modern democracy; the concept of representative government that has spread far and wide and has, at last, recently emerged triumphant over its most persistent adversary, communism.

Communism was born in the ashes of feudal systems and was embraced, in its early days, by idealists and utopians, near and far. It died with the Berlin Wall, with the death of the Ceauşescus, with the rise of Solidarity, with the Lithuanian declaration of independence and with many other acts throughout what had once seemed an impregnable empire.

It died with its utopian promises unfulfilled. Its ideals had long since given way to a totalitarian political system sustained by fear and repression. And despite years of optimistic fabrications, the truth about its failure as an economic system could no longer be hidden, for it could not provide for the people its creators had said it would nurture.

Last year the world was dazzled by a sequence of Communist collapses behind what Winston Churchill had aptly called the Iron Curtain. It all happened so swiftly. Yet, the seeds of communism's collapse had been fertilized by its own excesses and shortcomings. The flowers of freedom were only awaiting a few rays of bright light, in the form of trigger events, in order to burst forth in full bloom. Those events happened first in Poland, then East Germany, Hungary, Czechoslovakia, Bulgaria, Romania and, finally, in the Soviet Union itself.

That Marx and Lenin were false prophets is a fact now realized and appreciated almost everywhere people had once thought their ideas to be the wave of the future. Today, even Albania, once the most isolated and dogmatic of Communist states, is opening up and testing the waters of democracy.

In Africa, country after country that had embraced Marxist-Leninist politics and economics is abandoning both and moving toward multiparty democracy. The Congo has led the way, taking steps even five years ago to move from a centralized to a market economy and now declaring for multiparty democracy in the absence of pressure to do so. Others, such as Gabon, the Ivory Coast and Zaire, are moving in the same direction.

A free press is part of this process, of course, and in Zaire, for example, in the last year some sixty newspapers and magazines have begun publication, nearly all of them critical of the government. Yet the sky hasn't fallen and the sun still rises there every day.

Democracy can be heady stuff, especially if one not used to it can suddenly speak one's mind. It may come soon to Angola, too, a potentially rich country where negotiations continue with the objective of replacing fifteen years of civil strife with free and open multiparty elections.

In Central America, Marxist government gave way this spring to a democratically elected one. The former rulers, the Sandinistas, have done their best to throw sand in the gears since then and the new government of President Violeta Chamorro is struggling, but it is on its feet and determined to succeed.

The positive contagion of democracy is spreading far beyond former Communist domains, proving the universality of its appeal.

Military and authoritarian regimes throughout Latin America have given way to democratically elected governments. The economies of many of these countries are fragile and it may be some time before democracy gets firmly rooted, but the trend is unmistakable.

Across the Pacific, Taiwan, which has had a successful market economy for decades, has, in recent years, systematically opened its political system to vigorously contested multiparty elections and an energetic free press.

South Africa, too, is moving toward a new democratic order. The road is not easy and there is yet a long way to go, but the credentials of the principals are well established and the process is moving forward. This complex society will no doubt draw elements from various models to create a democratic system that is uniquely its own. Precisely how it will look we cannot know at this time, but we can be sure that when the process has completed its course, a new South Africa will emerge with a democratic system for all its people.

While democracy moves forward by inches or leaps in lands where it is largely a new experience, we who have long enjoyed its benefits must remember that it faces formidable obstacles in many countries. Divisions along ethnic, tribal, racial or geographic lines have bred centuries-old suspicions in many parts of the globe and these will not quickly or easily give way to face-value trust in the rule of law.

Those of us from the Western democracies have a great deal of work ahead of us, for we must be ready, when asked, to help those for whom democracy is a bold experiment, as it was for you in Britain centuries ago and for us in America when we declared our independence.

We must help as teachers, not preachers. Those in the emerging democracies are eager to learn, but they cannot put sound institutions in place without either experience or helping hands. They need to understand the linkage, on the one hand, between private property rights and the possibilities inherent in the market system, and the right to assemble, speak out, vote and serve the public, on the other.

While many countries in various parts of the world may welcome this help in time, at present it is the countries of the former Soviet empire that seek it most urgently. The help they seek is not so much in the form of money (although they welcome credits and investments from the West). What they seek most is knowledge, both of the institutions of democracy and the workings of the free market.

Some help is already on the way and I will return to that in a moment. First, though, let us examine the elements that have brought such dramatic changes in such a large part of the world in such a short time.

As World War II drew to a close we entered a period of tension with the Soviet Union that came to be known as the Cold War. From time to time it became a hot war, as the Soviet Union supplied its proxies, whose objective was to destabilize their neighbors or, in the case of recently freed colonies, to ensure that Marxist-Leninist partisans gained control.

The Soviets were obsessed with long memories of invasions of their land, so they set out to create for themselves a cordon sanitaire, a wall of buffer states between themselves and the West.

While the Soviet leaders in the late forties and the fifties may have believed fervently in the superiority of their system, they weren't taking any chances. In those days, as we now know, dissidence real or imagined brought a Soviet citizen a long visit to the gulag. Stalin had shown the way earlier with his ruthless extermination of the kulaks, the small farmers, and with the Moscow show trials, which eliminated potential critics and rivals.

Soviet bellicosity toward the West ranged from Khrushchev's bombastic "We shall bury you" claim to the real and massive military buildup achieved during the period known as détente.

Defense critics in the United States during those days were feeling the negative aftereffects of the Vietnam War and felt it was unnecessary, even outrageous, that national security outlays should take up 5 or 6 percent of the national budget. What they probably did not know at the time was the USSR was routinely spending close to or even more than 20 percent of its budget on military expansion.

Throughout the seventies fierce arguments were waged in the U.S. between those who believed a strong defense was a prerequisite to serious negotiations with the Soviets and those who felt that preemptive concessions and arms control treaties would reduce the chances of nuclear war.

The arms control group sought not to turn swords into plowshares, but rather to simply limit the growth of weaponry by treaty. The history of treaties throughout the centuries is such that one should not want to stake one's life on a treaty, but that is exactly what the arms control fraternity wanted to do.

I recall being severely criticized by many in that group for opposing the proposed Salt II Treaty in 1979. After being briefed by both the Carter administration and independent defense experts, I concluded that what was really needed was a round of arms *reduction* talks, not talks that aimed at only limiting the growth of arsenals. I said so, but the criticism did not abate, for it often flourished when those committed to a fixed position cannot look beyond it.

That same year, 1979, I visited NORAD headquarters, deep in a mountain in Colorado, where sophisticated equipment monitors our own missiles and tracks any hostile ones that might be fired our way. Among the things I learned on that visit was that we really had no defense against such missiles. Once alerted by all this equipment, all we could do was launch our missiles in retaliation. Hence the term "mutually assured destruction." That, of course, spells MAD. It seemed an apt name or concept that was basically a dangerous gamble.

The following year, in my campaign for the Presidency, I called for a rebuilding of our own national security system, which had been allowed to lag. My belief was—and had been for some time—that the rulers of the Soviet Union would respect strength but exploit weakness. The record reflected that, with their military buildup during the years of détente as the most recent example. In any case, a broader reading of history shows that appeasement, no matter how it is labeled, never fulfills the hopes of the appeasers.

As happens in campaigns, one must reduce full-length arguments to short phrases. My defense concept, therefore, became "peace through strength." That did not make me popular with some people in the foreign affairs establishment in the U.S. One of them described me as "a dumb cowboy actor." Others were less friendly.

After I had been elected, I conferred with defense experts and scientists and learned that we had some off-the-shelf technologies that could form part of a practical defense system against strategic weapons.

To be fully effective, such a system must have three stages: identifying and destroying missiles as they left their home base, intercepting them at the height of their trajectory and hitting them as they came down. The existing technologies could help put in place the third stage of such a system. For the first two our researchers would have to work at the frontiers of technology existing then, in order to come up with a complete system.

In a speech to the American people in March 1983, I described the concept of such a Strategic Defense Initiative, or SDI. I said we would proceed with research and development leading to the deployment of such a system.

In some quarters you might have thought I

had announced the beginning of World War III. For some of the proponents of mutually assured destruction, their cause had taken on the aspects of crusade. They mistrusted the motives of anyone not as committed as they to their scheme. They took the position that any approach other than theirs was not only doomed to failure but was likely to bring on a nuclear holocaust as well.

They wasted no time in attacking the Strategic Defense Initiative. Some sought to trivialize it by nicknaming it "Star Wars," after a science fiction movie. Others said it was unworkable because it would not prevent 100 percent of enemy missiles from reaching our soil. The critics missed the point. I was convinced, from the expert opinions I had gathered, that if such a system could be made, say, 85 or 90 percent effective, that was as good as 100 percent, for it would persuade the other side that it was hopeless—and self-defeating—to mount an attack at all.

What the critics did not know or chose to ignore was that the Soviets had nearly bankrupted their economy in their rush to outpace the West in armaments during the seventies.

The Soviets realized that the West in general and U.S. in particular had the financial, technical and production resources to create a successful strategic defense system. They knew that if we mustered the political will to do this, the arms race would be over. In announcing the Strategic Defense Initiative, my intention was to signal the Soviets that we had the political will to accomplish this, that we intended to proceed, and that serious talks aimed at reducing offensive weapons were the only sensible course to take.

The solidarity of the Western alliance was essential to the success of this approach. It was tested that same year when a well-coordinated and massive propaganda campaign was mounted against the Federal Republic of Germany and the United States with the aim of preventing the deployment of cruise missiles in West Germany. The German government stood firm and announced it would deploy the missiles. This, in effect, checkmated the Soviets. Coupled with the initiation of our SDI program, this event told the Soviets the game was up.

Thinking back again to 1979, the year before I was elected President, I recall a meeting with Mrs. Thatcher in her office in Parliament. It was December and she was not yet Prime Minister. We talked of the threat of Soviet missiles. She reminded me that while we in the United States were concerned about the prospect of intercontinental missiles, the Soviets already had in place powerful missiles aimed at every capital of Western Europe. "We *must* stand together," she said to me. Those four words embodied the very basis of the Western alliance and they were to return to mind many times in the years that followed.

Margaret Thatcher served with a resolute sense of mission and purpose. I admired this, and as President I knew I could always count on her to give sound advice and strong support

in matters that affected both our countries and the alliance.

A leader, once convinced a particular course of action is the right one, must have the determination to stick with it and be undaunted when the going gets rough. Those qualities well describe Mrs. Thatcher and I appreciated them on many occasions during my eight years in the White House.

Her counsel and support were especially valuable during those days when we were setting in place the strategy to get the USSR back to the negotiating table to begin the process of reducing arms. This was at the height of the propaganda campaign against the cruise missiles and the din of the doubters about the Strategic Defense Initiative.

Mrs. Thatcher's observations about Mikhail Gorbachev proved prescient, too. She met him before I did. She declared publicly that he was a man "we could do business with," and she conveyed that message to me privately as well. She was right.

Margaret Thatcher is a remarkable lady whose achievements will be appreciated more and more as time goes on. For me she has been a staunch ally and a good friend. I salute her.

In the fall of 1985, I met Mikhail Gorbachev for the first time, in Geneva. On meeting him, I, too, sensed that here was a man with whom one could be quite direct. He proved to be a complete realist. I liked the feeling of openness he conveyed and we conversed freely.

At one point I said to him, "We don't mistrust each other because we're armed. We are armed because we mistrust each other." I said we had two alternatives: to find a way to trust one another enough to begin to reduce arms or to have an all-out arms race. And I added that's a race you can't win. There is no way we are going to let you maintain arms superiority over us.

He did not agree outright, but neither did he dispute my assertion or turn down the peaceful alternative.

As events would later show, he had already concluded that his nation's economy was in such bad shape that it was useless to attempt to counter both the Strategic Defense Initiative and the cruise missile deployment. Glasnost was his answer to this knowledge.

As is always the case, once people who have been deprived of basic freedom taste a little of it, they want all of it. It was as if Gorbachev had uncorked a magic bottle and a genie floated out, never to be put back again. Glasnost was that genie.

In time, President Gorbachev sent his negotiators back to the table at Geneva and the sessions ultimately brought forth the first international agreement to eliminate an entire class of nuclear weapons. He and I signed the INF agreement in December 1987 and it was ratified soon after. The process of actually reversing the Cold War arms buildup had begun.

From the beginning of our relationship I respected Mikhail Gorbachev, for he was the leader of a great power and he had come to his position at a difficult time for his nation. Over the six times we met in our respective official

capacities, I came to think of him as a friend and one who shared my dream that the day would come when his people and those of the Western alliance would work together for common purposes, replacing the tensions, skirmishes and proxy wars that had dominated the relationship for nearly four decades.

That dream has begun to come true over the matter of Iraq's invasion of Kuwait, where we and the Soviets confer regularly and stand as allies.

Leaders of modern nations have efficient staffs and many technicians and experts on which to rely. Still, life at the top is frequently a lonely business. This knowledge President Gorbachev and I shared. I appreciated that whatever he said or did reflected a judgment reached after carefully weighing many interests.

He and I have met twice since I left the White House: once in June in San Francisco and again in September, when I visited him in the Kremlin. This time I saw him not only as a friend, but a friend in need, for his nation was—and is—going through a period of great uncertainty and turmoil.

The Soviet Union has lost its ideological underpinnings. The ruthless Stalin has long since been discredited. Marx has been assigned to dusty bookshelves and Lenin is no longer the icon of the Communist religion, for communism is shattered and its remnant forces scattered.

Gorbachev has released the state's grip on religion so that worshippers again congregate without looking over their shoulders. He has freed the press from being a propaganda machine of the state, and Soviet journalists are beginning to act like journalists elsewhere: inquiring and skeptical. Today they report the bad news with the good. Parliamentary debates, once conducted behind closed doors, are now fully covered, widely followed and vociferously commented upon. These products of glasnost are good omens for the shift of democracy.

On the economic side, however, the picture is a very dark one. Perestroika has not yet met the promise of its name, restructuring—at least so far as economic results are concerned.

Making the shift from a seventy-year-old command economy run by bureaucrats in Moscow to a market economy where individuals make thousands of economic decisions every day would not be easy under the best of circumstances. Unfortunately, the circumstances facing President Gorbachev are about as far from best as they can be.

While several thousand private-enterprise service businesses, called cooperatives, have sprung up during perestroika years, the people of the Soviet Union still mistrust profits, and most do not yet understand the link between productivity and reward because there are still so few opportunities for incentives to work.

Soviet industry must accelerate its conversion from arms production to consumer goods, and ownership must devolve from the state to private hands. All of this is a tall order in a state as large and complex as the USSR. Meanwhile, the distribution system, which is still operated on a centralized basis, has all the

logic of the Mad Hatter's tea party. Thus, we see television and newspaper pictures regularly of Soviet consumers queued up in stores with nearly empty shelves.

The Soviet republics are asserting varying degrees of independence from Moscow. Some are even restricting the sale of their products to within their own borders. This, in turn, complicates problems in a distribution system that must cover a land twelve thousand miles wide.

President Gorbachev has been trying to persuade the republics to adopt a new treaty of union. So far, this has been an uphill effort. It is likely to be some time before a definitive new relationship emerges between the central government and the republics.

The most hopeful scenario is one in which there is a relatively peaceful transition from what was, essentially, an imperial structure to a rather loose confederation of democratic republics that reserve to themselves much of the decisions that affect the lives and the livelihood of their people.

While it can be said that today President Gorbachev controls the Soviet Foreign Ministry and he commands the loyalty of the KGB and the military, he does not control the economy or the political direction of the fifteen republics.

Western business executives are finding it difficult to make binding agreements with central government ministries because so many economic decisions are now being made in the republics.

A new union or confederation that emerges would probably have a greatly reduced role for the central government. It might have the responsibility for foreign affairs, a central bank and national defense, but probably not international trade. We may see in what is today the USSR a decentralization of power far greater than what you in Britain or we in the United States are used to.

As a Californian I have sometimes noted that my state, were it a separate country, would be the seventh-largest economic power in the world. Although California has a large foreign trade, it cannot make treaties or conduct a foreign policy. These things are not possible under our Constitution; however, they very well may be for the republics of a reorganized Soviet Union.

The outcome of the fundamental changes now under way in the Soviet Union will, in one way or another, affect us all. It is in the interests of those of us in the West to do what we can to help the people of that vast nation make the transition to democracy.

For a long time I have been saying it would be far better to compete economically with the Soviet Union than to compete in an arms race. We now have that opportunity. The competition can be waged on a playing field where the rules are those of democracy and the free market, but first we must show them how the game is played.

Already, investments are beginning to trickle in to the USSR from countries of the European Community and the United States. These will probably remain a trickle until conditions appear more certain, although recent changes in Soviet law, prompted by Gorbachev, make it economically more attractive than before.

Other help is on the way. Recently, the New York Stock Exchange conducted a seminar in Moscow on capital markets. It agreed to send experts over to assist in the establishment of a stock exchange in the Soviet Union. For a stock exchange to work, of course, there must be shares in businesses available for purchase and sale. Under the economic reforms now under way, it is expected that a number of Soviet state enterprises will be converted soon to joint-stock companies.

Another way to broaden ownership and privatize elements of the Soviet economy would be to employ a concept now being used successfully by several thousand companies in the U.S. It involves what are called employee stock ownership plans, or ESOPs for short. Typically, a company starts an ESOP by creating a trust for its employees. The trust borrows money in order to buy shares in the company. The bank loan is paid back out of the earnings the employee trust gets from its company shares. In time the trust owns the shares free and clear. Thus, it can provide each employee in the program with a substantial family nest egg.

Human nature being what it is, when one has assets one has the incentive to protect them and make them grow. This translates into greater efficiency and productivity. Employees who own shares in their company identify their own well-being with the economic health of the enterprise. In Soviet industry, where incentives are lacking, such a system of employee ownership might work wonders in terms of productivity and morale.

Also lacking in Soviet industry are modern management techniques and competitive marketing know-how. New York University has a new unit, the Institute for East-West Business Dynamics, which is preparing to take groups of Soviet managers to New York for intensive courses in these subjects, thus preparing them for participation in a market economy.

There are pockets of resistance to President Gorbachev's economic reforms. Others argue that the reforms do not go far enough fast enough. The resisters tend to come from the nomenklatura, that privileged class of bureaucrats and professionals who lived lives of affluence in a supposedly classless society while most Soviet citizens did without. There is not a lot of sympathy for those people these days, but more than a few of them are still embedded in the apparatus of central government, fighting a rear-guard action against reform.

The economic reforms embrace the concepts of private property, a federal bank comprised of central banks of each of the republics and a convertible ruble. With production and the Soviet gross national product declining, will the people be patient long enough for the reforms to work?

We must hope so, for the alternatives are not desirable. It is conceivable that President Gorbachev will feel the need to invoke some of his more drastic powers, using the Army and the KGB to impose and maintain martial law. If he does so, I believe it would not be from some power-made impulse, but rather from a belief that such an action would be the only way to save his nation from instability.

In the peaceful-transition scenario does not succeed and if the martial-law scenario is played out and fails to push the transition forward, the so-called worst case may result. This would involve chaos, civil strife, perhaps anarchy and widespread famine. The spillover from such an upheaval would become everyone's business. There would be millions of starving refugees and there would be uncertainty about the control of the remaining nuclear weapons deployed about the Soviet countryside.

For all these reasons we in the West must take every effort to understand the current transition. We must understand the tensions between and among the various nationalities within the USSR, and we must assist the people of that vast land in making the transition to democracy and a market economy as peacefully as possible.

The world is still a dangerous place. Saddam Hussein has shown us that in recent weeks. Still, we have won the Cold War. There is no doubt about that. The evil leaders who once ruled a Soviet empire are gone and so is the empire, replaced by a modern realist at the top who has unleashed pent-up forces that yearned for freedom and democracy. As the victors, it is for us to hold out the hand of reconciliation and, as we did with fallen enemies after World War II, to tend to the sprouts and saplings of democracy in the former adversary's land until they can grow strong and tall on their own.

That brings me full circle, back to the 175th anniversary of the Cambridge Union Society. I understand the union was formed in 1815, not to celebrate victory at Waterloo, but to settle a brawl between a number of undergraduate debating clubs. It must have worked, for the merger of those clubs into the new Cambridge Union led to a movement that resulted in the formation of the Oxford Union and several dozen other debating societies throughout the United Kingdom.

For a century and three-quarters now you have passionately debated the issues of the day. Many of your members have gone on to positions of leadership in government and the professions.

The free and open expression of ideas—and debate over these ideas—is a heritage that Britain had given all of us in the democratic world. It has been an integral process of the long evolution of representative democracy since the knights confronted King John at Runnymede. It is an essential part of the British spirit, seemingly ingrained in all of you. I think I hear it in the music of Benjamin Britten, Elgar and Handel. I read it in the poetry of Shakespeare, Donne and Milton and the prose of Dickens. The passion for free expression seems to permeate your culture just as it does your union here.

But just as the development of representative democracy has flowed dynamically from Great Britain to other lands, so your union's commitment to free expression and open debate is reaching out in the form of your planned project with our Princeton University to teach debating at universities in the lands that were once behind the Iron Curtain.

As you celebrate your 175th anniversary, nothing could be more fitting than to undertake a project such as this, taking the British spirit of freedom of expression into lands which have known so little of it in the past.

I wish you year upon year of continued success and vigorous debate of issues yet unknown.

It has been a pleasure and an honor to be with you today. Thank you and God bless you.

Ronald Reagan is a man who knows who he is and what he stands for and is comfortable with both. He has never been driven to prove things to himself or to anyone else. He did not come into office as President with any grand scheme for the world. Rather, he came to office to pursue a few key goals based on some core principles about which he felt both strongly and deeply, and he set out to accomplish those goals with a steadfastness which knew no limits. He was not swayed from his course by temporary defeat or by criticism, whether from the Congress, the media or even large sectors of the public. It was this self-confident determination and perseverance which brought him success in areas important to him and to the country, and it was these qualities, also, which made him a great President.

*President Reagan and General Brent Scowcroft in the Oval Office, May 23, 1983.*

Ronald Reagan restored America's faith in itself and in its ability to change the world. And he used that faith to alter Soviet views about the "correlation of forces" in the world and hasten the end of the Cold War. He was successful in pushing through the Congress a challenging program to rebuild our defenses which would have been unimaginable only a few years earlier, thus forcing the Soviet leadership to realize that it had to change course because it could no longer compete.

I once asked President Reagan how he had happened to enter politics. He responded that he had been urged by friends to run for Governor of California. He told them he knew nothing about politics—he was an actor. "Now," he said, "I have discovered that 90 percent of politics is acting and I am a natural."

There is no doubt that Ronald Reagan had been an actor. And he certainly was a *great* politician. But he *never* mistook the Oval Office for the stage; he knew when it was time to act and when it was time to be real. His resolve, dedication, sincerity and humor, his unending optimism and, above all, simple, devout patriotism and commitment to America's role as a world leader will be forever lasting gifts to his country.

BRENT SCOWCROFT
*National Security Advisor, 1989–1993*

*I*T'S BEEN a difficult time for you, I know. Uncertainty about the future always carries with it anxiety and worry.

But I'm here to tell you that as a result of the sacrifices made by your father or mother, your husband or wife, your sister or brother, we've won this fight and your family members are heroes. These heroes have restored democracy and peace to the world. Talk about shooting for the moon!

And to take it one step further, I'd like to include you in this class of distinction also. *You,* too, are also heroes in your own right.

It's true you weren't on the battlefield or training for combat. You played a different position on the U.S. team.

You kept things operating, kept the households running. You prayed fervently, hoped, cared for the family. You wrote the letters, sent packages, walked the dog, cut the grass. You held things together in place of your absent loved one.

Well, congratulations on a job well done. Morale is high, hopes are soaring and the future is bright, very, very bright indeed.

The truth is that we had to persist. We could not be timid in our embrace of democracy. It was not the time to let our support wane.

We won this fight. Together, you and your spouse have provided a more peaceful world for your children and for your children's children. Soon your loved ones will return home and normal life will resume: weekend baseball games, birthday parties with ice cream cakes, vacations, movies—probably no chance you've seen any of mine, have you?—there will be lots of hugs, relief, thankful hearts overflowing with gratitude. There will be cause for great celebration.

America is great because of men and women and children like you—with big hearts and strong minds and with courage beyond the usual measure.

You know, someone wisely said that a hero isn't really braver than anyone else; he's just brave five minutes longer than anyone else.

We will continue praying for all involved in Operation Desert Storm—both Marines and their families. Our nation is behind you.

It's because of you that we can be sure that America will be *semper fidelis*—always faithful to her best hopes and highest ideals.

Thank you for your support of your loved ones and for your service to your country.

God bless you and God bless America.

*I*n 1969, when he was Governor of California, Ronald Reagan visited Singapore. We had a long discussion about the threat of communism in Europe, Asia and throughout the world. His attitude was robust, straightforward and clear-cut: communism had to be resisted and thwarted, whether in South Vietnam or in Eastern Europe.

After he became President in 1981, I found his views and policies were as robust, straightforward and clear-cut as those he had expressed when we met twelve years earlier. He never changed his principles. He did not have much time for complex or complicated sophistry. He knew that communism was a menace that had to be faced down, and he faced it down. His "Star Wars" program was mocked by the world's liberal intellectuals, but it left General Secretary Mikhail Gorbachev with no choice but to give up the military competition and attempt fundamental restructuring of the Soviet economy. This led to the unraveling of the Soviet Communist system and empire. Ronald Reagan had hastened its end.

In the United States itself he provided the same clear-cut leadership. He faced down the air traffic controllers and established the simple rule that the American nation was not open to blackmail. Although he did not have a mind that was retentive like a computer, he knew how to select and surrounded himself with outstanding men and women who made the Reagan years among the most successful in America's post–World War II history.

In every meeting with him I found him seeing the sunny side of any problem, and upbeat about the end result. As a result, Americans felt good about themselves. He inspired them to move America forward. He served America and the world well.

LEE KUAN YEW
*Senior Minister, Republic of Singapore*

*I* AM VERY HONORED to be here this evening to introduce a man for whom I have great admiration.

This great Polish patriot, in just ten years since he founded the Solidarity Movement, has brought about the end of communism's stifling grip on his country. He has successfully led the struggle for free, open and democratic elections and has paved the way for a market economy to replace the failed efforts of centralized planning and control.

Early in the movement a skeptical world looked on as Lech Walesa led his people over the wall back into the shipyard in Gdańsk, Poland, after the authorities closed it. I recall those days, when I was in the Oval Office, and how thrilling it was. One of man's most fundamental and implacable yearnings, the desire for freedom, was stirring to life behind the Iron Curtain—the first break in the totalitarian dike. In fact, had I been a little younger, I would have liked to follow him over the wall as well!

Since that time Lech Walesa and Solidarity have achieved what so many never thought possible: he has freed his country from the throes of communism and he has rejuvenated Poland's economy.

Of course, his struggle has not been easy. Imprisoned, tormented and battered, Lech Walesa has found additional strength for his fight. He is the lamp of freedom, the symbol of salvation for his people.

This brave worker from Gdańsk symbolizes the triumph of moral force over savage force and the victory of personal ideals over collective oppression.

Just a few months ago Nancy and I had the pleasure of meeting with Lech Walesa and participating in a wonderful rally in Gdańsk at the shipyard. How inspirational it was to see this courageous man who is the very heart and soul of the worldwide move toward democracy and hear him ask: "Tell us how we can become like the United States."

From humble beginnings he has been elevated to his nation's highest post.

His country is united in spirit and in solidarity with him—and so is the entire world.

Now, as Poland works to modernize its economy, many American companies are discovering that Poland is a sound place for investing. The Polish people are good, honorable people with a respect for free enterprise that decades of Communist rule could not stamp out. After years behind the Iron Curtain, Poland has joined the nations of Free Europe.

Today Poles and Americans are working side by side—not just in business, but also in human services. In fact, one program I am especially proud of involves a Polish-American effort to overhaul the Polish health-care system. Over the past few years Project Hope has sent hundreds of volunteer health-care specialists to Poland to work with the government in reforming the health-care delivery system.

Today, both in commerce and compassion, Poland is a nation the world can be proud of.

So at this time, it is my distinct honor and pleasure to introduce a champion of freedom and Nobel Prize winner who has captured our hearts and inspired the world, the President of the Republic of Poland, His Excellency, Lech Walesa.

*T*he Reagans and I first met at a Governors' conference in Sun Valley, Idaho, when he was Governor of California and I was to be on a press panel. We had been commended to each other by my friend the author Truman Capote, who had met them in California while he was studying the death penalty after writing *In Cold Blood.* We became good friends even though we did not share the same political views.

While President Reagan was in the White House, we saw each other at frequent intervals. They came to my house for dinners, and Nancy and I used to lunch informally. It is remarkable that our friendship was sustained throughout the eight years of the Reagan Presidency, despite criticism of the administration's policies that often appeared in the pages of the *Post.* That doesn't often happen in Washington. We remain friends to this day.

What I most admired about Ronald Reagan as President was his ability to lead, his dignity, courage and humor—even in difficult circumstances—and that he has never wavered from his strongly held beliefs. He has great personal charm and magnetism. The Reagans' marriage is extraordinarily close and sustaining, as they share so many interests and quiet pleasures.

KATHARINE GRAHAM
*Chairman of the Executive Committee,*
*The Washington Post Company*

OUT OF RESPECT for the students here today, I will keep my remarks fairly brief. You see, I figure half of the students here are cutting class and the other half didn't have one scheduled this period, and with that in mind I just didn't think it would be fair to subject them to another lecture.

But I will stay at this podium long enough to share a few thoughts at this very special day. First of all, I must admit I was a little worried when my staff told me that G.W. wanted me back on the tenth anniversary of my care here. At first I thought maybe it was for a ten-year checkup, but my doctors in L.A. told me there was no such thing. Then I wondered if it had something to do with my hospital bill. I could only imagine the interest on a decade-old bill. But I was all prepared to plead my case: I've recently lost my job, and before that I was in public housing for eight years.

But then I learned I was to be given an honorary degree and that only made matters worse. You see, I've been burdened by a sense of guilt that the first degree I received in 1932 was honorary! It's no great secret that when I was in college I sometimes was more interested in football practice than my schoolwork. Maybe if I had gone to school without the distraction of football, I would have done well and made something of my life!

In all seriousness, I am deeply humbled and honored to be recognized by George Washington University in this way. After all the time I spent with G.W. doctors, it seems fitting that I've now become one! And I am so flattered that you would name the Institute of Emergency Medicine for me. This is one of our country's true treasures and I know from personal experience how important it is, and not only because of the events of ten years ago.

This university is part of history. Many of your faculty and students have been key players in this town for decades. Our administration borrowed heavily from your talented family and I will always be grateful for that. All of you should be proud of the contribution G.W. is making to America.

I want you to know how much it means to me that you would honor Nancy, too. There are no words to describe what she means to me, and it makes me so proud to know that there will be a plaque in the emergency room to pay tribute to her and to help others who find themselves as she did that day ten years ago.

For me it was easy—I just got on the gurney and let the wonderfully talented and dedicated people at the George Washington University Hospital do what they do best. But for Nancy, it was the greatest challenge of her life. To get the word that there had been a shooting, to have been told that I was OK, to rush to the hospital and then be told that not only was I not OK, but that my life was in great danger; then the waiting, the worrying and yes, the praying—I can't even begin to imagine what it must have been like for her. But she held up. She was there at my side every moment—a source, as your plaque so eloquently states, of great comfort and strength. I couldn't have made it without her, and so I thank you from the bottom of my heart for recognizing her in this way.

It's hard to believe that a decade has passed since our lives came together in a way none of us could have ever imagined. You have all been told what happened on March 30, 1981. A seemingly routine public appearance came perilously close to being a very dark chapter in history. But the people at the George Wash-

ington Hospital would have none of that. With no warning or time to get ready, they got *the call*—the one they had practiced for and thought about, but probably never expected would ever come—and made history. With speed, precision and unmatched skill, they did what they do best. I do not think it is an exaggeration to say the Good Lord was looking out for Jim Brady, Tim McCarthy and me when He delivered us to the doors of G.W. Hospital. We were healed here and allowed to carry on. For that, we will always be grateful.

And speaking of Jim Brady, I want to tell all of you here today something that I'm not sure you know. You do know that I'm a member of the NRA, and my position on the right to bear arms is well known. But I want you to know something else, and I am going to say it in clear, unmistakable language: I support the Brady Bill and I urge the Congress to enact it without further delay. With the right to bear arms comes a great responsibly to use caution and common sense on handgun purchases. And it's just plain common sense that there be a waiting period to allow local law-enforcement officials to conduct background checks on those who wish to buy a handgun. The Brady Bill is good legislation and I hope my colleagues at the other end of Pennsylvania Avenue will do what's right for the people and that means enacting this bill. And I couldn't mention this bill without adding a special word about its most dedicated supporter, Sarah Brady. Nancy and I have the greatest respect and affection for Sarah, who is not only an effective and articulate advocate, but an inspiring woman who we are honored to call our friend.

It's been forty-three years since G.W. Hospital was built, and in that time it has earned a reputation for being one of the very best and most important in the country. Part of that, as you well know, is because of the hospital's special role in providing medical care to national leaders and visiting foreign guests. Your reputation for excellence also comes from what you do routinely as well, including contributing more than $30 million annually in uncompensated care, providing emergency room care to 50,000 patients per year and coordinating consortium training of District of Columbia emergency medical personnel, to name just a few.

More than just impressive numbers, the story of G.W. Hospital is one of excellent health care. Lives are saved. Sick people get well. Illnesses are prevented. Comfort and compassion are always in great abundance.

It is fitting that the hospital bearing the name of our country's first President is known for such excellence. As George Washington set the standard for how we govern ourselves, so G.W. Hospital sets the standard for how we heal our sick.

And the excellence of this institution is by no means restricted to the hospital. George Washington University is well known across the country and around the world as one of our very best. From all fifty states and from ninety countries, the students here are treated not only to one of the most distinguished and able faculties in college education, but to the uniquely enriching experience of studying in the nation's capital.

Where else can you walk out of your dorm, look down the street and see the White House complex? Where else can you live next door to an embassy? Where else can you be taught by policymakers and Congressional advisors? Where else do you have to choose between which cabinet member or Senator you want to see in the Marvin Center at night? This is no ordinary university. It is a special experience to teach and study here.

And it is to these fortunate young people who are studying here that I would like to direct my concluding comments today. Most of you—at least the undergraduates—were not even teenagers when I stopped by here on the way home from a speech ten years ago. Think of how much the world has changed since then. We have seen a space shuttle program recover from a tragic accident. We have seen the Soviet Union agree to an historic treaty calling for the elimination of an entire class of nuclear weapons. We have seen that same Soviet Union wrestle with the very foundations of its existence as it makes the painful but necessary changes toward democracy. We have seen the Berlin Wall torn down and communism crumble in Eastern and Western Europe. We have seen free elections in Nicaragua. We have seen the triumph of good over evil in the Persian Gulf. We have seen computers, faxes, VCRs and cellular phones in most places of business. And that's just part of what has changed in the last ten years.

I can't begin to tell you what changes I've

witnessed since my arrival on the scene more than eighty years ago. But what has always struck me about change is how quickly time passes. Do you remember when you first thought about college? Where did the time go?

In four short years you blink and college will be gone. You go to class, you study hard—even pulling an occasional all-nighter—you have a few burgers at the Bone or a few sodas at the Rat, some of you join fraternities or sororities, you fall in and out of love, you cheer for the Colonials, and before you know it you're in cap and gown. It's hard to believe it happens so fast, but it does.

In your short time here you become best friends with people you didn't even know before you came here. I'll bet you hardly remember when you did not know many of the people you are closest to today. The bonding which takes place in college is unlike any other experience.

My young friends, savor these moments. Keep the memories close to your heart. Cherish your family and friends. As I learned ten years ago, we never really know what the future will bring. Live each day to the fullest.

Live each day with the enthusiasm, optimism and hope that guided the man whose name this university bears. If you do, I am convinced that your contribution to this wonderful experiment we call America will be greater than George Washington or any of his successors could have ever imagined.

Thank you for the honor you have bestowed on Nancy and me today, and God bless you all.

$\mathcal{A}$s a reporter, I covered Ronald Reagan as candidate, Governor of California and President for a quarter of a century, and wrote three biographies about him. He was as unfailingly courteous after a critical story as after a story that pleased him. Reagan treated everyone with fairness and decency. He was a gentleman in the best sense of the word, and he set a high standard for civil discourse in an age when this quality is in short supply. While passionate about his beliefs, Reagan never treated political adversaries as enemies. In fact, he became friends with a number of these adversaries, such as the late House Speaker Tip O'Neill. In the words of the founding fathers, Ronald Reagan always showed a "decent respect to the opinions of mankind."

*President Reagan and Lou Cannon aboard Air Force One, September 8, 1982.*

Another commendable quality of Reagan was his modesty. He was never puffed up, and was a font of self-deprecating humor.

When first elected Governor, he was asked how he would do and responded, "I don't know; I never played a Governor." Some made fun of this quip, but it showed that Reagan was self-secure, proud of the acting profession in which he had succeeded and able to joke about his political inexperience. This self-deprecation caused adversaries to underestimate him, usually to their later regret. But it was a quality that ordinary people appreciated. Reagan understood that the source of his leadership was a connection with the American people that he always valued and never lost. On the eve of his election as President in 1980, a reporter asked Reagan what it was that people saw in him. "Would you laugh if I told you that I think, maybe, they see themselves and that I'm one of them?" he replied. "I've never been able to detach myself or think that I, somehow, am apart from them."

These words still ring true.

LOU CANNON
*Author of* Ronald Reagan: The Role of a Lifetime

*T*HANK YOU, Governor Wilson, and thank all of you for that typically warm California greeting. How generous you are, inviting me home to this magnificent chamber on what I have been told is Ronald Reagan Day. And I thought they only name a day after you—well, after you're gone, if you know what I mean. As you can see, I'm very much here.

On days such as today, memories crowd in, and it is easy to imagine this chamber full of illustrious spirits—legislative giants such as "Big Daddy" Jesse Unruh, the legendary speaker who I bantered with every January and who I debated for the rest of the year, and George Moscone and Bob Moretti, to name just a few. But they loved this state with an intensity that I hope never goes out of fashion.

Well, the world has turned over many times since a gangly midwestern kid from Dixon, Illinois, by way of Des Moines, Iowa, hitched his wagon to the star called Hollywood. That town, much maligned yet inescapably symbolic of the nation it entertains, has often been called a dream factory. In truth, California itself encourages the dreamer in all of us—bigger, brighter, more diverse, more creative and, yes, more complex than just about anyplace I know.

In our classrooms and on our street corners, in our churches, synagogues, temples and mosques, we reflect the rich mosaic of the human race. In our research laboratories, our operating rooms and our governing councils, we display what Justice Holmes called "an itch for superlatives." Indeed, while officeholders elsewhere content themselves with talking points, Californians move boldly to take advantage of turning points. Where others see only problems, we glimpse possibilities.

The spring of 1991 is such a time, and in Pete Wilson, California is fortunate to have such a leader. Pete and I began our political careers together in 1966. Of course, he was a little less experienced than I. But I was impressed with him from the start, all the more so once he, too, made that painful but—thank heaven—only temporary move from California to Washington, D.C. Come to think of it, Pete, we were both there for eight years. I don't know what your excuse was. As for me, I couldn't leave well enough alone after two terms as Governor, so I ran for the only job in America that's any tougher.

Not only was I forced to leave my beloved California, but on top of everything else I spent the next eight years living in public housing! Eventually, I came home and here I am—in the prime of life—and out of work. Back in the autumn of 1932, former President Calvin Coolidge was asked to fill out a membership form from the Washington Press Club. At the place marked "occupation" he wrote in "retired." Then he skipped down a line to the section marked "comments." Coolidge thought for a moment before writing, "and glad of it."

Pete, there may be days when you wish you could say the same thing. Certainly you've had no shortage of tests since taking office in January. First, you had the lingering aftermath of the big earthquake to deal with, then a continuing drought and an exploding deficit. What's next, Pete? A swarm of locusts?

Whatever it may be, I have confidence in Pete Wilson's ability to deal with it. Pete's a problem-solver, and when he talks about the need for "preventive government" he brings an innovative approach to social and economic ills that simply can't be cured by standard procedures. Quite simply, Pete is looking for the source of the problems *before* they become problems.

No doubt Pete has already discovered himself what I soon learned about our state, which, in truth, is a nation, 30 million strong, where the Governor and the legislature must contend daily with a host of challenges: how to keep California's economy strong and its citizens fully employed, how to expand opportunity for all in an atmosphere where business is competitive and prosperity is not strangled in regulatory red tape, how to extend a helping hand to those who cannot help themselves, how to assure that every Californian can go to sleep safe at night and wake up to a neighborhood that's free of crime and purged of the drug menace.

One area in which California is setting the example is in gun control. Now, I'm a supporter of the Second Amendment to the Constitution, which gives citizens the right to bear arms. But I also believe that something must be done to curb the level of violence in this country. This week Congress will vote on the Brady Bill, which mandates a nationwide seven-day waiting period for the purchase of handguns. It is good legislation and I urge all of you to encourage your national representatives to vote for it. For years California has had a waiting period for purchases of handguns and it's time for the rest of the country to catch up. The Brady Bill can and will work *now.*

Of course, international relations are as important as domestic ones to a state like California, for we import and export more than any other state—more than many nations. According to the mapmakers, it's a long way from Los Angeles to London. But distances have a way of vanishing when measured in shared values and the entrepreneurial spirit. My friend Margaret Thatcher has a saying: "It's easy to be a starter, but are you a sticker, too?" Californians are starters, to be sure, but we are also stickers.

Along with the rest of our fellow Americans, we stuck to our guns in the Persian Gulf; more important, we stuck to elemental principles of justice and self-determination that are as old as the American republic. We have stopped apologizing for America's vital interests, and we have started asserting them. Half a million heroes sped to brilliant victory, supported by the vast majority of Americans—people who displayed yellow ribbons, and a red-blooded patriotism that was never bellicose and that has its logical sequel in our humane efforts to help the Kurdish victims of a cruel dictator.

For an unforgettable season, we were a country united, a liberator striking the shackles from a far-off land. As much as we focused on the dangers facing our men and women in the Persian Gulf, our fears were—and are—far outweighed by our pride in their accomplishments and the joy of welcoming them home.

On the international front, what Churchill called the Iron Curtain is dissolving. The Berlin Wall exists only in museums and in thousands of souvenir collections. Cold War enemies are united in a new Germany. A Polish electrician has won the heart of the world—not to mention the Presidency of a non-Communist Poland. The world's largest country, the Soviet Union, is struggling to change its ways. My friend Mikhail Gorbachev has a tough row to hoe. Perestroika has not yet met the promise of restructuring for which it stands—not, at least, insofar as the price of bread is concerned or the availability of meat on the shelves.

It is a very different story for the promise of democracy, whose universal appeal grows more evident with every dictator humbled and every wall breached. In our own hemisphere, military and authoritarian regimes throughout Latin America have given way to the *real* power of the people. Yet we should not engage in premature celebration, for in many of these countries the economy is fragile and it may be some time before the democratic plant flowers. We who have long enjoyed the benefits of democracy must remember the formidable obstacles faced by many countries. We should not delude ourselves into expecting that centuries-old suspicions will vanish overnight; it is easier to demolish a wall than to build up faith in the rule of law.

At the same time we are not without challenges of our own back here in California. Balancing the state's budget is certainly right up at the top of the list. Well, I'm not here to tell either the Governor or the legislature how to do their work.

You've got a lot of debate before you. There will be victories and defeats on both sides of the aisle. The questions here are not *if* or *when* to balance the state budget, but *how*. Think of such built-in restraint as a constitutional air bag, a protective device installed by political engineers to ensure the safety of every Californian on the long road to tomorrow. Whatever the immediate costs of action, the cost of doing nothing would be greater still. No one wants to be held responsible for dashing the hopes of countless young people for whom California remains the same dream factory that I first encountered more than half a century ago.

In the spring of 1975, retiring Justice William O. Douglas prepared a letter to his brethren on the United States Supreme Court. Justice Douglas had grown older, but he was not old—not in spirit, not in temperament and most definitely not in the optimism with which even then he anticipated the future. As a lifelong conservationist, one who found God in a trout stream as well as a church pew, Justice Douglas told his colleagues that he was reminded of many a canoe trip: "Those who start down a water course may be strangers at the beginning," he wrote, "but almost inevitably are close friends at the end." He drew the same conclusion about his long journey with his fellow Justices, and I think it is not stretching a point to liken your journey to his. Whatever your political background and outlook, if you will always remember that what you all want at the end of the journey is a secure and prosperous tomorrow for the people of California, you will be friends at journey's end.

Today marks the latest stage in a journey that began a quarter century ago, when a citizen-politician tossed his hat into the arena and a promising young candidate named Pete Wilson lent stature to the ticket I happened to head. It is the latest stage, but by no means the last. When Woodrow Wilson was once accused of being an idealist, he replied with more than a trace of anger that *of course* he was an idealist—that's how he knew he was an American. As I look out over this audience, I see a room full of idealists, practical and visionary, conservative, moderate and, yes, even liberal.

As Californians we hail from many traditions; we adhere to many faiths. We realize that in order to compete in the modern world, society must encourage those innovative souls who would take risks so that we all might reap rewards. Yet in getting ahead we must not leave anyone behind. We must never put at risk vulnerable Californians—the very young, the very old, those impoverished in worldly wealth or those who simply find themselves on society's outskirts.

Whatever divides us, this much unites us. We care about one another—about California. And out of our concern rises a passionate belief in the democratic process. Some people are content to twiddle their thumbs; we prefer to roll up our sleeves. Some people let things happen to them; we choose to make things happen.

My fondest wish for you who have been entrusted with California's future is that you never forget to care *for* her and *about* her. May she be for you, as she has been for me, the love of a lifetime.

Thank you and God bless you.

$\mathcal{R}$onald Reagan is one of the most fascinating figures of twentieth-century America. His bedrock principles could not be shaken or reshaped by fashion or by elites. Yet, he was able to get things done politically while not losing sight of these core convictions. His innate American optimism enabled him to thrive despite several changes in careers. What other man, other than a war hero, could enter politics in his early fifties and, despite setbacks along the way, reach the pinnacle of the Presidency?

*President Reagan with Malcolm Forbes, Sr., and Malcolm Forbes, Jr., in the Oval Office, June 24, 1983.*

Part of the perpetual underestimation of this man comes from the fact that he made his feats look easy. He always seemed confident, vigorous, serene, buoyant. He actively practiced one of his favorite sayings: you can do much if you don't mind who gets the credit.

In 1964, on the Saturday before the elections, I was with a group of CEOs and their wives at a function hosted by my parents. By pure chance, we saw Reagan's powerful television appeal on behalf of Barry Goldwater. Even Tom Dewey, pillar of the Eastern Establishment, was impressed. After the Goldwater debacle, bereft conservatives turned to Reagan. Nonbelievers thought the man might run for Congress or the Senate, where he could get by just making speeches. Instead, Reagan ran for Governor of the largest state in the union, whose size and complexity exceeds that of most nations, and confounded skeptics and scoffers by turning in an impressive performance.

Even today some Republicans don't fully appreciate Reagan's Presidential achievements. He turned a dispirited nation into a confident one. He slew the inflationary dragon that had seriously sapped American morale and was undermining our willingness to contain the increasingly aggressive Soviet Union. His tax cuts and regulatory curbs enabled Americans to achieve their longest peacetime expansion. His foreign military policies not only broke the Soviet momentum but fatally undermined the evil empire itself. Reagan knew the importance of ideas. He always supported Radio Free Europe and Radio Liberty, which I had the privilege to head during his second term. While devoutly hoping never to have to use our growing military arsenal, Reagan recognized you could effectively engage the Soviet Union in the battle of ideas on a daily basis, an insight most diplomats lacked. Shortly after Reagan left office, to almost everyone's astonishment, the Cold War came to an abrupt end. Yet because the economy was expanding, the burgeoning military budget never consumed the level of national resources that it did in the fifties and sixties. Talk about guns and butter!

Americans always admired Reagan's sense of propriety and unstuffy dignity, an admiration that can only now grow.

He was an outstanding President, something someday even historians will recognize.

MALCOLM S. FORBES, JR.

*I* AM PLEASED to be here this afternoon at this prestigious event for the members and guests of the Los Angeles Junior Chamber of Commerce. I addressed this organization eighteen years ago, when I was Governor of California. Come to think of it, most of you were not even old enough to vote back then.

Today I plan on saying a few words and then we'll open this up for a dialogue.

It's great to see so many of you here. I understand you are the largest chapter in the United States—six hundred members strong. Probably most of you are about twenty-five or thirty years old. It seems like only yesterday—well, not exactly yesterday—that I was twenty-five and was sitting on the front porch talking to George Washington about things. No, that's not quite true, though I am a *bit* older than twenty-five. In fact, I have well exceeded my life expectancy, which is a source of annoyance to a lot of people!

I must admit I'm a fan of yours. The L.A. Junior Chamber nurtures the talents of so many future business leaders in this country. And your chapter, in particular, contributes generously to our community and our economy.

I have a tremendous respect for your group. Your philosophy stresses professional development in the public and private sectors, as well as community service. The L.A. Junior Chamber continues to open new windows of service, through your Nissan Los Angeles Open, the L.A. City Area Special Olympics, the Foster Family Picnic and so many other necessary volunteer programs.

Beyond the daily changes and issues facing us on the domestic front, the international scene continues to be an area of great turmoil as well as a continuing birthplace for democracy.

There were times when it looked as if the Cold War might go on forever. Yet, less than two years ago, the people of the old Soviet bloc began to take matters in their own hands and it was over in a matter of months.

It's true that a number of specific events led to this dramatic climax, but that takes nothing away from the breathtaking speed with which the Soviet bloc finally crumbled. When it did, we all breathed a sigh of relief, yet the easing of East-West tensions did not bring an end to human strife and struggle. Far from it.

These days the headlines tell of violence in Yugoslavia, Sri Lanka, India and elsewhere. Age-old disagreements over nationality, customs or religion boil over into armed conflict, assassinations, destructions. In a number of cases, distinct groups want to go their separate ways, but the central governments refuse to give them their freedom. There seems little room for compromise.

When I read or see the news of these tragic events I find myself thinking about our blessings as well as our unresolved problems here at home. American racial and ethnic minorities, for example, seek their place in the sun. We Americans read, write, talk, debate and argue about this place a great deal of the time. What is distinctly American about all this activity is that we aren't arguing whether these groups should have their full share of opportunity, but rather how to make it happen.

Nationalism and sectarian and ethnic strife in many parts of the world seem to be driven by fears of the participants that they are playing a zero-sum game in which advance by one group automatically means losses for another. That's not the case here in the United States, but why isn't it?

The reason lies in our uniqueness as a nation. We—or our ancestors—came to America as individuals, families or in small groups, not as entire nationalities. We came from every corner of the earth and we brought with us an array of cultural traditions.

From this we created a new entity, the American, a person of many parts, but whose whole was stronger than the sum of those parts. Those who came had one thing in common: a desire for freedom and hope for a better life. This was translated into our belief in the rule of law, law that emanates from the people and not law handed down from on high by government or kings.

We keep adding new Americans all the time, of course, and the diversity of their backgrounds makes us all richer. I'll confess to getting a lump in my throat when I witnessed a swearing-in ceremony for new citizens. Written on their faces was happiness, pride and a determination to pursue their vision of the American dream.

Despite all the blessings the Lord has given this land between the oceans and despite our unity of purpose in times of need, such as during the recent Persian Gulf war, there are 250 million of us and we represent a dazzling range of interests. The process of dealing fairly with all of these interests takes constant management and adjustment at the local, state and federal levels.

That takes leadership and that's where you come in. As members of the Junior Chamber, you are young, but you're not inexperienced in the world of business. Many of you have had the pleasures and pains of running a business: meeting payrolls, paying bills and taxes, balancing budgets. Some of you are managers, others are administrators, and others market products and services. What all of you have is experience in the daily life of America, and judging from the legendary energy level of the Junior Chamber, you have plenty of zest for what you do.

You are just what we need more of in public life. I hope some of you will seriously consider interrupting your business careers to seek public office.

For a long time we had a tradition of the citizen-politician, the person who would take time out of a career to do the public's business. In recent decades this tradition has given way to that of the career politician. Typically, this person will study public administration in college, then go to work for a legislator or legislative committee. Then, if the boss moves on, say, to Congress, the aide runs for his or her seat, and so on.

Now, most of these career politicians are earnestly dedicated to public service. The one thing they have missed, however, is that they went into it before first getting any experience in what is often referred to in Washington as the real world. As a result, it may be hard for them to put themselves in the shoes of those of you on Main Street.

We need to leaven this loaf with a good many more of you who are out there dealing with the ups and downs, the joys and sorrows, of life in the real world.

Now, this doesn't mean you have to rush out and declare your candidacy for some office this afternoon. I was in my mid-fifties when I first

ran for public office. What I hope you will do is actively think about getting involved in public policy issues as a citizen. If there is a particular officeholder or candidate you like, give him or her a hand in the next campaign. Or take a look at the various volunteer groups that support the parties. Or consider nonpartisan groups that take an interest in particular policy issues, such as taxes and the environment.

Although I held public office for a total of sixteen years, I also thought of myself as a citizen-politician, not a career one. Every now and then when I was in government, I would remind my associates that "when we start thinking of government as 'us' instead of 'them,' we've been here too long." By that I mean that elected officeholders need to retain a certain skepticism about the perfectibility of government.

The ancient Chinese philosopher Lao-tzu had words for today when he said, "Govern a great nation as you would cook a small fish; do no overdo it."

Several state governments, including our own here in California, have been finding themselves forced to take that sort of advice lately because their constitutions require balanced budgets. When times are tight, such mandates force elected officials to examine the value of various programs. This results in decisions that may be painful in the short run but, taken in a larger context, are healthy for the state and for representative government.

Unfortunately for all of us, there is no requirement for a balanced budget at the federal level. And one of my greatest disappointments as President was that I was not able to get the federal budget balanced. This was especially disappointing because I had made a pledge to the American people to do so, and I wasn't able to fulfill it—at least not yet.

I haven't forgotten that pledge, believe me. I'd like to see future Presidents get two essential tools they will need to bring the budget under control. One is a constitutional amendment that will require the federal government to balance its budget each year. The other is what's called a line-item veto.

Congress has been evading its duty to consider this important business of the people for quite some time.

At its best, Congress is the place where great national issues are debated. But it is not at its best when it refuses to debate and vote on issues as important as these.

Let's start by insisting that Congress go on record with a fair, up-or-down vote on the balanced budget amendment and the line-item veto. And let's not stop until they do so. You can help get the process rolling by writing your elected representatives in Washington, asking them these questions: Do you favor or oppose bringing these measures to the floor for a vote and, if not, why not?

I once heard a TV commentator say, "Ronald Reagan states he wants a balanced budget, yet he never submitted one to Congress." He was right. It's true. The reason it's true is that I understood the reality of the situation.

The budgets I sent to Capitol Hill were routinely declared dead on arrival, no matter how modest the cutbacks we proposed. In fact, in

most cases, we were calling for cutting the rates of growth of programs. This was usually translated by the programs' partisans as "cutting back on vital programs."

Believe me, sending a balanced budget proposal to Congress was an exercise in futility. I never found the Congress of the United States to be in a frame of mind to accept a balanced budget and I am convinced it won't be until the people demand a constitutional amendment requiring one. We, the people, can make that happen. We may not be able to make Congress see the light, but we can make them feel the heat!

Along with the balanced budget amendment, we need to give the President what forty-three state Governors already have: the line-item veto. I had it as Governor of California and I used it 943 times over eight years without once being overridden by the state legislature.

With the line-item veto, the President could go into the budget and veto out the pork and fat that adds so much to the deficit. With one stroke of the pen, the President could eliminate those items that Congress has no right forcing the American people to pay for.

Some recent examples are a proposed $25,000 study to decide whether or not to build a new workout gym for Congressional staffers since they can't use the facility used by the Congressmen. How about the million-dollar study by a Congressman which was supposed to discover the reason why people don't ride their bicycles to work.

There are many people who really need the

government's help. We should be using taxpayer money for programs that are important and that can help those people, not for things that are the pet project or a political payoff for some member of Congress.

As with the balanced budget amendment, Congress won't lessen its resistance to the line-item veto until the people demand that the issue be fully and openly debated, then voted on. The real reason Congress does not want to do this, of course, is that the outcome might reduce its power. Many in Congress have forgotten that power belongs to the people and that they are only the representatives of the people, not powers unto themselves.

There is another ancient Chinese proverb that I think fits this situation. That is, "Use power to curb power." Use the power of your voice, your pen and, ultimately, your vote to let your elected representatives know that you want a balanced budget amendment and the line-item veto so that we can make sure our representative democracy works the way it was intended to work. Once you've done that you will have become an activist. The next step is to become a citizen-politician. Once you've spoken out, it's an easy step to take. I know, I tried it, and it works.

Thank you and God bless you.

*The* year 1980 was, for the most part, a dark moment for America. At home, sluggish economic growth and skyrocketing prices had combined to produce stagflation, emptying American pocketbooks and sapping the American spirit of optimism. Malaise at home was matched by humiliation abroad. Terrorists in Tehran held fifty-five Americans hostage as the United States looked on in frustrated impotence. Soviet troops occupied Afghanistan. Moscow's surrogates were on the march in Africa and Central America. Morale in our military services was lower than at any period in memory. And everywhere—even among our most trusted friends in Western Europe and Japan—American prestige had reached a nadir unplumbed since our entry, nearly forty years before, into World War II.

*President Reagan and Jim Baker aboard Air Force One, March 25, 1981.*

All that changed with the election of Ronald Reagan as President. His infectious optimism simply made people feel good about themselves and their country at a time when it was desperately needed. His no-nonsense integrity, his unshakable belief in the values that made America great and his unapologetic pursuit of these time-tested principles were the corner-stones of his administrations. The Reagan revolution transformed the American landscape. In just a few years, our nation embarked on the most sustained noninflationary peacetime expansion in its economic history, creating tens of millions of new jobs and unleashing the energies of hundreds of thousands of new entrepreneurs. And just as surely as the Reagan revolution restored our prosperity, economic growth and flagging spirits at home, that revolution also restored our tarnished prestige abroad. America was once again respected by her allies and feared by her adversaries.

In short, America was back—and the verdict of history is clear: Ronald Reagan was the right man at the right time to revitalize our nation and make all of us proud once again.

JAMES A. BAKER III
*Secretary of State, 1989–1992*

*P*erhaps Ronald Reagan's greatest leadership characteristic was his unswerving conviction. We all knew the issues on which it was futile to argue: tax reduction, strong defense, the work ethic, abiding faith in a market economy and the democratic process. He often commented that the Oval Office was not his office; he was just a temporary occupant. It belonged to the people.

Probably no President was more approachable or more reserved at the same time. He was always available, and he always had the courage to make tough decisions and *stick with them.* But he seldom talked about his personal life other than to refer on occasion to his old role as a union negotiator.

History will judge Ronald Reagan for his vision and his strength of purpose in pursuing that vision. He knew that the way to peace was to negotiate, and that the only way to negotiate was through strength. Step one was to restore our strength and to label the USSR for what it was. Step two was then to engage them in serious negotiations on a number of fronts. George Shultz provided superb advice and great negotiating skills, but it was Ronald Reagan who supplied the determination and the leadership.

True, the USSR *might* have collapsed anyway. But there is no question that Ronald Reagan's policies hastened that collapse. Don't ask Ronald Reagan's political opponents about that, just ask the Russians.

FRANK C. CARLUCCI
*Chairman, The Carlyle Group*

*I* AM PLEASED to be here with you this evening in commemoration of Captive Nations Week. You know, if things continue the way they have been, maybe next year we'll have to call it Free Nations Week. Now, wouldn't that be something?

Remembering those nations which have lost—or newly won—their freedom is important to me, and I congratulate this event's co-sponsors: the Republic of China Chapter of the World League for Freedom and Democracy and the Claremont Institute for the Study of Statesmanship and Political Philosophy. In the purposes of these two organizations, we see reflected America's calling and her destiny—to nourish and defend freedom and democracy and to communicate these ideals everywhere we can.

We who are privileged to be Americans have had a rendezvous with destiny since that moment in 1630 when John Winthrop, standing on the deck of the tiny *Arbella* off the coast of Massachusetts, told the little band of Pilgrims,

"We shall be as a city upon a hill. The eyes of all people are upon us."

I have long believed that the guiding hand of Providence did not create this new nation of America for ourselves alone, but for a higher cause: the preservation and extension of the sacred fire of human liberty.

The Declaration of Independence and the Constitution of these United States are covenants we have made not only with ourselves, but with all of mankind. Our founding documents proclaim to the world that freedom is not the sole prerogative of a chosen few. It is the universal right of all God's children. As John Quincy Adams promised, "Whenever the standard of freedom and independence has been or shall be unfurled, there will be America's heart, her benedictions and her prayers."

Can we doubt that a Divine Providence placed this land, this continent of freedom, here as a refuge for all those peoples in the world who yearn to breathe free? Look around this room tonight. Among our number we have Cambodians who have escaped the cruel purges of Pol Pot. We have the boat people of Vietnam, who risked their lives to escape from a tyranny worse than death. We have the Hmong, who fought so bravely with us for their freedom, and who withdrew with honor to these shores when that struggle was concluded. We have the myriad of peoples of the Baltic states and Eastern Europe, who alike fled the dark descent of an Iron Curtain, in Winston Churchill's memorable phrase, over their homelands. We have the free Chinese, who found sanctuary here and on the island of Taiwan, there to create a beacon of hope for the mainland.

Never have our duties as a people been heavier than over the past few decades. A troubled and afflicted mankind has repeatedly looked to us—today's living Americans—to keep our rendezvous with destiny. True to our nation's calling, we have responded. No people on this earth has fought harder or paid a higher price to advance the cause of freedom, nor has met with greater success.

In Europe, in Asia, in Central America and the Caribbean, and recently in the Middle East, we have led nation after nation out of the wilderness of invasion and captivity to the broad sunlit plains of liberty. We stood shoulder to shoulder with our allies and friends in Europe until the Iron Curtain that artificially divided their continent was torn asunder and Germany was reunited. We held the line in Asia, buying time for countries like Korea, Taiwan and the Philippines to build the institutions of democracy.

My good friend Margaret Thatcher recently said that I, Ronald Reagan, single-handedly won the Cold War against communism. I cannot accept this honor. To begin with, I had the Iron Lady on my side.

The eighties were a decade when you and I and the vast majority of Americans courageously supported the struggle for liberty, self-government and free enterprise throughout the world. Together with our allies abroad we turned the tide of history away from totalitarian darkness and into the warm sunlight of human freedom.

There can be no doubt that the tide of freedom is rising. At the start of this century there were only a handful of democracies. Today more than half of the world's people, living in over sixty countries, govern themselves. Nations as varied as Lithuania, Croatia and Armenia have legislatures elected by the people and responsive to the people. One of the engines in this progress is the desire for economic development—the realization that it is free nations that prosper and free peoples who create better lives for themselves and their children. Another is the natural desire of disparate peoples for self-determination.

The cult of the state may be dying, but it is not yet dead. In Eastern Europe, Poland, Hungary and Czechoslovakia now have popularly elected governments. An unwelcome army of occupation will soon withdraw. These governments now face the difficult question of privatizing the vast resources accumulated by their totalitarian predecessors. How quickly and completely they move to a free-market econ-

PRESIDENT REAGAN *returning home to Los Angeles with the*
*Presidential Medal of Freedom, January 13, 1993.*

PRESIDENT REAGAN *presenting Mother Teresa with the*
*Presidential Medal of Freedom, June 20, 1985.*

*(facing page, top and bottom)*
PRESIDENT REAGAN *with General Secretary Mikhail*
*Gorbachev at Rancho del Cielo, May 3, 1992.*
PRESIDENT REAGAN *lending advice to President-Elect*
*Bill Clinton, November 27, 1992.*

PRESIDENT REAGAN *standing with Presidents Bush,*
*Carter, Ford and Nixon at the opening ceremony in dedication of the*
*Ronald Reagan Presidential Library, November 4, 1991.*

*(facing page)*
PRESIDENT *and Mrs. Reagan at the Ronald Reagan*
*Presidential Library.*

PRESIDENT REAGAN *with young visitors to the*
*Ronald Reagan Presidential Library.*

*(facing page)*
PRESIDENT REAGAN *with Princess Diana at a White House*
*dinner for her and Prince Charles, November 9, 1985.*

PRESIDENT REAGAN *on his last day in office, January 20, 1989.*

omy will determine the standard of living of their peoples for years to come.

Moving south, Bulgaria, Yugoslavia and Romania have yet to complete their democratic transitions. Bulgaria may be the first to achieve this if the current parliament resigns as promised later this month and free elections are held in September.

We find Yugoslavia on the brink of civil war. The Croatian and Slovenian peoples, by majorities in excess of 90 percent, have indicated their wish to withdraw their republics from the Yugoslavian state. The state seems equally determined to preserve its territorial integrity by force if necessary.

As Americans who believe in government by consent, our sympathies naturally lie with the breakaway republics. It is for the people, not the state, to determine where the boundaries of civil societies shall fall.

This same principle of self-determination applies to the Soviet Union's many republics. I am not speaking here of the Baltic states. Lithuania, Latvia and Estonia were illegally occupied by the Soviet Union at the opening of World War II. They are sovereign states by right and should be freed immediately. I am speaking of the Soviet Union's other republics.

America should not get into the business of preserving the artificial state structures established by monarchs and dictators.

Once the Soviet Union has dissolved into a loose confederation of nations, what then? Freed from the twin burdens of empire and communism, the Russian people will reassert their natural greatness. Their land will stretch seven thousand miles from Leningrad—excuse me, I meant St. Petersburg—to Vladivostok.

They will be a nation of 160 to 180 million people, bent upon repairing the economic and social ravages of totalitarianism. If they choose democracy and the free market—and we should be encouraging them to do so—this can be accomplished quickly. In five years their family farms will feed not only themselves, but many of the nations around them. In fifteen years their enterprises, taking advantage of Russia's vast natural resources and the foreign investment that will pour in, will number among the best in the world.

Moving to China, we have seen the brutal way the Beijing regime responded to the cries of the Chinese people for democracy in Tiananmen Square. They fail to realize that you cannot crush hope with the treads of tanks; you cannot drown democratic aspirations in a hail of bullets.

In our relationship with China, we should always remember what our Chinese friends on Taiwan have accomplished: a resource-poor island has become one of the major trading nations in the world; a political transformation no less dramatic than that of Europe has resulted in full-fledged democracy. The implications of these changes for China's future are profound. As President Li Teng-hui recently remarked, "We are building a prosperous democracy—not just for the Taiwan area itself, but for the whole of China. We are building a democracy for unification." We in America can never go wrong if we do what is morally right and keep our commitments to Taiwan.

Soviet colonies around the globe, abandoned by Moscow in its own quest for survival, are withering and dying. We have just marked the sixteenth anniversary of the death of freedom for Vietnam and Cambodia. Hanoi and Phnom Penh are both abandoning the socialist economic model and adopting a more market-oriented approach that will surely bring greater political freedom in its wake. The peace negotiations in Cambodia are making progress, but the participation of the ruthless Khmer Rouge in these talks gives many people pause.

As long as these struggles continue, freedom-loving people around the world must say, "I am a Chinese imprisoned for advocating democracy at Tiananmen, I am an Afghan fighting to liberate my country from the tyranny of Marxism-Leninism, I am a Vietnamese, a Cambodian, a Hmong. I, too, am a potential victim of totalitarianism."

Those who preach the supremacy of the state will be remembered for the sufferings their delusions caused their peoples. It is my hope that in the twenty-first century, which is only nine years away, human dignity will be everywhere respected; that the free flow of people and ideas will include not only the newly freed states of Eastern Europe, but those republics which are still struggling for their freedom.

America's solemn duty is to constantly renew its covenant with humanity to complete the grand work of human freedom that began two hundred years ago. This work, in its grandness and nobility, is not unlike the building of a magnificent cathedral. In the beginning, progress is slow and painstaking. The laying of the foundations and the raising of the walls is measured in decades rather than years. But as the arches and spires begin to emerge in the air, others join in, adding their faith and dedication and love, to speed the work to its completion.

My friends, the world is that cathedral. And our children, if not we ourselves, will see the completed work—the worldwide triumph of human freedom, the triumph of human freedom under God.

Thank you and God bless you.

*T*hose of us who have called the White House our home and have assumed the awesome responsibilities of leading this great nation share a special bond that withstands differences in political ideology. This is exemplified in my personal reflections of my relationship with President Ronald Reagan.

Understanding the significance of the opening of my Presidential Library, which houses the papers and other historically significant items from my administration, President Reagan honored me by delivering an eloquent and moving speech at the dedication ceremonies. It was personally gratifying to Rosalynn and me that the President and First Lady would give of their time in this way, and it underscored the importance of our shared commitment to the legacy of the Presidency.

*President Reagan and President Carter in the Oval Office, October 13, 1981.*

When the Reagan Library opened after he left office, we then had the pleasure of attending the dedication ceremonies in California. All of the five living Presidents were there, and an unprecedented photograph was made of us together. People who see this picture are awed by the message of solidarity that it conveys.

JIMMY CARTER
*Thirty-ninth President of the United States, 1977–1981*

*T*HANK YOU very much, Mr. President [George Bush], and all the other distinguished speakers who hold that exalted title. You know, I've been called a great communicator, but I have to admit it's hard for me to communicate the emotions that crowd in at such a moment and the humility that comes with tributes like those you have heard this morning—the pride I feel as I look out over this audience and see so many old friends for whom this library is a testimonial of love, loyalty and idealism.

To Lod Cook and the members of the Reagan Library Foundation, and to the thousands of donors the world over whose generosity is reflected in the building we dedicate this morning, there are no words to convey adequately the gratitude that both Nancy and I feel for all you have done.

Let me also thank President Bush and the former Presidents who have joined us. Today the exclusive fraternity of Presidents has grown, and although we don't get together very often, when we do—well, as you can see, it generates quite a bit of interest. At one time or another I've run against most of these gentlemen, and they've run against me. Yet here we are. Which just goes to show that above personal ideologies and party politics, we stand united as Americans.

I am proud and honored that so many of the great Presidential families are represented here today:

• the descendants of Franklin Delano Roosevelt, for whom I cast my first four votes and who has served as a personal inspiration to me as well as millions of Americans;

• Caroline and John Kennedy, Jr., who through their strength and courage have so proudly carried forward the flame of their father's legacy;

• Lady Bird Johnson, whose warmth and strength served as a tremendous source of inspiration to her husband, and whose personal efforts have inspired a whole new generation of Americans to "Keep America Beautiful." She is joined by her daughter Luci Johnson Turpin and Luci's husband, Ian Turpin.

The five Presidents on this platform span twenty-two years of challenge and triumph—from the first man on the moon to the last aggressor out of liberated Kuwait—two and a half decades forever stamped with the style and substance of:

- a grocer's son from Yorba Linda, California, who as a boy heard train whistles in the night and dreamed of traveling to distant places, and who as President would crisscross the globe to build a new and lasting structure of peace. And his lovely wife, Pat, whose splendor and grace has served as an inspiration to every First Lady that has followed her;
- an All-American from Michigan by way of Capitol Hill, who as an embodiment of midwestern decency and honor steered the ship of state through rough waters and won the affection of Americans everywhere. And his First Lady, Betty, who has been a shining example of personal strength to millions of Americans;
- a son of the South whose election did more than anything else to restore that great region to its rightful place in the American mainstream, and who devoted himself tirelessly to cleaning the blood of Abraham from the sands of the Middle East. And his "partner to the President," Rosalynn, who assists him to this day in his important efforts to improve the quality of life in nations around the world;

- and a Texan imbued with the "can do" optimism of that larger than life place—who in liberating a small nation half a world away has also freed the United States of America from the crippling legacy of Vietnam. And with us today, America's First Lady, Barbara, whose personal campaign for literacy has opened the minds and hearts of so many Americans;
- and, of course, my Nancy. I don't know how to begin to describe what she means to me, except to say I can't imagine life without her.

Would you please join me, ladies and gentlemen, in expressing our gratitude to these great Americans, not just for their presence here today, but for their historic contributions to a world where, to a greater extent than ever before in our century, no one wields a sword and no one drags a chain.

Today we gather for a single purpose: to give to the American people and the world a Presidential Library. There is, understandably, a great temptation to look back, to remember, to share warm and fond memories and to reflect on the events which brought us here. And as we do, I hope we do not unduly focus on one man, one political party or even one country. Instead, our focus should be on the enduring fundamental principles of life that ennoble mankind.

Ever since Franklin Delano Roosevelt, Presidents have built libraries amidst the surroundings that have shaped their characters and molded their values.

From West Branch, Iowa, to the Simi Valley of California, these institutions reflect the genius of the American people for self-government. Within their walls are housed millions of records for scholarly interpretation, along with thousands of objects that give both solid and symbolic substance to this nation's highest office and to the forty men who have occupied it since Washington took his oath.

Like the office they commemorate, Presidential Libraries are living institutions. Certainly it is my hope that the Reagan Library will become a dynamic intellectual forum where scholars interpret the past and policymakers debate the future.

It is said that after leaving the White House Harry Truman once came into his living room to discover his wife, Bess, tossing their old love letters into the fireplace. "Think of history!" said a horrified Mr. Truman.

"I have," said Bess.

Well, in a few days, more than 6 million pages of documentation pertaining to my administration will be released to the public. In time, more than 50 million pages will be made available for researchers.

But if the Reagan Library is anything like its counterparts, most of those who enter these doors will not be academics. No, they will be ordinary people of all ages, backgrounds and political persuasions, eager to examine their past and explore a history not always learned in school. For them, this institution will be a time capsule of American growth and greatness, covering more than a single Presidency, honoring more than a single President.

Here visitors will have a chance to tour and study at their leisure the accelerating changes in a fast-forward world. They will be able to trace the historic process by which mankind has stepped back from the narrow window ledge of mutually assured destruction.

They will observe an American President and a Soviet leader sitting in a boathouse on the shore of Lake Geneva, striving to banish the nuclear nightmare from the dreams of all our children. They will see tears of pride from the boys of Pointe du Hoc; they will hear the thrusting engines of *Challenger* lifting off on a heartbreaking final mission.

They will be introduced to a warm and selfless First Lady who reached out to a generation of young Americans threatened by the scourge of drugs, and who put a comforting arm around an older generation through the Foster Grandparents Program.

They will catch the sinister crackle of a would-be assassin's weapon, one that forever changed the lives of Jim and Sarah Brady while reconfirming my belief that whatever time remained to me was to be spent in service to the American people and in accord with the Lord's wishes.

No doubt many visitors will stand in the replica of my Oval Office. Perhaps they will sense a little of the loneliness that comes with decision making on a global scale, or the stabbing pain inflicted by a terrorist's bomb half a world away, or the dread sound of a telephone in the middle of the night, with news of hostile actions.

They will also feel some of the immense

pride that comes to any President in that office as he comes into daily contact with the American heroes whose faith in themselves, their mission and the mandate is a never-ending source of emotional renewal.

But then I was lucky. If I ever tired, all I had to do was look over my shoulder. Age has its privileges, and on this day of memory and reflection, I hope you will indulge me in recalling some very special people. I remember a small woman with auburn hair and unquenchable optimism. Her name was Nelle Reagan and she believed with all her heart that there was no such thing as accidents in this life. Everything was part of God's plan. If something went wrong you didn't wring your hands, you rolled up your sleeves.

And I remember a storytelling salesman with the Irish gift of laughter and a certain American restlessness. In the spirit of his forebears who had settled on the endless sea of grass that was the Illinois prairie before the turn of the century, Jack Reagan took his family to many new beginnings. Perhaps that was the root of my belief, shared with Thomas Paine, that we Americans of all people were uniquely equipped to begin the world over.

Jack had dreams. Nelle had drive. The Reagans of Dixon, Illinois, may have had little in material terms, but we were emotionally wealthy beyond imagination, for we were Americans, young people in a young land with the best days ahead. And we were part of a very special extended family. I grew up in a town where everyone cared about one another because everyone knew one another—not as statistics in a government program but as neighbors in need. Is that nostalgic? I don't think so. I think it is still what sets this nation apart from every other on the face of the earth.

Something else I learned, and that every generation of young Americans must discover for themselves. I learned to admire the entrepreneurial spirit of this pioneering land, where everyone has a chance to push out the boundaries of life. All this and more will greet visitors to this Library and Museum. If they are anything like me, they will arrive with the conviction—so reminiscent of what Nelle Reagan taught long ago in Dixon—that America itself is no accident of geography or political science, but part of God's plan to preserve and extend the sacred fire of human liberty.

I, too, have been described as an undying optimist, always seeing a glass half full when some see it as half empty. And, yes, it's true—I always see the sunny side of life. And that's not just because I've been blessed by achieving so many of my dreams. My optimism comes not just from my strong faith in God, but from my strong and enduring faith in man.

In my eighty years, I've seen what men can do for each other and do to each other. I've seen war and peace, feast and famine, depression and prosperity, sickness and health. I've seen the depths of suffering and peaks of triumph. And I know in my heart that man is good, that what is right will always eventually triumph and that there is purpose and worth to each and every life.

A dynamic people, by rolling their sleeves up and getting government off their backs, can achieve economic renewal. They can slay the beast of inflation and break the record book when it comes to sustained economic growth. They can create millions of new jobs and show a watching world the success of free enterprise.

I remember a time when the growth of American government seemed inexorable and the encroachment of that government on the lives and liberties of our citizens seemed unstoppable.

I also remember a time when America was advised to keep a low profile in the world, as if by hunkering down and muzzling her deepest beliefs she might avoid foreign criticism and placate her enemies.

And I remember a time when walls divided nations and human rights were trampled in the name of corrupt ideologies, a time when the arms race was spiraling out of control and distrust stood between us.

Eighty years is a long time to live, and yet within the course of only a few short years I have seen the world turned upside down and conventional wisdom utterly disproved. Visitors to this mountaintop will see a great jagged chunk of the Berlin Wall, hated symbol of yes, an evil empire, that spied on and lied to its citizens, denying them their freedom, their bread, even their faith.

Well, today that wall exists only in museums, souvenir collections and the memories of a people no longer oppressed. It is also a reminder that a strong America is always desirable—and necessary in our world.

Today a heroic people has cast off the chains of Marx and Lenin that gave rise to so much of this century's tensions. The Iron Curtain has rusted away. In churches and schools, in factories and on farms, the people of Eastern Europe have found their voice and with it a battering ram to knock down the walls of tyranny. Totalitarianism is melting like snow.

As the mythology of communism melts under the fierce heat of truth, our greatest enemy now may be complacency itself.

Meanwhile, let us joyously invade our former opponents—with Yankee ingenuity, entrepreneurs selling their wares, enthusiastic tourists—all spreading the gospel of human freedom.

Prosperous democracies don't declare war on each other—they simply let their citizens build better lives for themselves.

Western Europe soared like a phoenix from the ashes of World War II. So can Eastern Europe from the ruins of totalitarianism. And the American people can help show the way. What a happy challenge for those looking for something to do after the Cold War!

Today is the latest chapter in a story that began a quarter century ago, when the people of California entrusted me with the stewardship of their dreams. The latest—but far from the last. For ten years after we summoned America to a new beginning, we are beginning still. Every day brings fresh challenges and opportunities to match. With each sunrise we are reminded that millions of our citizens have yet to share in the abundance of American prosperity. Many languish in neighborhoods bereft of hope.

Still others hesitate to venture out on the

streets for fear of criminal violence. Can't we pledge ourselves to a new beginning for them?

Around the world, hope stirs in the Middle East, and our prayers are with the peacemakers as they strive to realize an historical opportunity to bring peace to that ancient cradle of faith. With the Cold War over, can't we achieve a new beginning wherever peace is threatened?

Proverbially, old men plant trees even though they do not expect to see their fruition. So it is with Presidents.

The doors of this library are open now and all are welcome. The judgment of history is left to you, the people. I have no fears of that, for we have done our best. And so I say, come and learn from it.

My fondest hope is that Americans will travel the road extending forward from the arch of experience, never forgetting our heroic origins, never failing to seek divine guidance as we march boldly, bravely into a future limited only by our capacity to dream.

May every day be a new beginning, and every dawn bring us closer to that shining city upon a hill.

Thank you. God bless you all. And God bless America.

*P*resident Reagan had a self-confidence and a self-esteem that many of his insecure predecessors would have envied. He had strong convictions and truly seemed to believe that everyone could have a Horatio Alger approach to a successful life.

On his desk in the Oval Office was a small wooden plaque with the inscription: "There is no limit to what a man can do or where he can go if he doesn't care who gets the credit." That was the way Ronald Reagan conducted his Presidency. He was at one with himself, and his ego did not dominate his decisions or his surroundings.

*President Reagan sharing a quip with UPI senior correspondent Helen Thomas, April 22, 1981.*

He talked tough to the "evil empire" but he was a gentle man, and moved the world toward peace with his then Soviet counterpart, Mikhail Gorbachev.

As President he played the role big. His self-deprecating humor was a saving grace.

There was a Reagan revolution, and with it Reagan left his mark on the twentieth century and future generations.

HELEN THOMAS
*Washington Bureau Chief, United Press International*

Someone once observed that a test of character is how one performs under difficult circumstances. But another test of character is how someone handles power.

Surely during the time Ronald Reagan was in the White House there was no more powerful office in the world than President of the United States. Yet he never forgot who he was without the trapping of that office and he was unfailingly kind and charitable to people he encountered, even to reporters who covered him and often wrote or said things about him he surely must not have liked.

In November 1981, President Reagan came to the Washington headquarters of ABC News to dedicate our new building. Quite an honor and all our top management was there, including news president Roone Arledge and ABC board chairman and founder of the network Leonard Goldenson.

After Mr. Reagan delivered short remarks dedicating the building I began firing questions at him about an embarrassing interview his budget director, David Stockman, had given. Uncomfortable under this assault, the President started dodging and weaving in his answers.

Arledge tried to smooth things over.

"I was just kidding when I said the first question would be by Sam Donaldson," he said, aware that the majesty of the occasion was quickly dissolving.

*President Reagan and ABC's Sam Donaldson laughing in the White House Colonnade, outside the Oval Office, July 20, 1983.*

137

"So fire me," I replied in what I hoped would be a lighthearted tone.

"You know, that's not a bad idea," shot back Arledge without a trace of lightheartedness.

The official party moved backstage, where one of the President's top aides started complaining that the President had been "mousetrapped."

"You told us this was to be a building dedication and you turned it into a press conference," the aide complained bitterly.

It was a terribly embarrassing moment for the top management of the American Broadcasting Company and a terribly dangerous moment for me.

Before Arledge could reply—thank God before he could reply—another voice interrupted.

"Oh, that's all right, that's just the way Sam is," said President Reagan with a chuckle, and my job was saved.

Ronald Reagan's power never went to his head. He was never vindictive, never petty, always charitable and a gentleman to those around him.

SAM DONALDSON
*ABC News*

138

*R*onald Reagan loved the annual dinners of the Washington Gridiron Club, an organization of newspaper journalists whose sole purpose is to lampoon the capital's politicians.

President Reagan so enjoyed these affairs because they were more like show business (which he adored) and less like politics (which he tolerated as a means to an end). His graceful remarks closing Gridiron dinners were typified by this one-liner: "I've heard that hard work never hurt anybody, but I sure didn't want to take a chance on it."

That typical Reagan self-deprecating humor, while pointing up that he was no workaholic, poked fun at a capital city that takes itself too seriously. He also demonstrated his firm belief that government and politics cannot solve the nation's or the individual's woes. To President Reagan, government was the problem, not the solution.

*President Reagan greeting syndicated columnist Robert Novak in the Oval Office, March 23, 1981.*

Unlike most politicians I have known, President Reagan did not like gossiping about politics. I found that out in 1975 during a long ride in a small plane from Jackson, Mississippi, to Boca Raton, Florida—alone with former Governor Reagan except for the pilots and two aides. I eagerly anticipated all I would learn about his Presidential plans for 1976.

But he was not talking politics. He told charming, occasionally ribald Hollywood anecdotes, and treated me to his store of politically incorrect dialect jokes.

So it went whenever I had private time with President Reagan. He was making clear that there is life outside of politics and government, dispelling the great illusion that our salvation lies in Washington.

ROBERT J. NOVAK
*Syndicated Columnist*

*I*'M DELIGHTED to join so many distinguished leaders in the radio and television community.

This is a beautiful award and a very special honor, all the more so because it involves a business that has been my heart and soul for so many years. As David Sarnoff, a great visionary in broadcasting, once said, "We have hitched our wagon to the electron."

I just happened to hitch my wagon a little earlier than you did. In fact, when I was a young lad Ben Franklin asked me to hold his kite for him. As lightning flashed across the sky, I said, "No, you go ahead, sir."

And that was the man who wanted to be "healthy, wealthy and wise"!

And, of course, Washington is in the throes of a political season—angry rhetoric, intricate parliamentary maneuvers, treacherous back stabbing. And that's just the debate over new broadcast licenses. Sounds like a good pilot for the new TV season!

You know, one thing you can always expect in our business is the unexpected. I probably wouldn't be standing here today if not for a strange twist of fate one day. When I graduated from college in Illinois in 1932, the Great Depression was at gale force. I was hired as a rookie announcer at a little 1,000-watt station in Iowa. The catch phrase was, "Station WOC, Davenport—where the West begins, in the state where the tall corn grows."

Later, I moved to WHO, our sister station in Des Moines. I spent four years there and they were among the most pleasant of my life. If I had stopped there, I believe I would have been happy the rest of my life.

I ended up doing play-by-play for the Chicago Cubs and even went with the Cubs for spring training in California in 1937. By the way, it was on that trip, just by chance, I met an agent who signed me up for the movies, and in Hollywood if you did not sing or dance you became an after-dinner speaker. Pretty soon I did more speaking than acting and found myself running for Governor. And not willing to leave bad enough alone, I ran for President.

So I want to thank all of you for giving this young fellow his start and for all the other things you do for your country. You provide not just news and entertainment but wisdom about the human condition.

You save countless lives by warning about floods, hurricanes and other natural disasters. And charities also save lives by using your stations to raise hundreds of millions of dollars every year.

Last year broadcasters relayed video messages from soldiers in Desert Storm to the United States. The cheerful words "Hi, Mom! I'm in the desert. I miss you!" brought together not just families but our whole country.

Broadcasting has transformed our universe. Radio and television waves are a sixth human sense—the extra dimension of the twentieth century. This invisible energy inspires humans to be human—to learn, laugh, love, hate, go to war or join together in peace. Instantly.

Radio and television waves are the Paul Reveres of the universe. They are liberators undeterred by the icy tundra or trackless desert. You tear down Berlin Walls, uproot Bamboo Curtains and destroy dictators.

Before radio most of the world was not free. Life, to quote Hobbes, was "brutish, nasty and short." Even a century ago our own nation was fragmented and isolated. We had over 20,000 newspapers, but almost every paper was confined to a particular city or town. Communications were so slow it took three days for Americans to learn about Dewey's landmark victory in Manila Bay in 1898.

The ancient Greeks discovered how to generate electricity—static electricity. But it was not until 1887 that a primitive radio wave was transmitted. Heinrich Hertz sent an electric current running through a wire with a gap in it. The electricity jumped off at a gap and landed on a wire on the other side of the room, like a bird flying from one perch to another.

In 1901, Marconi sent the dot-dash signal, and soon after Lee De Forest added voices and music to the airwaves, including a live concert by Enrico Caruso in 1912.

Americans rushed out to buy elegant Atwater Kent radios. Or they built their own receivers with a spool of wire, a crystal, an aerial and earphones.

The high-tech revolution touched every part of our lives. Radio helped the British Navy win the historic Battle of Jutland in 1916. Even so, a top naval officer wrote that "to trust . . . the wireless reports of cruisers which are out of sight is to run a needless risk."

That official later got over his skepticism. He used radio to offer his fellow citizens "nothing but blood, sweat and tears" and led Britain through its darkest and finest hour.

Back home, and a world away, I was announcing for the Chicago Cubs during their finest and not-so-finest hours. Which reminds me of a story. At my age everything reminds me of a story.

When I did baseball play-by-play in the thirties, I covered hundreds of baseball games played by the Chicago Cubs and the Chicago White Sox without going to the stadium.

Despite the baseball benefits some prominent observers actually lamented the arrival of instant communications. They feared the airways would carry the virus of the Russian Revolution to other nations.

Even President Woodrow Wilson warned his fellow Americans: "With the tongue of the wireless and the tongue of the telegraph, all the suggestions of disorder are now spread throughout the world."

Funny how years later radio would spread "disorder" in the Communist monolith itself.

Veteran newscaster Daniel Schorr tells a story about his visits to Eastern Europe. He says people didn't ask much about the President of the United States. They asked if he knew Willis Conover, the famed broadcaster for Voice of America.

In those early days, some well-meaning people also feared the rise of television. In a terrifying book called *1984*, George Orwell predicted Big Brother would use a "telescreen" to control his own subjects.

When *1984* was published shortly after World War II, Albania was becoming an Orwellian state. The tiny mountainous country was tightly controlled by the Communists, impoverished, cut off from the rest of the world.

Like Big Brother, dictator Enver Hoxha needed television for his propaganda. He also needed modern industry, so he electrified the Albanian countryside.

He then lost control of his subjects. Many people—risking severe punishment—secretly switched to Yugoslavian, Greek and Italian channels.

On television, Albanians saw Eastern Europe turn toward democracy and followed suit. Today television is often the only electrical appliance in an Albanian home. Foreign broadcasters are so common that many people in that underdeveloped country speak at least one foreign language. In fact, the *Los Angeles Times* recently had this headline: "STRESSED-OUT ALBANIANS ARE BECOMING COUCH POTATOES."

George Orwell, bless his heart, was wrong about the "telescreen." Look what happened when the long-dreaded year of 1984 finally arrived. A prominent political candidate made many public criticisms of the leader of the United States. But he was not imprisoned because America is a great and free country. Well, at least he lost forty-nine states!

Broadcasting now has another challenge—China.

Twenty years ago Ted Koppel was ABC's correspondent for China. Getting news from China was not easy in those days. He had to climb a hill in Hong Kong and try to pick up shortwave radio reports from the mainland.

But in the spring of 1989, shortly after the students rebelled in Beijing, Mr. Koppel did the impossible. He sent a live television report from one of the most tightly guarded places in the world—Tiananmen Square.

Like a spy in a movie, Mr. Koppel rode a bicycle under the noses of the Chinese authorities. A microphone was in his shirt and a miniature camera was mounted on his bicycle. A small truck behind him transmitted his commentary to a satellite many miles above. The satellite bounced Mr. Koppel's report back to New York and into the homes of millions of Americans.

No single man or group can control technology. No man can rule the satellites, transistor radios, camcorders, copy machines or notebook computers. Technology is literally in the hands of people—and so is the power.

And more electronic marvels are coming our way. Digital audio broadcasting—almost unheard of four years ago—brings crystal clear tones to the radio. High-definition television more than doubles the number of lines on screen and creates a stunning picture. Experts even predict that computer-generated images will bring back legendary performers in entirely new roles. Including Bonzo?

Pretty soon there could be a new device in your hand—a cellular telephone, personal computer, radio and television with an inflatable screen all rolled into one. You carry the magic box to the farthest desert or the highest mountain. Bounce your signals off a satellite. Catch the *60 Minutes* show on top of Mount Everest.

Rarely would a hiker get lost in a snowstorm or a driver in a dangerous part of town. Amelia Earhart—stranded on a deserted island—would reach in her pocket and ring up a rescue party. You wouldn't have to be E.T. to phone home.

America, the Cold War victor, stands triumphant on the world stage. Our culture is as powerful and transcendent as our military. In 1989, Americans made the top five movies in Greece, Ireland, Italy, the Netherlands, Norway, Switzerland, Hungary, Bolivia, Brazil, Australia and Japan. In October 1991, almost half of the top fifty entertainment programs in Italy and Spain were American, including programs like *Cheers* and *Golden Girls*.

Your collected work has escaped the earth and is speeding across the universe—even shows canceled after thirteen weeks. Can you imagine the reaction of aliens who pick up an episode of *Twin Peaks*?

But can our nation handle peace as well as war? Or will we become a self-absorbed nation of couch potatoes?

I may be old-fashioned on this subject, but I believe the communications business has a key role in strengthening the spiritual values that knit our society together.

For centuries after the birth of Christ, Bibles were copied by hand. A single Bible could take a year or more to produce.

Today the contents of the Bible are relayed instantly around the world. A spiritual revival is taking place in Eastern Europe, Russia, Latin America and other areas, nourished by radio and television.

In our secular age, our children are especially malleable and curious and vulnerable. The culture of their elders has lasting influence on their young minds.

The entertainment industry has taken commendable steps in the war against drugs. As you know, my wife, Nancy, has worked hard on this issue. And yes, references about drug use are far fewer these days than they were fifteen or twenty years ago. Alcohol abuse is also under sharp scrutiny, especially drinking and driving. And that's all to the good. But we must preserve and shelter and strengthen the American family. A strong family is the cradle of civilization.

As the twenty-first century comes swiftly upon us, broadcasting faces many other challenges—demographic changes, cable competition, government regulation and, of course, licensing of frequencies.

Some people may fear the future, the unknown. But our broadcasting industry shouldn't. We need only recall George Orwell and his misplaced fears about the "telescreen." And I know something else from my long experience: the people in this business aren't in the habit of shying away from challenges.

Certainly not the inventor Edwin Howard Armstrong. In the 1930s, Armstrong found an intriguing radio signal. But leading mathematicians and engineers scoffed at his discovery. They said the new wave was inconsequential and doomed to extinction.

Armstrong didn't realize he was supposed to fail. He went back to his tiny lab and perfected his invention. The result was FM radio—a clean, static-free sound used not just commercially but in police and fire stations, guided missiles, even for communicating in outer space.

That's the tale of broadcasting in this century. A pioneer's epic of hard work, a lot of luck and vivid imagination—and unexpected blessings beyond our dreams. And that will be the story of the next century as well.

*A*mong all the public figures that I have known in my life none were greater than Ronald Reagan and very few of them measured up to him.

He had a basic decency that was wholesomely impressive. The many pictures of this great leader in both of my homes are constant reminders of his fundamental goodness.

WALTER H. ANNENBERG
*Philanthropist*

*President Reagan presenting Walter Annenberg, the U.S. Ambassador to the Court of St. James, with the Ronald Reagan Distinguished Service Award.*

*T*HANK YOU ALL very much and welcome, consuls.

I am thrilled to host you here at the library today. You are distinguished representatives of your countries and I want you to know that our doors are always open to you here at this library.

I understand that you had the opportunity to tour the exhibits earlier. As you can well imagine, this is a very special place to Nancy and me. This building does not serve as a shrine to any one man or any one political party. Rather, it is a place where current and future generations can come to learn about what we accomplished and what the decade of the eighties meant to American and world history—a place where mothers and fathers can bring their children, where scholars can bring their notebooks, where friends from across the seas can come, too. Some would come to remember, some would come to look forward, but all would come because they sought knowledge. And it is the seeking of knowledge

that is man's noblest pursuit. I am pleased to know that you have had a chance to see it.

Perhaps you heard that a friend of mine is coming next week to visit. I have waited a long time to show Mikhail Gorbachev this library. It chronicles many of the historic steps he and I walked together, everything from our first meeting in front of that fireplace in Geneva to our last meeting in Moscow.

I'm also looking forward to taking Mikhail and Raisa up to our ranch in Santa Barbara on Saturday to show them the *real* American West!

So much has changed in his country in the past several months. During the failed coup last August the Soviet people spoke with one voice: The clock cannot be turned back; the ghost of Lenin will no longer haunt the nation. Boris Yeltsin stood on a tank—truly a man ten feet tall—and showed the world that the God of communism was finally dead.

Not surprisingly, democracy and the free market are only recent arrivals to Russia after centuries of czars, aristocrats and serfs—capped by the bloody reign of communism. The horrors of Stalin ended decades ago, but they were replaced by a heavy blanket of discouragement and cynicism.

Even after the modest reforms of perestroika in the 1980s, many Russians do not understand the link between productivity and reward, probably because there are so few opportunities to make money on their own.

But change will come, I am sure, with new generations of Russians. For all its challenges, the former Soviet Union is blessed with the richest resources in the world and a well-educated population.

Horace Greeley said, "Go west, young man." I have a feeling Russian youth will turn away from careers in the government and military to a new frontier—private enterprise. We see stories of urchins who earn more than their parents by selling newspapers on the street.

Those children will grow up understanding the value of hard work. And so will the fresh-scrubbed teenagers who work so hard in the first McDonald's in Moscow and other new Western enterprises.

Youth will be the salvation of Russian capitalism—irrepressible youth, without the enslaving memory of the past or fear of the future. Youth—and those young at heart—yearning to be the first on his or her block in Moscow, Kiev, St. Petersburg (the names change so fast), the first self-employed newspaper salesman, plumber, electrician, stockbroker, computer manufacturer, car dealer, doctor, banker. Change will come to Russia as

it comes to a world filled with social and political ferment.

The end of the Cold War was made possible by the unprecedented allied coalition that defeated Iraq and created a favorable climate for a landmark Middle East peace conference. Agreements growing out of the conference could mean lasting harmony and prosperity in that strife-torn region. The end of superpower tension paves the way for progress in many other regions as well.

But democracy can be heady stuff, especially if one not used to it can suddenly speak one's mind. The positive contagion of democracy is spreading far beyond former Communist domains, proving the universality of its appeal. Military and authoritarian regimes throughout Latin America and Asia have given way to freely elected governments. As nations take difficult steps toward the opportunities and responsibilities of democracy, we must help them remain strong and courageous.

Which reminds me of yet another story:

A very wealthy man bought a huge ranch and he invited some of his closest associates to see it. After touring many acres of mountains and rivers and grasslands, the owner brought everybody back to the house for lunch. The house was spectacular and out back was the largest swimming pool you have ever seen. The strange thing was, however, that it was filled with alligators.

The owner explained them by saying, "I value courage more than anything else. Courage is what made me a rich man. In fact, I think that courage is such a powerful virtue that if anybody is courageous enough to jump in that pool, swim through those alligators and make it to the other side, I'll give them anything they want, *anything*—my house, my land, my money."

Of course, everyone laughed at the absurd challenge and proceeded to follow the owner into the house for lunch.

Suddenly they heard a splash. Turning around they saw this fellow swimming for his life across the pool, thrashing at the water, as the alligators swarmed after him. After several death-defying seconds the man made it, unharmed, to the other side. The rich host was amazed but stuck to his promise, saying, "You are indeed a man of courage and I will stick to my word. What do you want? You can have anything: my house, my land, my money—just tell me what you want and it's yours."

The swimmer, breathing heavily, looked up at his host and said, "I just want to know one thing: who pushed me in that pool?"

Seriously, strength and courage have certainly contributed to changes in many areas. The economies of many of these countries are fragile and it may take some time before democracy gets firmly rooted.

We who have long enjoyed the fruits of liberty must remember that democracy faces formidable obstacles in many countries. Centuries of division and hostility—cultural, ethnic, tribal, racial, religious, geographic—make the rule of law difficult. Democracy requires trust between strangers, and trust cannot be earned overnight.

Those of us from democracies have a great deal of work ahead of us, for we must be ready when called to action by those for whom democracy is a bold, new, exciting experiment. And perhaps there's a role for you here today as representatives of so many countries with problems and issues that must be addressed.

I believe in the ideals of freedom, democracy and in the remarkable potential of the human being. Power is also spirit and that spirit has been unleashed upon the world.

Let us not be timid in our embrace of democracy. We should be as bold and brash and brave in our democratic ideals as ever. This is not the time to let our support for these budding democracies waver. We must press the advantage, for the work is not yet done. You see, their struggles are not theirs alone. Their struggle is our struggle—yours and mine.

The struggle for democracy does not end at the Battle of Midway, Normandy, Warsaw or Kuwait City. The struggle for freedom begins in the hearts and minds of all men and women and will not end—*must not end*—until all peoples everywhere are free.

Thank you and God bless you.

*I*n the summer of 1985 the President of the United States entered Bethesda Naval Hospital, where surgeons successfully operated on him after discovering a malignancy. In releasing this news to the public, the doctors made only one mistake: They didn't confer with their patient. As Ronald Reagan saw things, he didn't have cancer. "Something inside of me had cancer, and they removed it," said Reagan, with the same willful optimism that sustained his Presidency and drove his political adversaries to distraction.

No less unorthodox was President Reagan's view of the world. Historians, like generals, are prone to refight past battles. Many find it difficult to label the Reagan Presidency. In part this is because political bias clouds their perspective. But an even greater factor is the stubborn attempt to fit Reagan into existing academic models of the Presidential office, to apply conventional rules to the most unconventional leader of modern times.

Scholars of the Presidency typically celebrate so-called strong Presidents for the style as well as the substance of their leadership. Men like Theodore and Franklin Roosevelt, Woodrow Wilson and Harry Truman have been lionized for the way they dominated their age and dictated to Congress. They are admired as public educators who persuaded or cajoled Americans to accept their personal vision and public agenda. The most memorable Presidents speak words we cannot forget. And for most of this century—so runs the conventional argument—they have strengthened the Presidential office while centralizing authority in Washington, D.C.

Then came Ronald Reagan. By any measurement Reagan ranks among the strongest of Presidents. Indeed, one of his greatest accomplishments was to refute the popular doubts, widespread in 1980, that any one individual could master the demands of the office or channel the energies of the American people after a generation of failed or tragically shortened Presidencies. Yet, characteristically, Reagan did it his way. He stood conventional wisdom on its head. He used the tools of popular persuasion first fashioned by his boyhood idol, FDR, to *reverse* the flow of power to Washington that began with Roosevelt's New Deal.

A conventional leader would have hesitated to confront the basic assumption which has governed American politics since 1933—the idea that Washington must inevitably, irreversibly, assume more control over our lives. Ronald Reagan not only challenged such ideas—he demolished them. And the consensus he forged in their place governs his successors of both political parties. Not only did he reinvigorate American federalism. Through his appointments to the bench, President Reagan transformed the nation's judiciary in ways that will be felt well into the next century. By reversing the drift that characterized American foreign policy in the post-Vietnam era he reasserted America's claims to global leadership, never forgetting that great powers have responsibilities to match. And by restoring the nation's military capabilities he gave muscle to American diplomacy and pride to her Armed Forces.

A conventional leader would have taken for granted the existing superpower relationship, balanced on the equilibrium of Cold War hostility. Ronald Reagan insisted that the Soviet Union was a historical aberration, and that the Cold War could be won by the West in our lifetime. History will show that he was right—even if some historians are slow to accord him credit.

A conventional leader would have been satisfied with incremental progress on arms control, slowing the rate of increase in the world's nuclear stockpiles. Ronald Reagan believed that the arms race could be ended and the stockpiles eliminated. History will recognize and reward him for his breathtaking vision. And so will our grandchildren.

So forget the conventional academic models. The real question that should be asked of any President is, did he make a significant difference, not only in his time, but for a long time to come? Did the force of his personality and the power of ideas affect the way Americans live, how they see themselves, and how they relate to the rest of the world? Did he spend himself in causes larger than himself, for purposes nobler than re-election? Ronald Reagan did all this, in ways that have already made him a popular legend. The day is coming when historians, too, will acknowledge his enormous imprint on the Presidency and on the century he helped to define. The man who espoused timeless principles will find that time is on his side.

RICHARD NORTON SMITH

ON THE DAY that my forty-two classmates and I were graduated from Eureka, exactly sixty years ago, the sky was blue, the smell of freshly mowed grass was in the air, and there was a soft breeze. It was the kind of day when young men and women would normally enjoy the spring weather and then step out into the world, confident they could handle the future.

Well, the look of that day was deceiving. It wasn't all that normal. We were in the midst of what has gone down in the history books as the Great Depression.

There were only forty-two of us graduating that day. Many of our classmates had dropped out because of the hard times. Most of us still in school were nearly broke and in debt. The college was in bad financial shape, too. The previous autumn there hadn't been enough money to send the Golden Tornadoes to games away from home, so the only games we played were here in our own field.

Job prospects for those of us graduating that day looked pretty dim. Our then-new President, Clyde Lyon, sensed this. He gave a rousing speech to build our spirits. He said we shouldn't let the future "bully" us into non-achievement.

And I must tell you, it didn't. We made it, as you see by the fact that there are quite a few of us who graduated that day sixty years ago here today to see you get *your* degrees. We did many different things to get our start in the world beyond Eureka. I went home to Dixon, but couldn't find a job, then I tried Chicago and went on to Davenport, Iowa, where I landed a job as a sports announcer at station WOC for $5 a game. It may not seem like much to you, but in those days that seemed like a fortune!

One way or another we all survived. I think we turned out to be more resilient for the adversity we encountered in those early years. Luck played its part, but I think we took with us from Eureka College something else: strength born of a spirit of fellowship, willingness to work together for common goals and a deep faith in the word of God.

On that spring day in 1932 much that you have read about in history books was still in the future for us. Franklin Roosevelt was not yet President. The rise of Hitler and Nazism was not far off, but their fall and World War II were still years away. So were television, computers, fax machines, CAT scans, jet planes and nuclear weapons. So were the tearing down of the Berlin Wall, free elections in Nicaragua and the subjugation of Central and Eastern Europe by an evil empire. And, of course, so was the demise of that empire.

Still, a Frenchman was absolutely right when he coined the phrase that translates to: "The more things change, the more they stay the same."

Take your own situation. Lately, you've been thinking a lot about the future. You are probably asking yourself such questions as: What kind of job will I get? Am I choosing the right career path? Will I regret it in ten, twenty years from now, or will I be happy?

And you're also thinking about the past, especially the last four years here at Eureka. While those years may have held some disappointments for you, on balance they have been good years. Chances are, you're sad they're coming to an end. You don't want them to end and that's perfectly understandable. We didn't either, back sixty years ago.

These days, with companies in many fields downsizing, your biggest concern about the future may be focused on finding a job, period. I can appreciate the feeling that was a preoccupation of ours, too.

There is much to be said for setting priorities one at a time. The late, great British statesman Winston Churchill put it eloquently when he said, "It is a mistake to try to look too far ahead. The chain of destiny can only be grasped one link at a time."

He had in mind the fate of nations. Right now, your first concern has to be the fate of just yourself. If you don't have that job lined up already, don't lose heart. You'll get one, although it may not be your "dream job." If it isn't, don't wring your hands in disappointment. Instead, give that job everything you've got. Be the best at it you can possibly be. By doing so, you'll earn respect, including self-respect, and you can take time to plan ahead toward the next step in your career.

Now, as you think about your own future, there are some pitfalls to avoid. They come under three headings: too much planning, too little planning and letting complacency set in along the way.

As far as too much planning, I'll give you an example. Once, I heard a young man describe his life's plan. He was just a couple of years into his career and he had everything figured out. He was going to spend the next five years doing what he was doing; then the five years after that moving on to the next position; the next five years, something else again, and so on. Each five-year segment represented a methodical step up the corporate ladder. Don't know if he ever made it, but I do know that, other than frequent trips to the copy machine, he was in for a really dull life.

The opposite of that fellow is a person who is seduced by one particular aspect of youth, which is, it looks as if it's going to go on forever. For the person who is seduced by this temptation, the future seems to be something that will take care of itself, so he or she bobs like a cork in the river of life, not setting any goals, thus never achieving any. One day this person reaches forty and realizes he or she hasn't gotten anywhere toward satisfying the dreams of youth and isn't going anywhere now. Thus the seductive promise of endless youth has turned out to be a hollow one.

Now, I'm not suggesting you should close the door on youth because you are graduating from college today. Heck, I certainly haven't and I'm old enough to be your . . . father! Or his father! Or maybe even *his* father!

No, you should enjoy youth while you have it, still keeping in mind the fact that maturity is a matter of becoming comfortable with the world around you as time moves on and circumstances change.

I mentioned complacency as another pitfall to watch for. It sets in when you think of happiness as a fixed condition. You may have heard someone say something along these lines: "Once I make a certain amount of money, I'll be able to afford everything I need. I'll be content." That person, if he or she stops there, will be wasting talent and energy that could be put to use helping others or helping the community, thus gaining an even greater sense of personal fulfillment.

Setting interim goals is important, of course,

but don't let them become ends in themselves. It's better to stay a little restless each time you reach one of those goals. Push yourself to reach them, be courageous and reach your dreams.

Perseverance and courage are important ingredients for a successful future. A future that may bring surprises, uncertainty, good news or initial disappointments awaits you beyond the world of our alma mater. As you step forward to meet that future, I'm going to ask you to make a commitment to yourself, to Eureka, to your family and your nation. I am asking you to make the commitment to give something back, voluntarily, to this great and free country beyond becoming a productive adult member of our society. Volunteerism for us Americans almost runs in the blood. Alexis de Tocqueville, that astute French traveler, visiting our young country in the 1830s, marveled at the way neighbors pitched in to help one another and whole communities built projects seemingly overnight. He wrote, "America is a land of wonder, in which everything is in constant motion and every change seems an improvement."

We are older and wiser as a nation today and we know that not every change is an improvement, Yet, our spirit of optimism—of better tomorrows—is as strong as ever. And, to this day, we are the most generous people on earth. Through private sector initiatives, we give billions every year to philanthropic causes. Every time there is a natural disaster halfway around the world, money, food, clothing and medicine pour forth from Americans in every walk of life and every town, city and state.

Giving freely of some of your time to public service is simply a matter of paying your dues for living in the freest society on earth. For all its troubles, this nation is a remarkable achievement. It is the first and only one in which government derives its power from the people. And from the beginning, "the people" were a diverse lot, coming from many different places, but finding common ground as they created something entirely new, the American.

Where and how should you give of yourself? That's entirely up to you.

So find your project, then give it all you've got during the time you've set aside for it. Whatever it is—working with kids, helping old people, teaching someone to read—you'll be making our country work better, and you'll be a better you.

For some of you, this commitment might take the form of giving time to a business or professional association in connection with your career. That's worthwhile, too, for the betterment of the business and professional sectors of our society contributes to a more effective economy, which is good for all of us.

And down the road, a few of you may even seek public office. I say "down the road" because I hope none of you will set out to make the holding of elected office a lifetime career. First get your own life and career started. Then, if the elective office bug bites you later, you'll be much better able to understand the needs and problems of the people you seek to represent. One way to sample politics is to do your volunteer work helping your party or a candidate you favor. If there is a particular of-

ficeholder or candidate you like, give him or her a hand in the next campaign. Or take a look at the various volunteer groups that support the parties.

I have asked you to make one commitment. Now I am going to ask you to make another one. As you all know, life undoubtedly will present you with many challenges. You have received a solid foundation from your families, from your schools and from your churches which will prepare you for these obstacles.

Sometimes, however, the pressure can get pretty tough and you might consider giving up. What I want you to always remember is that even though you're sure things can't get any worse, you must always try to *keep your sense of humor.* It has certainly come in handy for *me* countless times over the years—helped me out of some pretty sticky situations!

The ability to laugh at yourself or laugh at life's unforeseen twists is often a better option than utter despair. It's a way of protecting yourself—with a smile!

I remember Tip O'Neill, the former Speaker of the House, and how our relationship evolved. Yes, he had different ideas about key issues but I felt we were developing a friendship. However, he would make remarks about my proposals and me personally, most of which weren't exactly flattering. One day I called him and said, "Tip, I just read in the paper what you said about me yesterday. I thought we were friends." His reply was, "Ol' buddy, that's politics. After six o'clock we can be friends. But before six, it's politics."

Tip could be sincere and friendly when he

wanted to be, but he could turn off his charm like a light switch. Until six o'clock I was the enemy and he never let me forget it. So, after a while, whenever I'd run into him, whatever time it was, I'd say, "Look, Tip, I'm resetting my watch. It's six o'clock."

I also used humor often with my friend Mikhail Gorbachev, the former head of the Soviet Union. There were times when we not only were not on the friendliest of terms, but I had great concerns about future relations between our countries. There were moments of frustration and disappointment. But there was always hope and our common ability to laugh. We could focus on what we had in common rather than what divided us.

As Frank Moore Colby once said, "Men will confess to treason, murder, arson, false teeth or a wig. But how many of them will own up to a lack of humor?"

You can't take life too seriously. And since you have what I hope will be long and productive lives ahead, you'll have a big advantage if you can laugh along the way.

My young friends, savor these moments. Keep the memories close to your heart. Cherish your family and friends because you never know what the future holds.

Live each day to the fullest. Live each day with enthusiasm, optimism and hope. If you do, I am convinced that your contribution to this wonderful experiment we call America will be profound.

Soon we will all come together in the ivy ceremony. Holding the vine together we will be reminded that Eureka will always be a part of us. As the dean cuts and gives you your piece, it will symbolize your separation from Eureka physically, but not in your heart, for it is there that fond memories steadily will burn.

Many speakers conclude their addresses with profound quotes from great historians. But if you will allow me, I would like to leave you with this. When I was in the White House, Nancy and I traveled to Ireland—the land where the Reagan family had its origins. A young guide was showing us through the ruins of an ancient cemetery. We came to a great tombstone and chiseled in the stone was an inscription. It read: "Remember me as you pass by for as you are, so once was I. But as I am you, too, will be. So be content to follow me." That was too much for some Irishman who had scratched in the stone underneath, "To follow you I am content. I wish I knew which way you went."

Thank you all very much. Congratulations, graduates, and God bless you.

*I* got to know Ronald Reagan when he left the White House to return to California. At first blush, he seemed uncomplicated, agreeable and not terribly concerned with traditional patriotic themes like individual rights and freedom that one might expect from a man who had played such a prominent role in the turbulent international politics of the 1980s.

My misperception was quickly made apparent. We happened to fall into a conversation about the Tiananmen Square protest of June 3–4, 1989, when the military brutally cut down student activists demonstrating for democracy in China. Perhaps, I suggested, the tragedy might have been avoided if those kids had been, well, a bit more patient. The steel in the ex-President's character flashed. Freedom, he said, is not something you can structure or manage. It is not neat and tidy. Often, it is rambunctious and boisterous, drawing its strength and vitality from such as those courageous young men and women who pitted their bodies against tanks in Tiananmen Square on the memorable occasion.

I suddenly saw the truth of his statement that "heroes may not be braver than anyone else—just braver five minutes longer." In every crisis of his career—from Qaddafi to Berlin to "Star Wars"—Ronald Reagan made good use of that five minutes.

LODWRICK M. COOK
*Chairman, Ronald Reagan Presidential Foundation*
*Board of Trustees*

*I* AM DELIGHTED to see all of you here this evening at the library, a place that is very special to Nancy and me.

Once again this year I would like to take this opportunity to thank all of you, the loyal members of the President's Forum, for joining us. I see so many familiar faces here. You are the backbone of the NRCC [National Republican Congressional Committee], the enormously generous patrons who continue to give, time after time, year after year. You are the people who are actively working to elect more Republicans to the House of Representatives.

Early on in my life I was a Democrat, as you've probably heard. My whole family were Democrats. As a matter of fact, I had an uncle from Chicago who won a medal once for never having missed voting in an election for fifteen years—and he had been dead for fourteen!

Seriously, I changed my tune, and one of the things that I wanted most when I was President was a Republican majority in the House.

In 1981, I went to Washington to change things. In fact, we worked tirelessly to make America stand tall again—strong at home and strong abroad. But at every turn I was met by a combative, Democratically controlled House that found it easier to play politics and fight *against* change than to be a forum *for* change.

George Bush has worked to carry on the programs and the progress that we made in the eighties. And as you've seen he's been stonewalled by the Democratic majority and its leadership over and over again. I know I sound like a broken record, but the American people want a change in the way Congress works. They are tired of ineffectual gridlock and the only way to break the gridlock is to bring more Republicans into the House. It's time for Republican control.

We need a Republican Congress to work with the President, rather than a Democratic one that's against him. We need a Republican Congress that will allow the American people to remove the straitjacket of rules and regulations and taxes so that people, not a government, can make the most of America's vast potential.

That's the point that the Democrats always seem to miss. They always want to take more and more away from what the American people earn and produce by raising taxes. The Democrats believe that America is great because of all the good things that government has been able to do for people and because America's greatness lies in government.

Those poor, misguided Democrats. They don't seem to understand that America isn't great because of what government did for the people. America is great because free people have had the chance and the incentive and the opportunity to dream, strive and work toward their goals. That's what has made America great.

Recently, the American people have seen what the Democratically controlled Congress can do when they put their minds to it. They pushed through a late-night pay raise for themselves. They defeated a much-needed balanced budget amendment—an issue I've been advocating for many years. And this may upset a few Democratic fat cats in Congress, but I still haven't given up on a balanced budget amendment. We saw them in action during the Clarence Thomas hearings and the American people didn't like what we saw. We want a change in the system and can you really blame us? Any system that puts Teddy Kennedy in charge of a sexual harassment case is a system that ought to be changed.

You see, Congress has been ruled by one party now for thirty-eight consecutive years,

and one-party rule, whether it be in Poland, Hungary, the Soviet Union or the U.S. House of Representatives, isn't conducive to innovation and change. One-party rule for too long breeds arrogance of power, a turning of the back on the will of the people. And the will of the people will not be ignored!

Now is the time to change a check-bouncing, pay-raising, budget-busting, liberal, Democratically controlled Congress!

With George Bush in for another term and a working majority in the House of Representatives, we will see a tremendous impact on the direction this country will take in the years ahead. We need a Congress that is firmly behind the President to implement the programs and policies we elected him to carry out in the first place.

Congressional redistricting, as a result of the 1990 census, has created eighteen new seats in the South and West—areas where Republicans are traditionally stronger than Democrats. Primary race losses and early retirements of House members have pushed the total number of Congressmen who will not be returning to the House next year to sixty-eight.

By the time of the November elections, it's possible that as many as a hundred or more members will not return to the 103rd Congress. The opportunity has never been greater and that is where your help is needed; the resources of the President's Forum members, your talents and determination can and will make the difference for the Republican Party in November.

Today our country is at a crossroads, just as we were twelve years ago and as we have been many times in our history. Just as we did then, the American people are clamoring for change. And the impetus behind that change is you.

Nancy and I want to thank each and every one of you for your continued support of the President's Forum—past, present and future—for your courage and your determination toward our cause.

You are making it possible for the Republican Party to make drastic gains in the House this fall. I am tremendously excited about the transformation that's sure to come.

I look forward to sharing the historic victory with each of you this November and celebrating the prospects of the coming years.

Thank you and God bless you.

*C*onqueror of communism, sworn enemy of statism, leader of unshakable conviction and contagious optimism, embodiment and culmination of conservative hopes, Ronald Reagan is one of history's heroes and the greatest of our great contemporaries. He transformed conservatism from an intellectual movement into a political revolution—a running revolt that continues to this day. He exposed the bankruptcy of modern liberalism and proved that true liberty is still a fighting faith. He saw the momentum of freedom in the sweep of history, and through the power of his words and the determination of his deeds placed the last shovel of dirt on the grave of Leninism. Reagan proved that conservatives can be idealists because our ideals are strong enough to justify our hopes.

*President Reagan greeting Heritage Foundation president Ed Feulner, June 20, 1985.*

I first saw Ronald Reagan close up when he testified on welfare reform before the Senate Finance Committee in 1973, displaying his unique ability to express conservative ideas in ways that Americans found compelling. In November 1978, my old friend Richard Allen, who was directing foreign policy research for candidate Reagan, asked whether I could set up a meeting between Reagan and journalists in London. Bill Deedes, the then-editor of the *Daily Telegraph,* moaned and groaned to me in advance about coming to a breakfast meeting—"a barbaric American custom"— with this man who used to be Governor of California. He left telling me it was one of the most interesting, fruitful and positive hour-and-a-half meetings he had ever attended on either side of the Atlantic.

Perhaps, however, the most memorable moment of my personal encounters with President Reagan occurred on October 3, 1983, at the "Heritage 10" anniversary dinner at the Shoreham Hotel in Washington, D.C. My wife, Linda, stood next to President Reagan on the dais. He was so moved by the color guard's presentation of the colors, and the Navy Band's playing of the "Heritage March" and the national anthem that when it was finished he whispered to Linda, "That was so moving, it makes me want to clap. Too bad no one else would join in." Linda immediately responded, "Mr. President, I bet if you did, everyone else would join in." "Do you really think so?" President Reagan asked, in genuine amazement, at which point the two of them began clapping for what became a standing ovation from the 1,400 people in attendance.

In Ronald Reagan's two terms as President he gave America a transfusion of his own optimism and hope. He saw the momentum of freedom in the sweep of history and restored a soaring sense of the possible—a revolution that rescued America from defeatism and much of the world from tyranny. In the end, he restored our confidence in the Presidency itself, proving that Jefferson's "splendid misery" could simply be splendid.

ED FEULNER

*President, the Heritage Foundation*

*I*'M THRILLED to see so many Senate candidates from around the country here. I commend you for accepting your party's challenge and I do hope you have better luck with the Congress than I did in eight years.

My friends, I'm truly delighted to speak to you tonight here at the Library. It is a very special place to Nancy and me, and we are always pleased to invite friends up here to the Simi Valley—it gives us an opportunity to show off a bit.

I must tell you that over the past several months I think I've spent more time up at this Presidential Library than I did at the Eureka College Library in my four years! It is truly spectacular and I'm thrilled that it's a place where current and future generations can come to learn about what we accomplished and what the decade of the eighties meant to American and world history.

If we look back even further, twenty years or so, events were occurring that would lead our nation and our party to a crisis point. Of course, few doubted that America, as strong and resilient a nation as ever existed, would rebound.

The prognosis for our party, though, was not nearly as optimistic. In fact, many people in this country hung the picture of our party mascot, the elephant, alongside the dinosaur in the gallery of extinct species. Many feared we wouldn't recover, but *we* never lost faith. And instead of panic, we not only got back on our feet, but we thrived.

Like Phil Gramm, early on in my life I was a Democrat. My whole family was Democrat. But all that changed and it wasn't too long ago that Nancy and I left our beloved California for Washington. And now, I find myself at the prime of my life, out of work!

Seriously, those days come to mind because of some of the startling similarities we see today. As it did twelve years ago, and as we have seen many times in our history, our country now stands at a crossroads. There is widespread doubt about our public institutions and profound concern, not merely about the economy but about the overall general direction of this great country.

And as they did then, the American people are clamoring for change and sweeping reform. The question we had to ask twelve years ago is the question we ask today: What kind of change can we Republicans offer the American people?

Step back a moment and consider the world today: The Berlin Wall, an unnatural, ugly, unwelcome, but undeniable symbol of the oppression of communism, has crumbled and exists only in museums and souvenir collections. In fact, we have a 6,000-pound piece of it on the west side of this Library. Today Germany is united. An unrelenting ideology has collapsed under its own weight, unifying Europe.

Across the world, our brave young men have been at last allowed to stand down from battle alert; children at home can go to sleep without the threat of nuclear devastation intruding upon their dreams. America stands alone as the preeminent superpower.

Don't let anyone fool you. This is *our* story. This is the fruit of Republican leadership. We cannot stand idly by and allow these events and accomplishments to be glossed over by the media.

Despite what some of our friends in the other party would have you believe, just because the Soviets are no longer a threat does not mean we should bury our heads in the sand. This world demands American leadership more than ever. We must never shirk that responsibility because it is in our best interest

to stay involved. Let us not forget that a safer world is a more stable world. A more stable world is a more productive one. We must not forget that peace opens up trade barriers around the world. As barriers fall, opportunity arises.

Today, as we remain secure on the international front, it is natural that we turn inward to confront the challenges that remain domestically. The American people are not content with the status quo. They look for change— and quite frankly, they deserve it.

But, my friends, we Republicans *are* the change. From the party's very conception we are the party dedicated to individuality, innovation and enterprise. In 1980 we faced economic disarray at home and crisis abroad. They were the twin evils sapping our nation's confidence. But the American people gave us a mandate for change and we followed through on it: We cut the growth of government. We cut taxes, gave workers back some of their hard-earned money. We rebuilt our defenses when liberals wanted us to tear them down. We created a defense strategy that Democrats said would unleash a nuclear holocaust. But while they complained, we laid a foundation for winning the Cold War.

Why did this happen? I would ask you to look around this library: Take in the books, look over these walls; how did they get here? You know, you can be the best author in the world, but if you don't have a pen, ink and a printing press, well, don't look to see your work on the best-seller list anytime soon. You can be the most creative architect, but without hammers, nails and people ready to do the heavy lifting, your dream house won't get off the paper the blueprint is drafted on.

In 1981 we succeeded in our quest because we were allowed to succeed and we were given the proper tools. More than the mandate for change, the American people gave us something even greater—legislators that worked *with* us, not *against* us, a Congress that looked forward, not backward. We had a Republican Senate. We had a House with enough Republicans to force action. This combination gave us the leverage we needed to bring tax cuts that jolted the economy into an eight-year expansion. Just having a Republican Senate allowed us to craft dramatic reform in the nation's tax system.

*George Bush* can build the vehicle of change the American people want, but he has to be given the proper tools. My friends, this is where you come in. You are leaders in your communities. You can make the case to those around you to elect a Republican Congress to work *with,* not *against,* a Republican President.

Let's take our record to the American people. Let's make our case for a unified government. Let's see a Republican Senate once more. Let's see what a Republican House can do on the domestic front when given the opportunity.

With a lot of perseverance across the coun-try, we can be the party of change. It is up to us to challenge the American people to give George Bush the mandate—and the tools—that they gave us in 1980. This will set the agenda of change for a resurgent America in the twenty-first century.

We need a President and a party who understand what the freedom revolution is all about. Republican leadership started the freedom revolution. Republican leadership alone can finish it.

So let's make our dream come true. Together, we will complete the shining city on the hill. We'll build it in poor neighborhoods afflicted today by drugs and crime; we'll build it in Kansas wheat fields; we'll build it in school classrooms, where children learn that great ideas and strong hearts can change the face and fate of the earth. It won't be easy and often the progress is discouragingly slow. But we must remain strong and courageous and ready for the fight.

You are making it possible for the Republican Party to make important gains in the elections this fall. I am tremendously excited about the transformation that's sure to come.

I look forward to sharing the historic victory with each of you this November and celebrating the prospects of the coming years.

Thank you, God bless you, and God bless America.

*T*he bilateral relationship between the United States and Mexico has improved markedly since the early 1980s. I believe the Reagan administration had much to do with this change.

Previously, because of the sometimes painful history between our two nations, some individuals in Mexico strove to use the United States as a whipping boy or scapegoat to advance their ideologies. When questioned, those who indulged in this activity disingenuously responded that it was "only for internal consumption" and should be ignored outside Mexico's territorial limits.

*President Reagan greeting John Gavin, the U.S. ambassador to Mexico, in the Oval Office, April 17, 1984.*

Most Mexicans proudly concurred with us that Mexico was too large and important to miss international notice and agreed that respect was a two-way street. The notion of the critics, however, was that—at least internally—they could prevent closer ties by campaigns of disinformation. That notion, while amusing, was not acceptable and we adopted a policy of responding firmly, albeit respectfully, to the nonsense and distortions leveled against the United States. Key to the success of this policy was the engagement and backing of our President.

On one occasion early in President Reagan's first term, I was invited to attend the National Security Advisor's morning briefing of the President to inform him on the current situation in Mexico. I closed a certain item by saying: "And, by the way, Mr. President, we have received an enormous amount of flak from the anti-U.S. elements on this issue." The President looked at me and said, with that wonderful grin of his: "Jack, if they don't do that at least once a month, you're not doing your job."

I dined out on this story for quite a while. Inside our mission and out, word got around that Ronnie Reagan was a stand-up guy and, more important, that he stood behind us in our work. It was just one more reason for making us proud to serve with him.

JOHN GAVIN
*U.S. Ambassador to Mexico, 1981–1986*

*I*T'S GREAT to see so many dynamic young entrepreneurs in one place.

I am proud of this place and I've wanted to share it with you young people since I met you last year at your conference in Mexico City. It was then that I became impressed with your organization, with your enthusiasm and your unique spirit. I am delighted that this conference has finally become a reality. Congratulations to you all.

I've always enjoyed meeting entrepreneurs. I remember, as if it were yesterday, when a friend showed me something he'd just invented—and he called it the printing press.

And soon after that came the first newspaper reporter. Well, that's progress, I suppose.

You hail from Vancouver, Toronto, Montreal, the Arctic Circle, Guadalajara, Mexico City, Monterrey, Detroit, New York, Chicago, Dallas and here in Los Angeles—wherever the human mind is inspired to dream and create and flourish.

Today I want to talk of the blessings—and obligations—of human freedom. Liberty is truly the greatest and most creative force on earth—as powerful and illuminating as sunshine itself.

Thanks to the bright light of freedom, the once-dreaded Berlin Wall decorates a thousand mantelpieces around the world—and this Library.

Free markets revitalized the Western economies and guided our socialist counterparts down the path to a brighter future. They created millions of jobs and new businesses, and set the stage for a twenty-first century of peace and prosperity.

Despite our current economic challenges—and they are many—consider the tremendous opportunities that are now presented to the entrepreneurs of North America.

The former Soviet Union—well endowed with iron, oil, coal and farmland, plus a well-educated population—could become one of our largest markets for consumer goods.

The European Community—EC '92—is

opening its borders and dismantling long-standing trade barriers. Euro-capitalism is replacing the closed-door socialism of the past.

The billion people of China sail on an irreversible course toward democracy and free markets, especially in the south of China. Ironically, their Communist leaders recognize that their political survival rests solely upon the ability of the free market to feed and clothe their huge population.

In Vietnam, the *New York Times* reports the North won the war but the capitalist South is winning the peace. Lifting price controls has made Vietnam the third largest exporter of rice in the world.

India—with the world's second largest population—has a growing middle class and is now self-sufficient in food production.

In Africa, country after country that had embraced Marxist-Leninist politics and economics are abandoning both.

Free markets and entrepreneurs have turned the world upside down—and transformed our daily lives.

The miracles of human ingenuity are never-ending. In five hundred years we've gone from Columbus to the moon, and soon to Mars. Laser surgery—quick, clean and painless—enables the blind to see. Doctors use high-tech beams to target and destroy cancer inside the brain. So-called designer bugs kill millions of pests and save crops without leaving a harmful residue. The march of progress has lifted the average human life span by some twenty to twenty-five years in this century.

Entrepreneurs have also revolutionized old

ways of thinking in this century. For many years, "bigness was best"—large companies with imposing hierarchies and vast economies of scale dominated. What was good for General Motors was good for America and the world. Government, business and union leaders pretty much ran things from the top down. Men in smoke-filled rooms negotiated and fine-tuned their way to prosperity.

But then the world moved too fast. Technology produced robots, "just in time" inventories and shorter research and development cycles. Many big companies could not adapt quickly enough. In 1979 sales by the largest five hundred companies in America represented well over half of our economy—58 percent. By 1989, the share fell to 42 percent, and employment in major corporations sank by nearly 4 million.

But at the same time, the eighties saw a tremendous outpouring of new jobs—19 million jobs in America. The jobs were being created by small businesses—nimble entrepreneurs finding niches in a booming economy. Organizations with twenty workers or less created two-thirds of the new jobs.

The new entrepreneurs came from all walks of life, from all ethnic and cultural backgrounds. The free market was no longer the playground of the rich. It was democracy in action.

In his classic work *Innovation and Entrepreneurship,* management scholar Peter Drucker explains why. He says the secret of success is not an advanced degree from Harvard, or an enormous amount of capital, or a large labor force, or twenty years of training. All of these factors can be important—but none is crucial. What is vital, according to Drucker, is the innovative spirit. That simply means the willingness to make small but necessary changes in the way you do business, even if the changes are not comfortable or popular. The needs of the customer come first, Drucker says. One must move steadily forward without falling back into complacency or bad habits.

In this dynamic new world, it doesn't matter where you came from. It's where you're going that really counts.

When I was President I heard story after story of someone taking an idea to the bank, borrowing, working hard and then experiencing the joy of seeing a business flourish.

One woman I met had graduated from college with plans to become a classical pianist. Then she developed arthritis in her hands and couldn't play anymore. So there she was, wondering what she would do with her life. One of her aunts said, "You've always made wonderful brownies, so why don't you make some and sell them down at the local grocery store?"

Well, she started doing that, and before long she was selling more than $1 million in brownies a year and had thirty-five employees.

Other Americans I met or corresponded with pursued their own unique dreams. A father-and-son team turned family recipes into a $10 million a year business making frozen Mexican dinners.

In a small town in Illinois, dozens of people lost their jobs when a factory closed. Then through their own determination and labor, and with a little capital from someone who placed faith in them, they created a thriving metal fabrication business. They were just a few quiet heroes who helped turn around our economy.

Then there's Sam Walton, the entrepreneur from Arkansas who drove around in a pickup truck. When he got into the department store business in the early 1960s, big chains dominated, selling their trendy products in the downtowns of larger cities.

Sam tried something different—and simple. One by one, he put stores in small towns. He tried permanent discounts instead of holding a sale once in a while as the big stores did. At first the big fancy stores paid no attention to Sam. They knew discount stores didn't have the style or sophistication customers wanted. The critics also said few people would drive out into the middle of nowhere just to shop.

But Ol' Sam had the last laugh. America's suburbs migrated out into the countryside. Consumers became more price-conscious in a highly competitive world. Sam became America's richest man—worth many billions of dollars. His once-mocked company—Wal-Mart—is now the largest department store chain in the United States.

If the key to business success is the innovative spirit, then it's government's job to stay out of the way.

That means lower taxes, limited regulations and restraint of government spending. Give people the freedom to tap their wells of ingenuity and entrepreneurial spirit. As I've often said, governments don't produce economic growth—people do.

Of course, the economic experts used to laugh at that idea, too.

Which reminds me of a story. At my age, everything reminds me of a story:

Three men, a surgeon, an engineer and an economist, passed away and approached Saint Peter at the gates of Heaven. Saint Peter approached them and said, "I'm very sorry, but there's only room for one of you."

Saint Peter thought for a moment, then said, "Which one of you is from the oldest profession?"

The surgeon spoke up and said, "That's me! God took Adam's rib and made Eve, so he was doing surgery."

"No," claimed the engineer. "Before that, God made the world out of chaos, and that took engineering."

The economist said, "Wait a minute! Who do you think *made* all that chaos?"

The simple formula of "freedom for the people" generated the longest peacetime recovery in the history of the United States along with low inflation and solid gains in manufacturing productivity. In Canada, tax cuts and deregulation spurred seven years of economic growth and prolific job creation.

More recently, free-market policies have caused an economic renaissance in Mexico. Under the visionary leadership of President Salinas, Mexico has cut tariffs, sold off hundreds of state-owned companies and got inflation under control. The Mexican stock market has soared—and "flight capital" has flowed back into the country—reflecting the faith people have in President Salinas and the future of Mexico.

Now comes the opportunity to lift the economies of North America to even higher levels. Last month the United States, Mexico and Canada signed an agreement in principle to create the largest free trade area the world has ever seen.

This builds on the historic trade agreement between the U.S. and Canada in 1988, which I reached with my good friend Prime Minister Brian Mulroney. The historic U.S.-Canada agreement cut tariffs and reduced other trade barriers.

As a result the world's longest undefined border got a lot busier. As a result our trade was a world-record $175 billion—and our two-way investment also reached record levels. It was not an easy task, but it was important and necessary, and it has proved a solid base upon which to build.

About what was to come, I always knew would eventually happen: the North American Free Trade Agreement. It is a good one—a very good one. When ratified by the legislatures of the U.S., Mexico and Canada, it will make us the largest, richest, most important and most dynamic free trade zone in the world.

The North American Free Trade Agreement, or NAFTA, is unique and new: It offers a combination of economic growth, opportunity, benefits to workers and environmental sensitivity never before seen in the world. NAFTA covers 360 million consumers and a $6 trillion economy.

I am proud that I had something to do with its inception. I am impressed by the determination and commitment of Presidents Bush and Salinas and Prime Minister Mulroney to successfully conclude the NAFTA negotiations. They tapped that abundance of North American creativity, imagination, hard work and determination, and did the job in record time.

NAFTA clears away the tangled underbrush of old trade barriers. The North American people can now construct the houses and factories of the future. From Mexico City to Minneapolis to Montreal, new markets will open up—in banking, insurance, telecommunications, trucking, automobiles, textiles, energy, agriculture, intellectual property and investment.

For instance, if you make petrochemical equipment in Texas, you'll have more markets. If you raise corn in Iowa, you'll be able to sell more of it. If you design software in the Silicon Valley, you'll have more protection against pirates.

If you're from Vermont, where 83 percent of the state's total exports go to Mexico and Canada, you may have one of the 11,000 new jobs created in that state since 1987.

By the year 2000, we could have a dynamic Mexican economy with over 100 million consumers, and more growth and jobs in the U.S. and Canada. We would be an export powerhouse from the Yukon to the Yucatán.

Achieving freedom and prosperity in North America—and throughout the world—is a bold, exciting experiment. Every day we're challenged to think new thoughts, to work diligently, to innovate and to go where no entrepreneur has gone before. But to ensure success in this great task, we must also nurture the values that make our society whole and strong.

Each of us has a unique profession, business or talent to lend a hand to this endeavor. Together, we are the most powerful force in nature—a free society, united in the belief of the capacity of men and women to overcome challenges and build better lives for themselves and their children. You are young, our nations are young—and even our continent is young—but I feel confident that the world, with its constant changes and transformations, is in good hands—your hands.

Thank you all for coming today and God bless you.

173

$\mathcal{R}$onald Reagan is perhaps the most Presidential person I have known. He was sharply focused on his central core of conviction. He was not diverted by trivia and detail. He was not afraid to have strong people around him. And he fully understood the duality of his role as Chief Executive and Head of State. He was a great President.

*President Reagan meeting with Senator Howard Baker in the Cabinet Room, March 21, 1988.*

HOWARD H. BAKER, JR.
*Republican Senator from Tennessee, 1967–1985*

*I* AM HAPPY to return again this year for this unique conference. I know you've been treated to an impressive lineup of speakers throughout the day. I've been doing quite a bit of speaking myself lately—talking about some of my favorite themes: free enterprise, the American dream and the strength of this great nation.

As you know, I've been around America a very long time! There's probably no one here today as "mature" as I am, and you should all be thankful for that.

But when I was a boy growing up in the Midwest, I was taught the value of toughness, resourcefulness and integrity. I learned about pride in country and that freedom is something to be cherished. I learned the value of hard work and the importance of giving something back. I was taught that America was a place of opportunities where dreams can come true.

So I dared to dream, and believed, as I still do, that our remarkable spirit makes this nation unique—an example to every nation around the globe.

Now, maybe a few of you heard my remarks at the Republican Convention a few months ago. I spoke of America's promising future, of her accomplishments and of her uniqueness among the world powers—and the pride that we as Americans can share in our victories around the world in the past decade.

Before I go any further, however, I do have to correct one thing I said at the convention: The truth is, I really did not *know* Thomas Jefferson.

I couldn't possibly have.

You see, we lived in different states!

Seriously—and I know this is not a political rally for one candidate or another and I'm going to do my best not to make any statements that might be, well, too partisan—but it's difficult for a fellow like me who feels so passionately about this country and about the importance of good leadership to keep quiet.

Because, as you know, the future of our country is at stake.

In less than two weeks we as Americans will have an important decision to make. Electing a President is always an important decision. But *this* election will have profound consequences for the future of our country.

Yes, you and I know that America's future is one of great promise. Yet today we hear the despairing voices of the doomsday Democrats, who gave us the turmoil of the 1960s and the malaise of the 1970s, telling us how bleak things are. To hear them, things are so bad that down at McDonald's, even the Happy Meals are depressed!

In 1980 you, the American people, gave me the honor of a lifetime by electing me President and entrusting me with the stewardship of your dreams.

In 1988 you elected George Bush to continue that work—to carry on the mission we had begun.

Today some would like us to believe that the last twelve years were not good for America and the world. Well, I'm here to tell you that they're absolutely wrong!

As unwelcome as facts might be to some, I think it's time we set the record straight on a few things:

With your help, a demoralized, underfunded and unappreciated military was revitalized into the most modern and respected military force in world history.

Inflation was brought down from double digits to the lowest rate in twenty-five years. Interest rates fell to their lowest level in two decades. And the stifling tax burden on American families was dramatically eased.

Our children are now able to go to bed at night without the fear of nuclear annihilation because entire classes of nuclear weapons have been eliminated from the face of the earth.

And after decades of struggle, democracy won the Cold War and the Berlin Wall came tumbling down.

Today America stands alone as the preeminent superpower.

That—and much, much more—is the record of the past twelve years. Don't let anyone tell you that this happened by itself. This is America's doing—the fruit of our leadership among nations.

We have every reason to be proud of what we have accomplished together. And despite our great victories of the past, I firmly believe *America's best days are yet to come.*

I want you to know that my optimism comes not just from my strong faith in God but from my strong and enduring faith in man. The possibilities are endless.

America's economy, even with its problems, is still the strongest and most competitive in the world. So, don't let them tell you America's economy is hopeless. The fact is, if *they* were elected and *their* plan of tax and spend was put into effect, we'd be looking back on today's economic times and calling them the good old days.

Now, more than ever, this world demands American leadership and I feel that George Bush is that leader. He is the man who can lead the United States and work to a period of greater economic prosperity. He has laid out an agenda which can mean the dawning of the new day for America. It is an agenda true to the hopes of all of us who seek a better tomorrow.

Let us not forget that a safe world is a more stable world. A more stable world is a more productive one. We must always remember that peace opens up trade barriers around the world. As barriers fall, opportunity arises.

Today, as we remain secure on the international front, it is natural that we turn inward to confront the challenges that remain domestically. The American people are not content with the status quo. They look for change—and quite frankly, they deserve it.

But we must be careful about the type of change we ask for. We need the type of change that will improve the quality of life for working Americans.

And speaking of change—if we really want to clean up the mess in Washington—we've *got* to change the United States Congress, where post offices double as pharmacies, and where members of Congress bounce more checks than Magic Johnson bounces basketballs! Let's find legislators who will work *with,* not *against,* our President.

I've never been able to hide what's in my heart, and I hope you know that I've always had the highest regard for America.

Now, I always hate to disappoint my loyal friends and supporters. And I always welcome your new ideas. But over the years the one thing I've learned in politics is that timing is everything. So I'm afraid I'm going to have to

decline your proposal that I become a candidate for President again in 1996. However, I have *not* ruled out the possibility of running in the year 2000!

But until then, I am devoting my time to helping George Bush and future Presidents to get more of the tools they need to bring the budget under control. And those tools are a line-item veto and a constitutional amendment calling for a balanced budget.

Recently, we came very close to passing that amendment for a balanced budget and I was right in the thick of it—twisting arms and talking to anyone who would listen.

If I remember correctly, the first American to favor a balanced-federal-budget amendment was the founder of the Democratic Party, my old friend Thomas Jefferson. After the Constitutional Convention was over and the Constitution was approved, signed and ratified, he pointed out a glaring omission: there was no provision to prevent the federal government from borrowing money and going into debt. Times haven't changed; that's still a glaring omission in the Constitution.

Every year I was President I asked Congress for a constitutional amendment that would require the federal government—like any well-run business or family household—to balance its budget.

As the debt soars toward $4 trillion, not surprisingly, Congress suffers from its lowest approval rating in decades. This year Congress had a chance to restore public faith in our government. Unfortunately, they were unable to rise to the challenge . . . this time.

In the past they have also refused to give the President a line-item veto, which most Governors already have. I had it as Governor of California and I used it 943 times without ever being overridden once. When the state legislators sent me a budget, I could take a blue pencil and reduce spending on individual items to a level taxpayers could afford.

Until Presidents have these things, I think the country is likely to face never-ending deficits piled up by a Congress unable or unwilling to make the hard decisions necessary to bring down spending to a level the country can afford.

There are so many battles ahead for you and me as private citizens. And they're important not just because the outcomes are critical, but because it's important simply to care enough to be in the fray.

Certainly, there's much to look forward to for Americans. And as excited as I am about the future of this country, this election is not about my generation. Nor is it about George Bush, really. It is about the magnificent young people across this great land of ours. It is about whether we will leave to them the type of country we have enjoyed—a country of unlimited opportunity where dreams come true— or whether we toss aside everything we have accomplished and opt for more government control, more spending, less freedom and dashed hopes.

Your support and tremendous enthusiasm is an important start, but it cannot end here. I'm asking you, as leaders in your communities, to spread the word.

America's greatest hope is the strength of her people. And we must see to it that America remains the envy of the world, where dreams come true.

Let us have faith that God will continue to give us grace sufficient to our needs—that working together, looking to his guidance, we will yet preserve and make brighter still this shining city on a hill that we are blessed to call our home.

Thank you for inviting me here today, God bless you, and God bless America.

$O$f all the times I've had the privilege of his company, the best memory of all is Ronald Reagan's appearance at the May 1981 commencement exercises of the University of Notre Dame. It was his first trip outside Washington since being shot six weeks earlier, and I recall there being some concern over whether the President was really up to the journey.

The worriers should have known better. The event was vintage Reagan—even, in a word I heard used by a member of the audience, magical. Striding onto the stage, the President was as robust and buoyant as could be, and appeared to gain even more strength from the thunderous Irish welcome. Accepting the day's honor made him feel a little guilty, he said; after all, "I thought the first degree I was given was honorary." It brought the house down. For Notre Dame and America, the Gipper was back.

In an eloquent address, President Reagan gave the graduating class a warm and inspiring send-off, painting a vivid picture of the future and outlining the principles that would guide his administration over the next eight years. His would be an era of slower growth of government, a transfer of power from Washington to the states and the people, a revival of the free enterprise system and, most important, a confident and purposeful challenge to enemies of freedom around the world.

"For the West—for America," he said, "the time has come to dare to show to the world that our civilized ideas, our traditions, our values, are not—like the ideology and war machine of totalitarian societies—just a facade of strength. It is time for the world to know our intellectual and spiritual values are rooted in the source of all strength, a belief in a Supreme Being, and a law higher than our own."

For the remainder of the 1980s, President Reagan carried those themes to fruition, making America proud again and setting the stage for the spectacular fall of imperial communism. And when his tenure ended, he saw the American people elect his own Vice President to succeed him—a deeply symbolic honor that is shared only by Presidents Washington, Adams and Jackson.

Ronald Reagan is an uncomplicated man with an uncomplicated formula for success. He was a leader who loved his country and trusted its people. He prayed to do God's will. He set his priorities honestly and pursued them intently. He respected the Presidential office and left it stronger than he found it. In him, people across the globe saw the best of America and our ideals, and he is directly responsible for the largest, fastest expansion of freedom in human history. There's no arguing with results: as was said of his hero, Franklin D. Roosevelt, "the world was lucky to see him born."

DAN QUAYLE
*Forty-fourth Vice President of the United States, 1989–1993*

*Roswell, New Mexico*
*October 30, 1992*

*I*'M DELIGHTED to be back in the land of enchantment today. Heck, at my age I'm delighted to be anywhere!

The people of Roswell have been very kind to me over the years—through thick and thin I knew I could always count on you.

I remember my visit here as your President a decade ago. Back then I spoke of many important issues facing America and today I speak to you with similar concerns—concerns that are important not only for the future of New Mexico, but also for the future of our great nation.

We simply can't afford to put an inexperienced fellow in the White House, particularly one with a dismal track record as a small-state Governor.

You may have noticed that in Presidential races, the Democrats prefer to nominate unknown Democratic Governors. The reason for this is that Democrats who *are* known couldn't possibly win.

And now that the election is just around the corner, Americans are looking closely at the Democratic alternative. They're looking at his record. They're looking at his character. And they're looking at his tax-and-spend programs. And you know what? They're saying, *no thank you!*

Throughout his life George Bush has been there for America. When our country faced great and trying times, George Bush fought his way into the military, gave true service to America and became a war hero.

And when it comes to the issues facing America today, we know where George Bush stands. He's been willing to make the tough and, yes, not always the popular decisions.

But what it all comes down to, beyond all the rhetoric and the hype, is *who* can we trust with the enormous responsibilities of the Presidency? Who can we trust to protect our national security? Who can we trust in a time of crisis? And who can we leave our children's future to?

As excited as I am about the future of this country, this election is not about my generation. Nor is it about George Bush, really. It is about the magnificent young people across this great land of ours. It is about whether we will leave to them the type of country we have enjoyed—a country of unlimited opportunity where dreams come true—or whether we toss aside everything we have accomplished and opt for more government control, more spending, less freedom and dashed hopes.

Your show of support here today is an important start, but it cannot end here. I'm asking you, as leaders in your communities, to spread the word. America's greatest hope is with George Bush. He will see to it that America remains the envy of the world.

I know that tomorrow is Halloween—a time for ghosts, goblins and other scary creatures. But this year, be on the lookout for a couple of tricksters who have been on the prowl for months. They've been masquerading as *new* Democrats with *new* ideas, telling us they're different from the rest.

Well, let me tell you something: they may have the best costumes we've seen in a while, but behind those masks are a couple of tax-and-spenders who will scare the *daylights* out of your pocketbook!

Yes, in just a few days we will once again choose our leader. And that leader *must* be George Bush. We can't afford to risk everything we've worked for. So please join me in supporting George Bush on Tuesday.

Thank you all for coming today, God bless you, and God bless America.

*I*t would not surprise me if most of the brief tributes to our fortieth President turned out to be very similar, for those traits and skills President Reagan demonstrated to some of those close to him were the same traits all of those privileged to work with him also saw.

He is optimistic, particularly about America; he is bold and courageous, always willing to test and, if necessary, to violate the conventional wisdom; and his great liking of people and his understanding of how Americans think and feel illuminated all his actions. These were the attributes that rebuilt our economy.

*President Reagan with Secretary of Defense Caspar Weinberger in the Situation Room, May 18, 1987.*

He also rebuilt America's defensive strength and used that regained strength to exercise the leadership that only a strong America can give the world—a leadership that is one of the strongest forces for peace in the world.

History will be kind and respectful toward President Reagan, and I believe history will record the great debt that all peace-loving and freedom-loving people owe to him.

CASPAR W. WEINBERGER
*Secretary of Defense, 1981–1987*

R. PRESIDENT, Mr. Chancellor, honorable members:

In my long and crowded life I have enjoyed more than my share of honors, few of which can match the experience of standing at this podium, speaking to this audience.

For one thing, it gives me the chance to see where an American President went to school. More flattering still, however, is the opportunity to be part of this union's long, distinguished and occasionally ferocious tradition of intellectual swordplay.

Needless to say, I enjoy the cut and thrust of public debate, although, I must say, after watching a few such spirited encounters during the recent campaign in my own country, I was reminded of the newspaper columnist who compared political debates to stock car races—no one really cares who wins; they just want to see the crashes.

Well, America survived the debates and a former Oxford student won the Presidency. So I congratulate you all. In the words of Benjamin Disraeli, "A university should be a place of light, of liberty and of learning." Long before my country existed, Oxford was all this and more. Here one develops a sense of self, even while realizing that in the modern world self alone is never enough. There must be a higher yearning equal to the higher learning.

A university is a paradoxical place where ancient tradition thrives alongside the most revolutionary hypothesis. Perhaps as no other institution, a university is simultaneously committed to the day before yesterday and the day after tomorrow. Here, too, one soon learns that so long as books are kept open then minds can never be closed. And with that unceasing curiosity that distinguishes youth (even among the elderly), Oxford's Union embodies the bracing clash of argument and the heroic struggles of ideas. Here the sharpest weapons are a rapier wit and well-honed disdain for what we in America call political correctness.

I consider it a tragedy that at some campuses in my own country those who hold unfashionable ideas are hooted off the stage or denied a forum in the first place. What a travesty of intellectual inquiry; what a perversion of the great, chaotic yet essential marketplace of ideas that we call democracy. But then, I have always believed that the only cure for what ails democracy is—more democracy.

The last major speech I gave in Great Britain focused on the toppling of that massive, creaking machine of oppression known as communism. And what a dry, rotted system it turned out to be. The fight against totalitarianism was a grand and noble cause, one that united the entire civilized world. Ironically, the end of Communist tyranny has robbed much of the West of its uplifting, common purpose. In the aftermath of victory, we grope not for new enemies, but for a renewed sense of mission.

With the Soviet empire defeated, will we fall into petty, self-absorbed economic rivalries? Will we squander the moral capital of half a century? Will we turn inward, lulled by a dangerous complacency and the shortsighted view that the end of one evil empire means the permanent banishment of evil in all its forms?

Among the many questions which cry out for our attention, none is more important than this: What will arise from the ashes of the old world order? Will it be a phoenix of freedom or a phoenix of fear?

At the end of 1992 there is no obvious answer. Indeed, if you look around the globe, the new world looks increasingly like disorder. According to a Russian institute, 160 border disputes rage in the former Soviet Union alone. If

you can bear it, you might cast your glance over the unspeakable horrors of Yugoslavia and Sudan.

Confronted with such realities, we might well wonder if we are trading a single, monolithic threat to the world's peace for a host of smaller, yet no less deadly flash points. Assume the latter to be true. Some will claim that the West has no immediate interest in the mean streets of Sarajevo or the arid wastelands of the Sudan.

Such an attitude only raises a second, morally unavoidable question. Quite simply, are the current threats to human dignity any less destructive because they are confined to relatively small geographic areas or in many cases affect non-Western peoples?

Let us be frank. Evil still stalks the planet. It may have no ideology more complicated than bloodlust; no program more complex than economic plunder or military aggrandizement. But it is evil all the same. And wherever there are forces that would destroy the human spirit and diminish human potential they must be recognized and they must be countered.

My young friends, no doubt many of you will go on to shape the events of your time. And what a time it is!

Wherever we look in this momentous season of change, old oppressions are crumbling even as new possibilities struggle for acceptance. Everywhere free men and free markets are on the march—from the Moscow City Council to the formerly one-party states of Africa. Yet the work of freedom is never done. We inhabit a time in some ways reminiscent of what Churchill called the locust years after World War I and the tense standoff that followed World War II. Twice in this century the community of nations has grappled with the structure of peace.

As a young man I saw the tragedy of Woodrow Wilson, as my country failed to seize the moment and a Europe shattered by war unwittingly sowed the seeds of a still greater conflict to come.

Sixty years ago this winter students debating in this very hall renounced the use of military force to repel the enemies of freedom. Winston Churchill, then deep in his wilderness years, provoked mocking laughter when he told Oxford students that rearmament was the unavoidable price of survival in a world overrun by dictators. Time proved him right, at a cost of untold suffering. In the wake of the Second World War, a resolute West stood up for individual freedom and stood up to those who would put the soul itself into bondage. It was, as young John Kennedy said, a long twilight struggle in which we were engaged.

Standing before Parliament in 1982, I predicted that Marxism-Leninism would end up on the ash heap of history. For my pains I was called a dreamer and an ideologue, out of touch with reality. Some foreign affairs experts regarded me not unlike the way the German poet Heine viewed a certain ambassador: "Ordinarily, he is insane, but he has lucid moments when he is only stupid."

You know what? Wherever I hear such comments I know I must be on to something. At the very least I'm encouraged to continue questioning conventional wisdom, for there are worse things to be called than a dreamer.

So let me tell you of another dream I have, as achievable as my much-maligned forecast about the collapse of the Soviet Union. It's a dream I have long had, but one that only *you* can hope to realize.

Just as the world's democracies banded together to advance the cause of freedom in the face of totalitarianism, might we not now unite to impose civilized standards of behavior on those who flout every measure of human decency? Are we not nearing a point in world history where civilized nations can in unison prosecute crimes against humanity, such as those now defacing Somalia and Bosnia?

Already we have seen the potential for such action in the unprecedented coalition against Saddam Hussein and in the pivotal role played by multinational U.N. peacekeeping forces in trouble spots around the globe.

In my view the time has come for the world community to behave as such. It is not enough to provide emergency assistance to victims of tyranny. We must look for ways to prevent victimization in the first place. What I propose, then, is nothing less than a humanitarian velvet glove backed by a steel fist of military force.

Consider that cauldron of hatred that was once Yugoslavia. What is being done to the people of Bosnia-Herzegovina shreds every definition of human decency and morality. Ethnic cleansing is a hateful euphemism for an evil we've seen before in Europe. Concentration camps are a form of real estate I did not expect to witness again on European soil.

Quite frankly, the average American is perplexed, to put it mildly, that such atrocities can occur in Yugoslavia while a Europe moving toward union refrains from action. While the term "sphere of influence" has fallen into disfavor, it is an unescapable fact that Bosnia is within Europe's sphere of *conscience*.

I've seen estimates that across this continent and the former USSR the potential exists for anywhere from five to twenty other Yugoslavias to erupt in ethnic bloodshed. As one observer put it, after looking at the facts that contribute to such tensions, "Why should they *not* happen?" But there is an antidote to chaos and a structure for humanitarian intervention already in place. Its name is NATO. More than four decades after it was founded as a bulwark against Soviet expansionism, NATO must again be made relevant to European peacekeeping. It must reinvent itself to deal with the kind of inhuman situations we now see along the Adriatic.

As my fellow conservative former U.N. Ambassador Jeane Kirkpatrick has pointed out, NATO forces are present, they are trained, they are available, and they are armed. Yet they are also, tragically, inactive.

Is NATO's current posture toward Bosnia so very different from that of the policeman who won't cross the street to stop a murder because it's not in his jurisdiction? But Europe was supposed to be NATO's jurisdiction. The U.N. has voted that humanitarian assistance to civilian populations may be delivered through all necessary means. NATO *has* those means. NATO *is* the means.

When it comes to the ordeal of Yugoslavia, I agree with Ambassador Kirkpatrick and former Prime Minister Thatcher. The Serbs must be told that if they threaten the Yugoslav region of Kosovo—an action likely to enlarge the conflict to Albania, Greece, Bulgaria and Turkey—then the civilized nations would begin "sharply focused bombing" against Serbian military supplies and targets. To do less is to silently acquiesce in wholesale slaughter.

Our multilateral organizations must declare ethnic cleaning and the slaughter of civilians by military forces totally unacceptable. And we must be prepared to put weapons behind our words. We must extend NATO protections and the NATO framework to those who desire to be part of our alliance. Room must be made in NATO for the democracies of Central and Eastern Europe, beginning with Poland and not excluding bloodied refugees from the tinpot tyranny called Greater Serbia.

It is not only the Balkans that can be saved from perpetual conflict. So can other regions torn by ethnic or political violence. An African recipient of the Nobel Prize has asked, why does the world ignore ethnic cleansing in Africa? And he is right—African genocide is no less a crime against humanity than mass murder in the heart of Europe. Yet that is exactly what is happening today in Somalia and Sudan.

The photos coming out of Africa are all but incomprehensible. In Sudan, 700,000 people have been killed and another 3 to 4 million driven from their homes as warring factions battle. According to one relief official, "I have never seen anything like it. If you left the town of Bor now, you would be walking on the bones of the dead." As reported by yet another journalist, thousands of innocent people began a desperate migration last month, walking south in search of food, pausing to eat grass and leaves, drinking from mud puddles in the road.

In Somalia, there is no government and no political structure. The U.N. estimates 300,000 people have already died in the man-made famine, with 2 million more in danger of starvation. Tons of food fill warehouses in Mogadishu while countless people starve because it's not safe for relief workers to make deliveries. In short, famine has become a weapon of war. Yet no government has the right to eradicate its peoples. No regime has the right to drive out its own citizens.

Sixty years ago Western democracies chose inaction rather than confront a Nazi tyrant. In the midst of Churchill's "locust year" the poet T. S. Eliot wrote eloquently of the dangers of appeasement.

As he put it:

Footfalls echo in the memory,
Down the passage which we did not take
Towards the door we never opened
Into the rose-garden.

What door leads to modern Africa? Facing conditions of absolute inhumanity such as now exist in Sudan and Somalia, does not the world have a moral responsibility to act? To choose the right to passage, to impose minimum order and provide sanctuaries of relief?

In parts of Africa today, mankind is an endangered species. Have we come to the point where we must set up human preserves as we have for rhinos and elephants? If so, then let us do it, and do it now.

Last year, largely in reaction to Iraq's murderous treatment of the Kurds, the U.N. changed the mandate of its world food program, enabling it to operate without the consent of host governments. I believe the precedent bears repeating, albeit on an even larger scale, in sub-Sahara Africa. But that is only the beginning of what must be done. We must work toward a standing U.N. force—an army of conscience—that is fully equipped and prepared to carve out human sanctuaries through force if necessary. When the nations of the U.N. commit themselves to medical and food relief, they should also commit the resources and above all the will to deliver those supplies, regardless of roaming bandits or tinhorn dictators who would thwart the international consensus.

Such a course is not without risk. Clearly, governments that contribute troops to such efforts would face the possibility of casualties. But I can think of no more honorable mission for a soldier or his country. Indeed, I believe every soldier would eagerly volunteer to undertake so noble a duty.

Ladies and gentlemen, everyone in this room wishes for the day when tyrants are no more. We all wish for a world in which military adventures are confined to the imagined ramparts of childhood. We wish for a time when every nation is free to develop its own resources and realize its own possibilities unmindful of threats from abroad. But it is a sad, undeniable fact of modern life that wishes are no substitute for national will. And wishful thinking only encourages the tyrants for whom human rights are as easily trampled as protesters in a city square.

It is a fashionable assertion in these troubled times that nations must focus on economic not military strength. Over the long run, it is true, no nation can remain militarily strong while economically exhausted. But I would remind you that defeats on the battlefield occur in the short run.

As the tragedies of Bosnia, Somalia and Sudan demonstrate all too well, power still matters. More precisely, economic power is not a replacement for military power.

Lest we forget, Kuwait's economic wealth did not protect it from the predatory Saddam Hussein; quite the opposite. Nor was the Iraqi dictator finally driven from Kuwait because his GNP was smaller than that of the U.S., Britain or Japan. It is not the industrial productivity of democracies that is feared by the armed bandits of Somalia but the kill rates of their gunships.

As long as military power remains a necessary fact of modern existence, then we should use it as a humanitarian tool. At the same time I believe that we should rely more on multilateral institutions such as NATO, the U.N. and other organizations to sanction the reasoned and concerted use of the power available.

And to strengthen the United Nations, I would strongly urge the admission of Japan and Germany as permanent members of the Security Council. These are superpowers, both economically and in their domestic influence, and it makes no sense to exclude them from the highest councils of international peacekeeping.

Earlier I mentioned the shameful episode of February 1933, when this union declared its unwillingness to fight for king or country. Of course, it later changed its mind, and a great many Oxford students did a great deal of fighting and a tragic amount of dying for king and country in the war that followed.

Besides, I don't want to suggest that undergraduates are the only ones capable of error, or willing to own up to a mistake in judgment. Take this graduate of Eureka College, class of 1932, for example. At times in the past I failed to adequately value international organizations like the U.N. I used to regard them as, if you will pardon the expression, nothing more than debating societies. Their sole purpose seemed to be to blame the United States for the world's ills.

But with the fall of the Soviet Union, obstruction has been replaced by cooperation. And with it the noble vision of the U.N.'s founders is measurably closer to realization. It was the British historian Arnold Toynbee who defined life as a voyage of discovery and not a safe harbor. How true.

After a lifetime spanning most of this tumultuous century, my voyage is drawing to a close. It has been an extraordinary trip by any standard. With my own eyes I have witnessed the birth of communism and the death of communism. I have seen the rise and fall of Nazi tyranny, the subsequent Cold War and the nuclear nightmare that for fifty years haunted the dreams of children everywhere.

During that time my generation defeated totalitarianism, and more recently we have begun to destroy the weapons of mass destruction. As a result, your world is poised for better tomorrows. What will you do on your journey?

As I see it, you have the opportunity to set and enforce international standards of civilized behavior. Does that sound unrealistic? It is not any larger a challenge than what my generation confronted. In any event it is part of the great legacy of Oxford that rings down through the centuries—the power to effect change when it is needed and the wisdom to resist change when it is unwise.

Because I believe in you and in your ability to influence a world worth influencing, I cannot leave this place without repeating some other words from T. S. Eliot. "Old men ought to be explorers," he wrote, before adding, "Not fare well, but fare forward, voyagers."

My fondest hope is that your generation's voyage will be as momentous in peace as mine has been heroic in war. At the height of World War II, Sir Winston Churchill reminded Britons that "these are not dark days; these are great days—the greatest days our country has ever lived; and we must all thank God that we have been allowed, each of us according to our stations, to play a part in making these days memorable in the history of our race."

Do not forget those who suffer under tyranny and violence. Do not abandon them to the evils of totalitarian rule or democratic neglect, for the freedom we celebrate is not the freedom to starve, or the freedom to languish in a long, starless night of the soul. This, at least, is something that should be beyond debate.

Thank you and may God bless you all.

*President Reagan with Vice President Bush on the patio behind the Oval Office, July 7, 1988.*

*K*nowing Ronald Reagan has been one of the great joys in my life—Barbara's, too.

As Vice President I sat at Ronald Reagan's side, learning every single day about the good things in life. I learned about character, about humility, about kindness.

I saw how humor can really make a difference—kind humor, sometimes self-deprecating, never hurtful.

I learned from Ronald Reagan about adherence to principle and about leadership.

I treasure the friendship that started and grew over the eight years when Ronald Reagan was President of the United States.

GEORGE BUSH
*Forty-first President of the United States, 1989–1993*

$\mathcal{M}$R. PRESIDENT, Barbara, thank you
so much for your kindness in recognizing me
in this way.

From time to time I have been called the
Great Communicator. But I'll tell you, it's no
easy thing to communicate what I feel right
now.

Receiving the Presidential Medal of Freedom is a great honor anytime, but it is especially meaningful for me to receive it from a
friend and in the presence of people who have
meant so much to Nancy and me over the years.

Each occupant of the Office of President
leaves his personal stamp upon both the institution and the nation that he is sworn to serve.

Over the years Americans have witnessed an
incredible example of service to our nation.
George, I join your countrymen in conveying
our deepest thanks for all you have done for
America.

And Barbara, you will long be remembered
for your dedicated efforts to give all Americans
the gift of literacy.

Twelve years ago the American people gave
me the honor of a lifetime in allowing me to
serve as their President. When we came to
Washington on that bright sunny day we
shared a dream for America.

Back then, the reach of big government had
become intolerable. It was a time of rampant
inflation and crushing interest rates—when
hope was scarce.

It was a time when cold, ugly walls divided
nations and human rights were trampled in
the name of corrupt ideologies. It was a time
when a nuclear arms race was spiraling out of
control and a blinding distrust stood between
East and West.

We believed that for the future of America
and the free world, this could not stand. And
together, we insisted that this great nation
must once again behave as such.

We saw an America where most people still
believed in the power of a better tomorrow.
Together, we got the government off the backs
of the American people. We created millions

of new jobs and showed a watching world the power of free enterprise.

America shined brightly as a beacon of hope to oppressed peoples everywhere. And we welcomed so many of them to our shores to breathe the air of liberty.

Together, we did make a better future. We rebuilt our national defenses because we knew that our adversaries respected strength and exploited weakness.

And, by standing firm and asserting our principles, we were able to reach the first treaty ever to eliminate nuclear weapons from the face of the earth.

We have every reason to be proud of what we accomplished together. But I've never forgotten that it's not the acts of any one man that can change the direction of a country. It is *ordinary* men and women across this land, performing *extraordinary* deeds that make America unique in this world. And so it seems fitting on this occasion to express my heartfelt appreciation to the people of this great nation.

As I reflect on my life, I recall the fact that I am a simple man from modest beginnings. The Reagans of Illinois had little in material terms, that's for sure, but we were emotionally healthy beyond imagination, for we were Americans, young people in a young land with the best days ahead. We admired the pioneering spirit of this hopeful land, where everyone has a chance to push out the boundaries of life.

America has been very kind to me in my long and fulfilling life. What better time and place to thank this great country for its blessings on me than here today in America's House.

This year marks the two hundredth anniversary of the laying of the cornerstone of the White House. By the way, my back is *still* killing me!

But seriously, though, I cannot begin to tell you the emotions that flood back to Nancy and me as we return to the White House today. It will always be America's House, but for eight years it was *home* to us.

Many of you were sworn into office in this very room twelve years ago. And it was here that two cold warriors came together, not in hostility but in friendship, to sign the INF Treaty.

I can assure you that Nancy and I have been reliving *many* memories today. In fact, four years ago in this room Nancy, with tears in her eyes, and I, with a lump in my throat, said goodbye to all of you.

But although we may be a bit sentimental today, my point is a serious one. My point is that Presidents come and go. History comes and goes, but *principles* endure and inspire future generations to defend liberty not as a gift from government, but a blessing from our Creator. Here the lamp of individual conscience burns bright. By that light I know we will all be guided to that dreamed-of day when no one wields a sword and no one drags a chain.

Like a runner nearing the end of his course, I will hand off the baton to all those who share my hopes for the future and my reverence for this blessed country.

Some may try and tell us that this is the end of an era. But what they overlook is that in America, every day is a new beginning, and every sunset is merely the latest milestone on a voyage that never ends, for this is the land that has never become, but is always in the act of becoming. Emerson was right: America *is* the land of tomorrow.

Our work is not yet done. A great cause remains because the task of the peacemaker is never complete. Although we've certainly fought our share of battles, my fondest hope is that our nation's day will continue to be great not on the battlefield, but in the science labs, the operating rooms, performing arts halls and wherever empires of the mind can be assembled. And that we will collectively make our contribution to the age-old battle for individual freedom with the belief that America's best days are yet to come.

Thank you very much, Mr. President. May God bless each and every man and woman that may occupy this great house. And may God bless the United States of America.

*I* had the privilege of working closely with President Reagan. He was a visionary who believed in breaking down walls to freedom and barriers to trade. His success is now there for history to judge—from the collapse of communism to the Canada-U.S. Free Trade Agreement, the precursor to NAFTA and genuine hemispheric free trade.

I think Ronald Reagan was successful because the American people saw exactly the same person in public that we saw in private. He was principled and fair, resolute and just. Most of all, he was secure: He knew himself well, he had had time to reflect carefully on his principal policy thrusts, he understood his countrymen and had an instinctive appreciation of America's role in the world. He also had the capacity, with eloquence and good humor, to define a national and international agenda in a manner that persuaded others to follow him because they felt challenged and energized. It's called leadership.

I will always think of him as a friend with a warm Irish heart, a man of good nature and deep beliefs, a person free from malice and filled with devotion to America and to the cause of freedom around the world.

*President Reagan greeting Canadian Prime Minister Brian Mulroney on the South Lawn of the White House, March 18, 1986.*

BRIAN MULRONEY
*Prime Minister of Canada, 1984–1993*

*I*T'S A PLEASURE to welcome you all to Simi Valley and the Ronald Reagan Presidential Library and Center for Public Affairs.

Many of the events we've hosted here have honored the outstanding men and women who have been instrumental in forging a new era of freedom for the world. And today is certainly one of those occasions.

I can think of few places more peaceful or symbolic for old friends to gather than here, in the mountains of Simi Valley, for it is here that we can escape the frantic pace of the city. It is here that we can step away from the never-ending conflicts and demands which our lives place on us. Here we can look out onto the grand North American landscape from whence we came and reflect on how we arrived at this moment and this place.

As you can imagine, when I'm here I often find myself thinking about the many people and events which have made my life so full. I also reflect on the immense privilege the American people bestowed upon me in electing me as their President.

I've heard some political pundits say that it is only calculated political maneuvers and jockeying that allows the modern man or woman to ascend to the highest positions of leadership. But I've always defined a "leader" as "someone who sees a cause worth fighting for and unites people in his efforts." And so it is with our distinguished guest.

Brian, *you* are a leader to believe in—a man with a grand vision of freedom and the dignity and courage to carry out that vision.

And through it all, you have had at your side a dedicated partner, wife and mother. On this day we also pay special tribute to Mila Mulroney. Her strength and grace have made her an international figure in her own right, as well as a valued friend to Nancy and me.

Which reminds me of a story about Mila and another lovely woman I know:

As President I was visiting Canada for one of our many summits. Brian and I had finished

196

our working session and were standing together, waiting for our wives to arrive. Finally we saw them walking toward us from some distance and I just couldn't resist: I turned to Brian and quietly said, "For a couple of Irishmen, we certainly married up, didn't we?!" He wholeheartedly agreed.

Brian Mulroney rose to the pinnacle of power because he never forgot where he came from. He never lost the basic values of hard work, personal integrity and unfailing respect for others.

As the grandson of an Irish immigrant, I, too, know the land from whence he came. And I'd wager that the banks of the Saint Lawrence River, where he swam as a child, were not much different from the banks of the Rock River, where I was a lifeguard in my youth.

Brian Mulroney spent his early years in a working-class home in a small industrial town. He grew up watching and seeking to understand the complicated relationship between two different cultures. He learned not only how to speak the two languages, but how to unify and lead an entire country.

Brian Mulroney spent his nights as a teenager with his ear pressed to a transistor radio in an effort to hear news about the wondrous events taking place beyond his small town. He knew then that he wanted to play a role in the *Canada* of the future.

And as Prime Minister he played a key role in creating a new *world* of freedom. Brian Mulroney led Canada during a remarkable time—a time rarely noted by historians—when conservative leaders dominated the free

world. It was a closely knit circle—Mulroney, Margaret Thatcher, Helmut Kohl and a U.S. President named Reagan.

We shared a strong antipathy toward communism and those who advanced its causes. We also held a staunch commitment to free-market economies, a distaste for creeping socialism and a common belief in the simple credo "freedom works."

We opposed arms control agreements that would merely limit the growth of nuclear arsenals. We *demanded* radical reductions in these weapons—even the elimination of classes of nuclear arms—and we *got them*. Together, we turned the century of totalitarianism into an era of liberty and opportunity.

The United States and Canada stood steadfast with the other nations of NATO and NORAD in defending freedom not only in North America, but around the world.

The Soviet empire collapsed. The Berlin Wall came down. Germany reunited. And Eastern Europe, at long last, regained its freedom.

Even today, despite the political turmoil in Russia, democracy is taking root and thousands of new small businesses are making sure communism never rears its ugly head again.

Brian Mulroney would never say that he played a significant personal role in this remarkable string of events, *but I sure will*. His commitment to world freedom and peace was demonstrated just yesterday as he hosted the summit between the democratically elected Presidents of the United States and Russia.

On that note, I would like to convey my

wholehearted support for our government's plan to provide economic aid to Russia and the independent states. While government spending is something we certainly need to resist these days, I believe that we must nurture that fledgling democracy. Our aid today can give a tremendous boost to their efforts to succeed with a free-market economy. If we fail to act now, we risk a future we just cannot afford.

This Prime Minister has also energized the free market on the North American continent. His tax cuts and deregulation in the 1980s spurred seven years of economic growth and unprecedented job creation in Canada.

In 1988 we signed an historic agreement to eliminate all tariffs and many other trade barriers in our economies. Since then our trade has risen to record heights and is the richest trading partnership in the world.

But Brian Mulroney has not stopped there. He has worked diligently to see the day when the people of our continent engage in free trade—from Mexico City to Minneapolis to Montreal. This day, I believe, is fast approaching and much of the credit will go to the man we honor today.

And, of course, for almost three thousand miles we share the same lands and water. We enjoy their majestic beauty and prosper from their unlimited wealth.

We had some tough discussions early on, but our commitment to work together resulted ultimately in the historic agreement to curtail harmful emissions. And the common environment we share is better for it.

I believe that history will salute you for skillfully steering the ship of state through challenging and uncharted waters.

You fearlessly confronted both internal difficulties and economic hardships imposed by the global recession. As you near the end of your term as Prime Minister, Canada is stronger, more confident and more secure than when you began your stewardship.

You can be very proud of your legacy as Prime Minister and your lasting contributions to the great nation that you cherish and serve.

Brian, let me again say how delighted we are that you and Mila are with us today. I know that the coming weeks will be ones of enormous change not only for your nation, but for you, Mila and your family.

And soon you are bound to find some time to climb your own mountains. You can reflect on the years past and remember how much we dared, how hard we worked, and how far we came.

And when you do, I'd like you to think of the accomplishments I've mentioned today. And of something I said to you during our summit in Quebec in 1985: "History's verdict will depend on us—on our courage and our faith, on our wisdom and our love. It'll depend on what we do or fail to do for the cause of millions who carry just one dream in their hearts: to live lives like ours, in this special land between the seas, where each day a new adventure begins in a revolution that never ends." Well, Brian, today I think it can be said that we didn't let them down.

*P*resident Ronald Reagan always reminded me of the time-honored definition used at the infantry school to define a leader—"Someone you will follow, if only out of curiosity."

Someone in whom you have total confidence. Someone who possesses a vision. Someone who is above the daily hassles and tactical battles that tie people to the transient crises of the day. President Reagan's vision was a simple one—America is a good place with good people. Our destiny is to let our light shine before the world. Communism is bad. We must help Communists see the errors of their ways and the benefits of democracy and capitalism. While waiting for them to see the errors of their ways, we will remain strong. We are a nation of destiny.

President Reagan's message was a simple one. It was sometimes seen as naive, simplistic and lacking sophistication. It had the sole redeeming virtue of being right. And the world is a better place for his having been right.

*President Reagan with General Colin Powell, who received the 1993 Ronald Reagan Freedom Award, by the Berlin Wall, at the Ronald Reagan Presidential Library, November 9, 1993.*

COLIN L. POWELL
*General, U.S.A. (Retired), Chairman of the*
*Joint Chiefs of Staff, 1989–1993*

*I*'M DELIGHTED to be here on this glorious day of hope and promise.

It is indeed an honor to have the privilege of speaking to you today and to receive an honorary degree from this distinguished institution.

Surely my service record alone can't explain my presence here. More than half a century ago I was made a second lieutenant in the Horse Cavalry Reserve. That's hardly enough to warrant the honor you do me today.

But I do have to confess to you that during my Presidency I had an idea that I could never get anyone to support—I wanted to reinstate the Horse Cavalry in the Armed Forces.

Frankly, my being here cannot be based on my academic achievements either. Yes it's true that my alma mater, Eureka College, awarded me an honorary degree twenty-five years after my graduation. That only aggravated a sense of guilt I'd nursed for twenty-five years. I've always suspected the first degree they'd given me was honorary.

Truthfully, I am very proud to receive this degree today and my prayer is that I can somehow be deserving of it.

It is a special pleasure to address the graduating class of 1993, as together we mark the culmination of The Citadel's sesquicentennial year.

My goodness—one hundred and fifty years. Has it really been that long? It seems like only yesterday that Colonel Harvey Dick and I were watching the first twenty members of the Corps of Cadets report for duty.

You know, the military college had been created that past December, and we weren't quite sure how things would turn out. I remember asking him, "Colonel Dick, do you think these 'original knobs' will make the grade?"

Well, a week later, ten of them were serving confinements; the other ten were finishing up tours; and all twenty had turned in at least one E.R.W. [written response after being accused of an offense]. You see, some things never change.

Come to think of it, I seem to recall the colonel was even driving the same station wagon around Charleston. The only difference was that back then, that wagon had *real* horsepower.

Seriously, on my way to Charleston I took a peek at "The Guide-On," which they tell me is the Bible of the knobs. The more I read that little booklet, the better I like it. For example, I learned the three permissible knob answers: "Sir, *yes,* sir" and "Sir, *no,* sir" and—I liked this third one best of all—"Sir, *no excuse,* sir." By golly, I think we ought to send the entire U.S. Congress down here to learn answer number three.

Then I read this friendly advice in the book: "When you receive an order, carry it out to the best of your ability. Never argue or offer suggestions which you think might be better. This is not in your best interest." Well, it seems to me that The Citadel has a few things to teach the cabinet and the executive branch, too! In fact, maybe we should just put the whole federal government through cadet training!

But then I remembered the last time the Corps of Cadets and good people of Charleston decided the federal government was taking too active an interest in their affairs. Before you knew it, Cadet George Haynsworth and the other "boys behind the gun" had fired the famous "first shot" at the Yankee steamer *Star of the West.* Well, we all know what happened after that.

As I recall, it took a good four years before everything calmed down again. Just think of the E.R.W. *those* fellas would have had to write!

In fact, of course, the "boys behind the gun" served valiantly the cause to which they had pledged their devotion. In this, they exemplified a Citadel tradition—a tradition that would transcend the divisions of our nation's bloodiest internal struggle and inspire generations of future cadets to courageous service to a nation reunited.

The Citadel's roll of honor today stretches unblemished from the Ardennes to the 38th parallel, from Grenada to the Persian Gulf, with name after name of those who have served our country bravely in time of war—names like General Charles Summerall, General Mark Clark and your current president, General Bud Watts.

Yes, countless soldiers have distinguished themselves on fields of valor and are part of the century-and-a-half tradition of duty and honor we celebrate today.

But for me, there is one name that will always come to mind whenever I think of The Citadel and the Corps of Cadets. It is a name that appears in no military histories; its owner won no glory on the field of battle.

No, his moment of truth came not in combat but on a snow-driven, peacetime day in the nation's capital in January of 1982. That is the day that the civilian airliner on which he was a passenger crashed into a Washington bridge, then plunged into the rough waters of the icy Potomac.

He survived the impact of the crash and found himself with a small group of other survivors struggling to stay afloat in the near-frozen river. And then, suddenly, there was hope: A Park Police helicopter appeared overhead, trailing a lifeline to the outstretched hands below, a lifeline that could carry but a few of the victims to the safety of the shore. News cameramen, watching helplessly, recorded the scene as the man in the water repeatedly handed the rope to the others, refusing to save himself until first one, then two, then three and four, and finally five of his fellow passengers had been rescued.

But when the helicopter returned for one final trip, the trip that would rescue the man who had passed the rope, it was too late. He had slipped at last beneath the waves with the sinking wreckage—the only one of seventy-nine fatalities in the disaster who lost his life after the accident itself.

For months thereafter we knew him only as the Unknown Hero. And then an exhaustive coast guard investigation conclusively established his identity. Many of your here today know his name as well as I do, for his portrait now hangs with honor—as indeed it should—on this very campus; the campus where he once walked, as you have, through the Summerall Gate and along the Avenue of Remembrance.

He was a young first-classman with a crisp uniform and a confident stride on a bright spring morning, full of hopes and plans for the future. He never dreamed that his life's supreme challenge would come in its final moments some twenty-five years later, adrift in the bone-chilling waters of an ice-strewn river and surrounded by others who desperately needed help.

But when the challenge came, he was ready.

His name was Arland D. Williams, Jr., The Citadel class of 1957. He brought honor to his alma mater and honor to his nation.

I was never more proud as President than on that day in June 1983 when his parents and his children joined me in the Oval Office, for then I was able, on behalf of the nation, to pay posthumous honor to him. Greater love, as the Bible tells us, hath no man than to lay down his life for a friend.

I have spoken of Arland Williams in part to honor him anew in your presence, here at this special institution that helped mold his character. It is the same institution that has now put its final imprint on you, the graduating seniors of its 150th year.

But I have also retold his story because I believe it has something important to teach to you as graduates about the challenges that life inevitably seems to present—and about what it is that prepares us to meet them.

Sometimes, you see, life gives us what we think is fair warning of the choices that will shape our future. On such occasions we are able to look far along the path, up ahead to that distant point in the woods where the poet's "two roads" diverge. And then, if we are wise, we will take time to think and reflect before choosing which road to take before the junction is reached.

But such occasions, in fact, are rather rare—far rarer, I suspect, than the confident eyes of one's early twenties can quite perceive. Far more often than we can comfortably admit, the most crucial of life's moments come like the scriptural "thief in the night." Suddenly and without notice, the crisis is upon us and the moment of choice is at hand—a moment fraught with import for ourselves, and for all who are depending on the choice we make. We find ourselves, if you will, plunged without warning into the icy water, where the currents of moral consequence run swift and deep, and where our fellow man and yes, I believe, our Maker are waiting to see *whether we will pass the rope.*

These are the moments when instinct and character take command, as they took command for Arland Williams on the day our Lord would call him home, for there is no time, at such moments, for anything but fortitude and integrity. Debate and reflection and a leisurely weighing of the alternatives are luxuries we do not have. The only question is what *kind* of responsibility will come to the fore.

And now we come to the heart of the matter, to the core lesson taught by the heroism of Arland Williams on January 13, 1982, for, you see, the character that takes command in moments of crucial choices has *already* been determined.

It has been determined by a thousand other choices made earlier in seemingly unimportant moments. It has been determined by all the little choices of years past—by all those times when the voice of conscience was at war with the voice of temptation—whispering the lie that "it really doesn't matter."

It has been determined by all the day-to-day decisions made when life seemed easy and crises seemed far away—the decisions that, piece by piece, bit by bit, developed habits of discipline or of laziness; habits of self-sacrifice or of self-indulgence; habits of duty and honor and integrity—or dishonor and shame.

Because when life *does* get tough, and the crisis is undeniably at hand—when we must, in an instant, look inward for strength of character to see us through—we will find *nothing* inside ourselves that we have not already put there.

And, you know, it turns out that much the same thing is also true for our country. Indeed, I believe this is especially so in the most crucial area of all—America's ability, when necessary, to defend her citizens and her freedoms and her vital interests by force of arms. For here, too, the crisis is often upon us in an instant. Here, too, our instincts and character must be equal to challenges we can scarcely predict.

But here, even character and instinct will not be enough. We must also have the tools—the military capability—ready in advance of the crisis that may demand their use.

Yes, it's true that today the world is a different, better place than it was a decade ago, but it is not an entirely safe place. A multitude of terrorists and international hoodlums are working night and day to do us harm. U.S. troops have been called into action over a dozen times in the last four years. And dozens of deadly conflicts still plague the globe, from Central Europe to the former Soviet Union to the Middle East.

Yet, our nation is calling the watchman down from the tower. There are some who want to send Paul Revere into retirement. And I fear it is much too early for that.

By the mid-1990s, defense spending will be

well under 4 percent of our economy. That's down to pre–Pearl Harbor levels.

Some members of the "blame the military crowd" in Washington want to cut defense even faster—almost recklessly. They think military weapons and, yes, military people are somehow akin to warmongers.

But just recently we've seen an incredible example of the great humanitarian duties performed by the U.S. Armed Forces. You don't hear too much about it from that "blame the military crowd," but I think history will record it as one of the great humanitarian projects of our era.

Not too long ago, our forces went into Somalia, a country suffering from daily violence and intense starvation. I'm sure you remember the horrifying pictures on television of the starving children there. Our country made the bold and difficult decision to take the lead in this effort. And our troops were sent because it was the right thing to do. They performed brilliantly and restored order to that desperate country, and when the mission was successfully completed they came home. It was a proud moment for our country, and I, for one, commend those young heroes for their valor.

Senator Dick Lugar of Indiana has put it simply and put it well: "The role of the United States should be to lead the world. Our country has the wisdom, the political will, the military capability and the economic strength to perform that role better than any other." I would add only this: It is freedom itself that still hangs in the balance—and freedom is never more than one generation from extinction.

Some continue to think of the world's best military as a laboratory for social experiments. Well, I'm here to tell you that nothing could be further from the truth. We are at peace today and we have that peace through *strength,* and you, our military, are the providers of that strength. Most importantly of all, you are *not* wagers of wars, but keepers of peace.

I'm tired of listening to those naysayers—I heard them often during my own years as Commander in Chief. Our military buildup, we were told, threatened a dangerous escalation of tensions. Our deploying of Pershings and cruise missiles in Europe would destroy any hope for negotiations with the Soviet Union, they said. Our insistence on SDI would scuttle the INF Treaty. And what kind of fool would call the Soviet Union an evil empire and say that communism was destined for the ash heap of history?

You know, I have to wonder: Just how many times do some people have to be wrong, on so many crucial points, before they start asking themselves a few questions? But you know what some of those critics are saying today? Some of the same people who said our policies were doomed to failure because the Soviets were supposedly too strong are *now* trying to argue that our policies made no difference because the "evil empire" was doomed to collapse no matter what we did! Looks to me like it ought to be time again for knob answer three: "Sir, *no excuse,* sir."

Today, having achieved the victory over communism that some said we were foolish to even seek, America faces the question of military preparedness in a post–Cold War era. And we are hearing some of the same old voices of the "blame the military crowd," but they're uttering a slightly different message. Before, their theme was that American military might was too costly and too dangerous. Now, they claim that it is too costly and largely unnecessary—that danger is past and the war is won.

It is said that the price of freedom is eternal vigilance. And I'd like to offer several reasons why we must stay strong militarily:

First, despite the spread of democracy and capitalism, human nature has not changed. It is still an unpredictable mixture of good and evil. Our enemies may be irrational, even outright insane—driven by nationalism, religion, ethnicity or ideology. They do not fear the United States for its diplomatic skills or the number of automobiles and software programs it produces. They respect only the firepower of our tanks, planes and helicopter gunships.

Second, the Soviet Union may be gone, but even small powers can destroy global peace and security.

The modern world is filled with vulnerable choke points—military, geographic, political and economic. The actual lives at stake may be few in number. But, in an era of mass communications, a well-aimed assault can topple governments, cause economic dislocations and spark international conflict.

Iraq came close to taking over two-thirds of the world's oil reserves. Terrorists have attacked airplanes, boats, government buildings, the Olympic Games and even the World Trade Center.

Third, technology—for all its blessings—can enable new enemies to rise up overnight. Scientific information flows to ambitious dictators faster than ever.

The research and development cycle for new products has shrunk from ten years to five years to two years or even shorter. Technology turns the world upside down.

When I was a boy in Illinois, Henry Ford and the Wright Brothers dominated the global marketplace with their marvelous machines. But I was not long out of college when Adolf Hitler's sophisticated tanks and bombers overran Europe. Nazi Germany also built the first jet plane and it came frightfully close to inventing the atomic bomb before we did.

The Soviet Union was devastated by Hitler's invasion in the early 1940s. Yet the Communist nation quickly rose from the ashes and developed the hydrogen bomb. And few people expected Iraq to recover so quickly from its horrendous war with Iran in the 1980s.

And who can predict what will be the blitzkriegs of tomorrow? Nearly two dozen nations will be able to produce ballistic missiles by the year 2000. On top of that, thousands of nuclear weapons and poorly paid nuclear technicians float around the former Soviet Union, available to the highest bidder.

Over the past few months we've heard quite a few odd announcements coming out of Washington. Just this week the new administration announced plans to slash the Strategic Defense Initiative program.

They have been all too eager to denounce this program for years and they have been proven wrong, time and time again. I am quite proud of the SDI program we launched a decade ago. I feel it played an instrumental role in our victory over communism.

Now I may not be a Rhodes scholar, but I *do* know this: if we can protect America with a defensive shield from incoming missile attacks, we should *by all means* do so!

And if the new administration in Washington thinks we are no longer at risk, they need to *open their eyes and take a long, hard look at the world.*

The Romans warned long ago, "Let him who desires peace prepare for war." Washington would echo these words in the very first State of the Union address, reiterating to his countrymen one of the simple truths of the ages—"To be prepared for war is one of the effectual means of preserving peace." Yet it seems we must relearn this lesson time and time again, often at terrible cost.

I know. In my eighty-two years I've seen America drop her guard time and time again— and each time with tragic consequences.

In 1916, Woodrow Wilson won the election on a promise that he would keep the nation out of war. Shortly afterwards, an unprepared America was sucked into World War I.

In 1940, President Roosevelt won re-election on a peace platform. That peace platform soon crumbled under the bombs of Pearl Harbor.

After World War II we disarmed virtually overnight. Before you knew it our Army was being pushed around by ragtag troops in Korea. And later, the Soviets shocked us by launching *Sputnik* and by invading Afghanistan.

Today the United States dominates the world arena. Once again our noble first instinct is to seek peace. And that's why America needs the brave and skilled soldiers of The Citadel more than ever—just in case.

As General Colin Powell, my former National Security Advisor and now Chairman of the Joint Chiefs of Staff, has noted, we need a powerful military that can solve small problems before they become big, bloody ones.

We cannot allow another Saddam Hussein to grab every oil patch in the Middle East.

It would be difficult to sit on the sidelines in Bosnia and watch the slaughter of innocent men, women and children and allow war to spread elsewhere in Europe, for let us not forget that that is the exact place that the First World War began.

When I was about your age President Roosevelt said we had "nothing to fear but fear itself." Today, in much different times, our prosperous nation has little to fear but *complacency* itself. We must stay strong and flexible. We *must* keep our powder dry.

And this venerable academic institution has an historic obligation to preserve the liberty of America.

Savor these moments. Keep these memories close to your heart. Cherish your families and friends because we never know what the future will bring. Live each day to the fullest because it is you who will lay the solid foundations of a free society.

You are ready to build the homes, the neighborhoods and businesses of the twenty-first century.

A noble defender of freedom, General Douglas MacArthur, knew well the qualities of a soldier patriot. During the desperate early days of World War II, when our victory in the Pacific was by no means assured, he wrote a prayer for someone he loved dearly—his young son. Perhaps it could have been written by any father or mother here today.

Here is part of the general's prayer:

Build me a son, O Lord, who will be strong enough to know when he is weak, and brave enough to face himself when he is afraid; one who will be proud and unbending in honest defeat, and humble and gentle in victory.

Build me a son whose wishes will not take the place of deeds; a son who will know Thee—and that to know himself is the foundation stone of knowledge.

. . . Give him humility, so that he may always remember the simplicity of true greatness, the open mind of true wisdom, and the weakness of true strength.

Then I, his father, will dare to whisper, "I have not lived in vain."

Cadets, live each day with enthusiasm, optimism, hope and honor. If you do, I am convinced that your contribution to this wonderful experiment we call America will be greater than we ever imagined.

In closing, let me say that nothing made me prouder as President than America's young people in uniform. And no decision was ever more difficult for me to make than the time I ordered our military forces into action. Each time I issued such an order, I reminded myself that it wasn't just a nameless, faceless soldier I was dispatching, but a child of loving parents, the partner of an adoring spouse or perhaps the parent and provider for some happy children.

I reminded myself that if things should go wrong, and casualties did occur, it wouldn't just be a day of flag-draped coffins coming home. There would permanently be empty chairs at family tables, vacant seats in Little League baseball bleachers and teary-eyed explanations to young children about why their daddy wouldn't be coming home again.

So I felt then, as I feel now, America owes a special thanks to those who are willing to make the ultimate sacrifice for their country. We must honor them and respect them, not just when they are in battle, but every day they wear the proud uniform of our country.

When I met with each of my successors prior to beginning their Presidencies, I strongly offered a bit of personal advice. I told them, even though you don't wear a uniform, as President you are the Commander in Chief. And when you are saluted by a member of the Armed Forces, don't just smile or wave. I said, stop and salute them back. And, from what I've seen, they've followed that advice.

So today, as an old cavalry officer and your Commander in Chief, I hope you will allow me once again to show you how proud I am. . . . [salute].

Thank you, again, for having me here today. Congratulations and God bless you.

*I*t was my privilege to serve at Ronald Reagan's side for nearly seven years—first as Assistant to the President and head of the White House Office of Public Liaison and then as Secretary of Transportation. And as I look back on those years, not only was President Reagan a visionary leader who turned America around and brought freedom to millions of men and women around the world, he was one of the most genuine and gracious individuals I have ever met.

*President Reagan greeting Secretary of Transportation Elizabeth Dole, November 20, 1986.*

The countless Americans I escorted into the Oval Office to see President Reagan shared two things in common. They were very nervous before meeting the President. And they were all immediately put at ease by his warm humor and his genuine modesty—a modesty summed up by the sign he kept on his White House desk declaring there is no limit to what someone can accomplish if he doesn't mind who gets the credit.

And I shall always remember the moment early in his Presidency when President Reagan told me about his days as Governor of California. "Each morning began with someone standing before my desk describing yet another disaster," he said. "The feeling of stress became almost unbearable. I had the urge to look over my shoulder for someone I could pass the problem to. One day it came to me that I was looking in the wrong direction. I looked up instead of back. I'm still looking up.

I couldn't face one more day in this office if I didn't know I could ask God's help and it would be given."

Both Bob and I have had the honor of seeing and speaking with President Reagan on several occasions in recent years. And we know that sustained by his beloved Nancy and the abiding affection of his countrymen, he faces the future with a serenity born of faith in God. Few men could ask for more.

ELIZABETH DOLE
*President, American Red Cross*

*T*HIS IS A SPECIAL day for my family and me, not only because my mother meant so much to *us,* but because she also meant a great deal to *you* and this institution.

You've already been told today, Nelle was quite a remarkable woman—tiny in stature, but with enormous optimism and a huge heart. And she believed with all her heart that there was no such thing as accidents in this life. Everything was part of God's plan.

Growing up, the Reagans had little in material wealth. And although we were poor, the government didn't come around and tell us we were, so we didn't know it. And we probably didn't know it because Nelle was always finding someone who was worse off than we were that needed help.

Nelle always felt that if something went wrong, you didn't wring your hands, you rolled up your sleeves. And that's just what she did here at Olive View.

Which reminds me of a story I'd like to tell you relating to that:

Some years after I was in Hollywood, I was able to bring my parents out here, and Nelle immediately started to adapt to her new home. She found this wonderful place and went to work, visiting regularly. She arranged for movies to be shown and for television and things of that kind that they never had before.

And one night I was a speaker at one of the Olive View banquets. Now, banquet food wasn't of the same quality that it is today. And the waiter came along, leaned over to me and whispered, "Would you rather have a bigger steak than what we're serving here?"

"Well," I said, "if that's possible, yes." Well, he arrived back with the biggest, fattest, juiciest T-bone steak you ever saw. Now, in the meantime, I had decided that he *had* to be a motion picture fan, and he must have liked my pictures. And I was basking in that kind of reflected glory.

As he put the steak down, I thanked him and he leaned down and whispered in my ear, "Anything for a relative of Nelle Reagan's. I used to be a patient at Olive View Sanitarium."

Seriously, as you've heard today, my mother, like countless others, embodied the spirit of volunteerism. Throughout our history Americans have reached out in service to others.

And it was that great American spirit that got this hospital started and keeps it going today. This generous spirit is the backbone of our country—Americans helping themselves, and each other, reaching out and finding solutions, solutions that governments and huge institutions can't find.

And so today we recognize Nelle Reagan and all the volunteers around the world. We recognize this precious resource, this strength of our nation—people who, through love and hard work, have made the American family the envy of the world.

I've gone on longer than I intended here today. Thank you for honoring Nelle. If she were here today, she would probably have been a bit embarrassed by this ceremony. But I suspect she is looking down on this occasion today and her heart is touched to know that her work continues.

Thank you, on behalf of our entire family, for honoring her in this way.

$\mathcal{R}$onald Reagan was a doer, a pragmatist, a man who enjoyed hard physical tasks, as in the ranch work he loved to do. But that brush clearing and fence fixing was a symbol, too; he wanted to be doing it himself because from the land came not only strength and clarity, but a vision—the vision of the West and the endless horizon. The American people liked Ronald Reagan and re-elected him in one of the biggest landslides in history because he

*President Reagan with Secretary of State George Shultz, December 4, 1986.*

trusted them and he conveyed to them that they need not be bound, tied down by class, or race, or childhood misfortune, or poverty, or bureaucracy. They, the people, could make something of themselves; indeed, they could remake themselves, endlessly.

But beneath this pragmatic attitude lay a bedrock of principle and purpose with which I was proud to be associated. Ronald Reagan believed in being strong enough to defend one's interests, but he viewed that strength as a means, not an end in itself. He was ready to negotiate with his adversaries.

He was a fervent anti-Communist who could comprehend and believe that people everywhere would choose to throw off the Communist system if they ever had the chance. And he worked hard to give them that chance. He favored open trade because he had confidence in the ability of Americans to compete, and he had confidence that an integrated world economy would benefit America. He stuck to his agenda.

The world learned when Ronald Reagan faced down the air-traffic controllers in 1981 that he could dig in and fight to win. The world learned in Grenada that he would use military force if needed. He did not accept that extensive political opposition doomed an attractive idea. He would fight resolutely for an idea, believing that, if it was valid, he could persuade the American people to support it. He changed the national and international agenda on issue after issue. He was an optimist; he spoke the vocabulary of opportunity. He had a vision of what he stood for and what we aspire to as a nation.

The points he made, however consummate the delivery, were unmistakably real in his mind and heart, an American creed: Defend your country, value your family, make something of yourself, tell the government to get off your back, tell the tyrants to watch their step.

Reagan was President as a Republican, a conservative, a man of the right. But these labels will mislead historians who do not see beyond them, for Americans could see some of Ronald Reagan in themselves. He came from the heartland of the country, where people could be down-to-earth yet feel that the sky is the limit—not ashamed of, or cynical about, the American dream. Not far from Ronald Reagan's small town of Dixon, Illinois, is Jane Addams's small town of Cedarville; not far from Cedarville is Ulysses Grant's small town of Galena. And not far from Galena is Carl Sandburg's Galesburg. Ronald Reagan has something of them all: his heart going out to the people; his will ready to fight for the country; his voice able to move the nation. And, as Carl Sandburg wrote it,

> The republic is a dream.
> Nothing happens unless first a dream.

GEORGE SHULTZ
*Secretary of State, 1982–1989*

*T*ODAY WE HAVE gathered to celebrate the powerful, refreshing tides of freedom and democracy. In doing so, we pay tribute to an outstanding American leader and dedicated worker for human freedom.

Before we do that, however, I want to say a few words about something that has been in the minds and hearts of Californians these past few weeks. It's about the brave men and women—American heroes in the purest sense—who risked their lives and displayed the utmost courage fighting the fires of recent days.

From the unified ground forces to the helicopter pilots who dodged the deadly flames— and everyone in between—we applaud you. You performed valiantly and have earned the respect and lasting appreciation of your fellow citizens everywhere.

In the past few weeks there have been fires in virtually every community that surrounds this Presidential Library. We have seen firsthand the heroic acts of bravery performed by these young men and women and we will forever be in their debt.

I am pleased to announce that on Saturday, November 20, Nancy and I will join the local communities here at the Library in a special ceremony honoring the heroic firefighters and their families.

And as a small gesture of our appreciation, for the rest of this year, the doors of this Library will be open without charge to any firefighter or member of their family.

Today, as we honor a great American, I would like to take a few moments to talk of a pending issue of great importance to our nation and our state: the North American Free Trade Agreement.

There was once a time when national boundaries formed natural barriers to the flow of commerce and ideas, but no more. Everywhere we look we find free men and free markets are on the march. Old barriers fall with each passing day and new opportunities define themselves with the speed of light. In a few days the United States Congress will face a momentous decision. It can approve a North American Free Trade Agreement that creates the largest free-trading bloc on the face of the earth or can succumb to timidity and factionalism.

It is the shrill cry of fear that says the United States cannot compete on the world market; it is the voice of reason and experience that argues otherwise.

Here in California, we are inescapably linked to markets around the globe. We want no barriers to our ingenuity, no obstacles to our prosperity, for we know that truly free trade is fair trade—a good deal for Americans and a great source of jobs in the emerging economies of tomorrow.

It is my fervent hope that on November 17th, members of Congress will display the courage which has so characterized the man we honor this morning. I hope that they will take the long view and do what we know to be right for our children and ourselves.

Today it is indeed a pleasure to welcome a special American hero to the library: Colin Powell, the soldier, the patriot, the visionary.

We are so happy to have the Powells with us today. To Alma, we are grateful to you for being such an important partner to Colin all these years. You, too, in so many ways, have been called to serve your country. You have done it with grace, compassion and courage, and for that our nation is eternally grateful.

For those of you who may not know, today is a special day, an anniversary of sorts. On this day just a few years ago, we turned a page in human history. The cold and unsightly symbol of oppression that divided East and West Germany crumbled to the ground.

On this day four years ago freedom's bells rang resolutely throughout the world, claiming victory for mankind against tyranny. Families were, at long last, reunited, and people everywhere joined hands in support and celebration. I recall the images vividly as the events in Germany unfolded. I remember a certain trip I made to Berlin not long before, when I called on Mr. Gorbachev to tear down that evil wall. I knew it would happen someday, but I never dreamed then that it would come down so soon—or that a huge piece of it would end up sitting in our front yard.

But there it is, just outside this Library—a 6,000-pound section of that divisive, once-dreaded Iron Curtain. Scribbled all over that cement slab are vibrant artistic expressions from the German people that tell the tale of hard-won freedom. It is here so that future generations will forever be reminded that freedom must always be cherished and constantly defended.

The story of the man we honor today is also one of liberation and hope. It is a story of strength, courage, perseverance and success. As the son of Jamaican immigrants, he grew up on the tough streets of the South Bronx, where most roads were dead-end streets.

Many of his peers were led astray by crime and drugs. But Colin was raised on the values of faith, family and love of country. He chose a path where talent had the better chance—the United States military.

It was there that he matured into a devoted soldier and responsible citizen. He lived each day serving valiantly the cause of "duty, honor, country," and, as a result, was a highly decorated combat veteran, a four-star general, and a distinguished leader of men and women.

As for my own relationship with Colin, we hit it off right away. He was my immediate choice for the position of National Security Advisor to the President—a powerful and highly demanding position.

I had immense respect for his perception, insights, cool-headed judgment during a crisis and extensive military experience.

Colin was a refreshing addition to our foreign policy team—someone I could rely on for straight talk. Any of you who have been in Washington know that straight talk can be a rare and valuable thing in that town. I especially appreciated his commonsense approach to military strength. Colin followed the maxim of a legendary Roman general who said, "To preserve peace, prepare for war."

Colin's philosophy was directly in line with my own. I'd always believed in the importance of peace through strength. And the military is the provider of that strength, so we must equip them, train them and support them.

Over the years American military leadership has brought us to even greater heights than we could ever imagine. In times of peace and in times of war, America's military power has led our nation to many great victories.

Colin Powell has been at the center of virtually every American victory in recent years—from the ending of the Cold War to Operation Desert Storm. During his four years as Chairman of the Joint Chiefs, Colin smoothly coordinated American military action in over two dozen crisis situations around the world. He managed with consummate professionalism the dramatic restructuring of our defense forces after the Cold War. He has guided the American eagle to greater heights than ever before.

And I think Colin himself summed it up best when he prepared to retire and delivered one of his final speeches. He said, "Our forces have been called on to fight wars, to restore and preserve peace, to relieve pain, to provide hope and deter aggression. . . . And in every instance, they've gone about their job with a competency and with a spirit too rarely seen in our country—proud, patriotic, selfless, drug-free, the best and brightest of American youth."

I believe Colin himself has become that rare individual who is respected by Americans everywhere across the political spectrum, from the inner city to the corporate boardroom to the floor of Congress to the battlefield. Just watch the young troops swarm him with warmth and affection wherever he goes. He is one of them, and they will always be at his side.

I have no doubt that thousands of young people across our great nation have been inspired by Colin Powell's story. They may have watched his briefings on television during the Gulf war or admired the well-deserved medals on his chest.

Who knows how many young men and

women have walked into an Army recruiting office with Colin Powell on their minds? And how many more youngsters will emulate his exemplary code of honor, will work hard and study with diligence, and create a better life for themselves and their families?

One of Colin's favorite Biblical passages comes from the prophet Isaiah. It reads, "And the Lord God asked, 'Whom shall I send? Who will go for us?'" And the prophet Isaiah replied, "Here I am, send me."

For several decades—during dark and dangerous days of global struggle—America has often looked to this brave soldier for help. And he never hesitated to say, "Here I am, send me."

Because you, Colin, have answered the call of duty without fail, America is stronger and safer and better than before. Thanks to America's military strength and moral vision, more people than ever are basking in freedom's light.

And so today it is my great honor and pleasure to bestow this freedom award upon General Colin Powell for a lifetime of dedicated service to the protection of liberty and peace, for extraordinary leadership of our nation's military, and for promoting the ideals of freedom and democracy throughout the world.

*T*wo examples vividly illustrate the exemplary qualities of President Ronald Reagan and why he still occupies a rare and special place in the memory of millions of Americans. First, in 1985 right after he had been at Fort Campbell, Kentucky, comforting the families of the 101st Airborne Division whose loved ones had been killed in a plane crash. The quiet courage and calm manner in which he led the nation and shared a burden of pain was an inspiration to all of us.

*President Reagan and Congressman Newt Gingrich aboard Air Force One, August 1, 1983.*

I also remember the night a few years earlier when he walked into the House of Representatives chamber just weeks after having been shot. It was the most electrifying single moment I have seen in the House as people cheered him for his courage and his remarkable ability to lead and exhibit his warm sense of humor, even in the face of the most difficult of circumstances.

It was this capacity to combine a deep love of country, a philosophical understanding of what works, a passionate sense of life with a very balanced, disciplined approach that made him such a remarkable leader.

NEWT GINGRICH
*Speaker, U.S. House of Representatives*

*I* CAN'T TELL YOU how thrilled Nancy and I are to be here with you today and to welcome you to *your* Presidential Library. Although it bears my name, it is *your* library every bit as much as it is mine. It is a monument to the talent and energy of each one of you who shared our dream of a better, stronger America and worked hard to make it possible.

I have no intention of making a lengthy speech—I suspect you've heard one or two over the years anyway.

I know many of you have taken time off from hectic schedules and traveled great distances to be here and we are so happy that you did.

Come to think of it, it's a good thing we decided to get together *this* year. After Clinton's tax plan takes effect next April, who knows if *any* of us will be able to afford a plane ticket to go anywhere!

I suspect you probably didn't have an easy time flying out *this* year either. With the White House Travel Office now requiring all flights to lay over in Arkansas, the trip to L.A. takes a bit longer than it used to. And with Presidential barbers doubling as air-traffic controllers, it's a wonder *anyone* gets *anywhere* these days!

Seriously, as I look around this gathering, I am filled with countless warm and fond memories. Many of you go back with us a number of years. Others of you are more recent additions to the family. Regardless of when you came, you have been a big part of our lives. For that, we are so grateful and feel so blessed.

Now, as most of you know, I'm not one for looking back. I figure there will be plenty of time for that when I'm *old!*

But I know you will have the opportunity to tour this Library and Museum shortly. As you walk through these exhibits, you will find yourselves reliving moments of history—large and small—that you helped to create and shape. You will see all around you the evidence of the ideas, accomplishments and events we shared together for so many years.

As this Library reminds us, every great nation must cherish and preserve its past. And the same is true for our movement that began so many years ago.

When we came to Washington on that bright sunny day in January of 1981, we shared a dream for America.

Back then, the reach of big government had become intolerable. It was a time of rampant inflation and crushing interest rates—when hope was scarce.

It was a time when cold, ugly walls divided nations and human rights were trampled in the name of evil and corrupt ideologies.

It was a time when the nuclear arms race was spiraling out of control and a blinding mistrust stood between the East and West.

We believed that for the future of America *and* the free world, this could not stand. And *together* we insisted that this great nation must once again behave as such.

We saw an America where most people still believed in the power of a better tomorrow. And together we got the government off the backs of the American people.

We created millions of new jobs for Americans at all income levels.

And it may shock many in Washington to discover that most of the economic gains during the 1980s were made by low- and middle-income citizens, *not* the wealthiest of Americans.

We knew that individual Americans could save or spend their money much more wisely than the government could. We cut taxes and freed the people from the shackles of too much government. And the economy burst loose in the longest peacetime expansion ever. We brought America *back*—bigger and better than ever.

In the 1980s, America shone brightly as a beacon of hope and freedom to oppressed people everywhere. The world looked to us not only because of our military might, but also because of our ideas of liberty and freedom. We helped fledgling democracies from every corner of the earth take root and flourish.

We revitalized a demoralized, underfunded and unappreciated military, and we built it into the most modern and respected force in the world.

Finally, after decades of struggle, democracy won the Cold War and the Berlin Wall came tumbling down.

Well, the world watched with amazement as we put our house in order and took our rightful place as the most powerful country in the world. And I *firmly* believe that *history* will record our era as one of peace and global prosperity.

However, our task is far from over. Our friends in the other party will never forgive us for our success and are doing everything in their power to rewrite history. Listening to the liberals in the White House, you'd think that the 1980s were the worst period since the Great Depression—filled with greed and despair.

Well, you and I know better than that. I've seen and heard many of you out there, busy setting the record straight *whenever* and *wherever* you can. You've been fighting for the truth. You've been writing letters to the editor and speaking up on television. You've been standing up for the 1980s and for the great things that together we did for America. Your efforts are making a difference, so I say to you: *Please keep it up!*

It was often said during the Communist years that he who controls the past also controls the future. Well, *we* are the ones who must preserve the principles of our noble past— free markets, a strong defense and traditional values. These eternal principles are the solid foundation of any future Republican platform.

The values of free markets in the 1980s were the values of American independence in 1776. And they will be the values of a strong and prosperous America in the twenty-first century.

But leave that for another day. Today we celebrate your accomplishments and salute the valiant political warriors and bold visionaries here in this audience.

You should never underestimate what you have done for America. It is a rare man—or woman—who steps forward and shapes the destiny of an entire nation.

Now before I go, I don't think a reunion of this kind would be complete without, well, something that you probably got used to while we were living in Washington—and no, I'm not talking about the cheese soup in the White House mess!

I thought to close today with one of my stories:

It's a story about a woman who walked into a bridal shop one day and told the sales clerk that she was looking for a wedding gown for her *fourth* wedding.

"Well," the saleswoman asked, "just exactly what type of dress are you looking for?"

"A long, flowing white dress with a veil," she responded with assurance.

Not totally convinced, but afraid to offend the woman, the saleslady said, "You know, dresses of that nature are usually appropriate for brides who are being married for the *first* time—for those a bit more *'innocent,'* if you know what I mean."

"Well," the lady retorted and put her hand on her hip, "I *do* know what you mean and I can assure you I'm as *innocent* as the rest of them. Despite all my marriages I remain as *innocent* as any first-time bride.

"You see, my first husband was a dear sweet man. It was a terrible tragedy. Actually, all the excitement of the wedding was simply too much for him and he died as we checked into the hotel on our wedding night."

"I'm sorry to hear that," said the clerk. "But what about the others?"

"Well, my second husband and I got into a terrible fight in the limousine on the way to our wedding reception. We haven't spoken since and got the marriage quickly annulled."

"What about your *third* husband?" asked the store clerk.

"Well . . . ," the woman replied, "he was a *Democrat*. And every night for four years he just sat on the edge of the bed and told me how *good* it was going to be!"

Sorry, I just couldn't resist telling that!

I will conclude by saying the only words I can to convey how grateful Nancy and I are to *each* and every one of you: *Thank you;* and until we meet again, God bless you, my friends.

*I*n my view, the fortieth President of the United States will go down in history for his rare perception.

We worked together to end the Cold War and the arms race. This achievement—the end of the long and damaging era of confrontation—will benefit all nations. The challenge that we faced was to discard old stereotypes and break with the inertia of past policies and practices. It is to the great and lasting credit of President Reagan that he responded to our initiatives and worked with foresight and determination to negotiate the first agreements that resulted in real arms reductions, putting the world on the road toward nuclear disarmament. What is even more important, once our agreements were concluded, Ronald Reagan stood by them and worked hard to make sure they were ratified.

*President Reagan with General Secretary Mikhail Gorbachev in Geneva, November 19, 1985.*

Such things do not happen by themselves. There were many forks in the road and difficult moments, both when we started our dialogue in Geneva and when we continued it in Reykjavík. What I particularly appreciated then, as I do now, is that Ronald Reagan never broke off that dialogue.

Ronald Reagan is a man committed to conservative values— the values that, among others, are important for humankind's survival and well-being. As I see it, however, he was never a prisoner to any ideology. In real life, he was not dogmatic; rather, he was ready to work out the differences and reach a reasonable compromise.

With President Reagan, we traveled the road from confrontation to cooperation. I join in the tribute to this remarkable man and salute him.

MIKHAIL GORBACHEV
*General Secretary of the Communist Party*
*of the Soviet Union, 1985–1991*

*N*OVEMBER 19th, 1985, was a day I had looked forward to for five years. In a sense, it was a day I had prepared for all my life. For forty years a nuclear cloud had hung over the world. Presidents since Harry Truman had labored to contain a spiraling arms race, aware that a single misstep could be fatal to the survival of mankind.

Over the years, both sides in this deadly contest had developed a policy known as mutual assured destruction, or MAD. And that's exactly what it was—madness on a global scale. Simply put, it called for each side to have enough nuclear weapons to obliterate the other in a matter of minutes.

In theory, this was deterrence at the point of a gun. In practice, it meant that we lived a mere push button away from oblivion.

As President I was determined to end this madness and, if humanly possible, to rid the world of nuclear cancer. I had no illusions that it would be easy.

I had learned long ago that the only way to bargain is from a position of strength. Yet when I came into office our bargaining position had been weakened by devastating cuts in America's defenses.

In 1981 we had planes that couldn't fly and ships that couldn't sail because they lacked the necessary spare parts. Because we had neglected our volunteer Army, we were losing some of our best soldiers.

Most ominous of all, we had allowed the Soviet Union to create a war machine that threatened not only its neighbors, but the equilibrium of deterrence itself.

My administration undertook a massive rebuilding program, both to redress the current imbalance and to convince the Soviets of the need to return to the bargaining table. It was a controversial move.

But in November 1985 it finally paid off here in a boathouse beside Lake Geneva where the President of the United States and the General Secretary of the Soviet Union come together to bridge four decades of mutual hostility.

The night before our first meeting at the Villa Fleur d'Eau, I confided to my diary, "Lord, I hope I'm ready."

When I shook hands with Mikhail Gorbachev on the steps of the villa, I had a plan in mind. As our technical experts began their work, I said to the General Secretary, "Why don't you and I step outside and get some fresh air?"

Gorbachev was out of his chair before I could finish the sentence. We walked together about one hundred yards down to the boathouse, where a fire had already been lit.

For the next ninety minutes we were alone, accompanied only by our interpreters. It was an extraordinary encounter—two men from opposite sides of the globe, believing in different ideologies, but with a common interest in saving mankind from the nuclear nightmare that haunted the dreams of children in every land.

I spoke first. "Here you and I are," I said, "probably the only two men in the world who could bring about World War III.

"But by the same token, we may be the only two men in the world who could perhaps bring about peace in the world.

"Mr. General Secretary," I continued, "we don't mistrust each other because we're armed; we are armed because we distrust each other. It's fine that the two of us and our people are talking about arms reductions, but isn't it also important that you and I should be talking about how we could reduce the mistrust between us?"

And so we did. In that one conversation, we cut through a lifetime of distrust.

On our way back to the main house, I invited the General Secretary to come to the United States and see our country for himself. Not only did he agree on the spot, he invited me to visit the Soviet Union. A corner had been turned. One meeting designed to break the ice had turned into three full-scale summits. It was better than we had dared to hope.

As a result the way was open for the first genuine arms reduction ever. On the flight home I couldn't help but think back to the dawn of the atomic age and to all the crises and flash points that had made ours an age of anxiety.

I hadn't changed all that much over those forty years, but the world had. And after our meeting in a Geneva boathouse, things would never be the same.

*I* first met Ronald Reagan, who was to become such a good friend and such a great President, when he was Governor of California and I was leader of the Opposition. Both of us in our different ways were fighting the same battle of ideas for freedom and we immediately found in each other kindred spirits.

*President Reagan walking with Prime Minister Margaret Thatcher, June 23, 1982.*

Ronald Reagan's qualities were easily underrated by his contemporaries, just as his huge achievements are often foolishly undervalued today. This may be because his easygoing charm, open friendliness and ability to express in the simplest terms truths of enormous importance made him seem just another "ordinary" American. But President Reagan is not at all ordinary, though he has a natural insight into what ordinary people—particularly ordinary Americans, who are indeed the salt of the earth—think. Ronald Reagan's basic beliefs were truly that—beliefs. And because he was a believer he did not suffer from the dismal plague of doubts which has assailed so many politicians in our times and which has rendered them incapable of clear decisions. But President Reagan was also an extremely effective politician because he took the greatest care about everything he did—whether it was in picking a sound, effective team, or in working out his position on the great issues of war and peace he daily faced as the leader of the most powerful country on earth, or in explaining his intentions to the American public. Let me give just one personal recollection.

On one occasion, when as Prime Minister I was visiting the President at Camp David, I learned that he was due to give a five-minute radio broadcast to the nation, so I asked to sit in and listen. He showed me the script he had prepared, carefully marked up in manuscript with indications for speed and emphasis. He had also noted the point he must have reached by the end of each minute. There were no run-throughs, no false starts, just perfect timing, while from time to time the master consulted his watch as he spoke his lines. I was told afterwards that it was always the same: faultless.

There were many heroic moments in President Reagan's tenure of the Presidency, surely the most significant and triumphant period of recent American history. But those few minutes watching the Great Communicator at work reminded me that no matter how prodigious one's talents or how passionate one's views, it is the exacting attention of supreme professionalism that provides the vital ingredient for political success.

LADY THATCHER
*Prime Minister of Great Britain, 1979–1990*

BEFORE I GET started here I want to thank my dear friend Margaret Thatcher for being part of yet another important milestone in my life and for those very kind words.

As most of you know, Margaret and I go back quite a ways. We met at a time before she became Prime Minister and I became President. From the moment we met we discovered that we shared quite similar views of government and freedom. Margaret ended our first meeting by telling me, "We must stand together." And that's exactly what we've done in years since—as friends *and* as political allies.

Margaret Thatcher is one of the giants of our century. Her many achievements will be appreciated more and more as time goes on and history is written. For me, she has been a staunch ally, my political soulmate, a great visionary and a dear, dear friend. Thank you, Margaret, for being with us tonight.

I would also like to convey my personal appreciation to Haley Barbour. Haley, you and the entire Republican National Committee are doing an excellent job keeping the heat on the Democrats at *both* ends of Pennsylvania Avenue. Haley, back when I hired you to work on my White House staff, I *suspected* you might amount to something someday!

I must say that returning to Washington today really brought back memories:

As our plane headed toward the airport, I looked down on the White House, and it was just like the good old days . . . the South Lawn, the Rose Garden . . . *David Gergen.*

I looked over a couple of blocks, and there was the Internal Revenue Service—*bigger* than I ever remembered it.

Then I looked down at the enormous United States Post Office Building. I could just *see* the excitement on the faces of the bureaucrats, knowing *they* would soon be managing our national health-care system!

Up on Capitol Hill, I saw that big white dome, bulging with new tax revenues. I instinctively reached for my veto pen and thought to myself, Go ahead, make my day.

You may have seen President Clinton draw his *own* veto pen on television just last week. The difference is that *his* pen doesn't have any ink in it—unless, of course, you're talking about *red* ink. And we all know the Democrats have *plenty* of *that!*

All of *you* have made *our* day just by being here. It's a pleasure to see so many familiar faces and those who work so hard for the Grand Old Party.

Birthdays often serve as the rare moments when we can pause from the bustle of our daily lives to reflect on the years that have passed, the accomplishments and people that have made them special.

As I look around this gathering, I am filled with countless warm and fond memories. Many of you go back with us as far as my two terms as California Governor. Others of you are more recent additions to the family. Regardless of when you came, you have been a big part of our lives. For that, we are so grateful and feel so blessed.

Now, as most of you know, I'm not one for looking back. I figure there will be plenty of time for that when I get *old!*

But rather what I take from the past is inspiration for the future. And what we accomplished during our years in the White House must never be lost amid the rhetoric of political revisionists.

It was a time when America was a bright beacon of hope and freedom to oppressed people everywhere. The world looked to us not just because of our military might, but because of our ideas of liberty and freedom. And

they knew *we* were willing to defend and promote those ideas in every corner of the earth.

We rebuilt a demoralized, underfunded and unappreciated military. And we made it the most modern and respected force in the world.

And who can forget those so-called experts who said our military buildup threatened a dangerous escalation of tensions?

What kind of fool, they asked, would call the Soviet Union an evil empire?

I'm tempted to say, there's *no* fool like an *old* fool! But as events have shown, there was nothing foolish in my prediction that communism was destined for the *ash heap* of history.

However, our task is far from over. Our friends in the other party will never forgive us for our success and are doing everything in their power to rewrite history. Listening to the liberals, you'd think that the 1980s were the worst period since the Great Depression—filled with greed and despair. Well, you and I know better than that: *we were there!*

Although the political landscape has changed, the bold ideas of the 1980s are alive and well. Republican candidates swept every major election across the country last year, from New York to Texas—from New Jersey to my home state of California.

And as a result it seems that our opponents have finally realized how *unpopular* liberalism really is. So now they're trying to dress their *liberal* agenda in a *conservative* overcoat.

After watching the State of the Union address the other night, I'm reminded of the old adage that imitation is the sincerest form of flattery. Only in *this* case, it's *not* flattery, but *grand larceny*—the intellectual theft of ideas that you and I recognize as our own.

Speech delivery counts for little on the world stage unless you have convictions and, yes, the *vision* to see beyond the front-row seats. The Democrats may remember their lines, but how quickly they forget the lessons of the past.

I have witnessed five major wars in my lifetime, and I know how swiftly storm clouds can gather on a peaceful horizon. The next time a Saddam Hussein takes over Kuwait or North Korea brandishes a nuclear weapon, will we be ready to respond?

In the end, it all comes down to leadership. That is what this country is looking for now.

It was leadership here at home that gave us strong American influence abroad and the collapse of imperial communism. Great nations have responsibilities to lead and we should always be cautious of those who would lower our profile because they might just wind up lowering our flag.

My friends, I would like to end by telling you something that Nancy and I have wanted to say to you for a long time.

During our years together here, as you know, things were always on the move. As soon as we accomplished *one* objective, we were quickly on to the next. There was rarely time to celebrate victory or recall all the people who made it possible.

Well, one of the benefits of retirement is you get a chance to reflect back over the years. Since Nancy and I have returned to California, we've spent many occasions looking back at what we did here and remembering the extraordinary people who worked so hard to make those great days possible. And we've wondered if we would ever get the chance to thank them. Well, *you* are those people—those great individuals who gave so much of yourselves—who sacrificed and supported us and helped us achieve everything we did.

So, I will conclude tonight by saying that the greatest gift I could receive on my birthday is to be able to stand before *each* and every one of you and convey in the only words I can how grateful Nancy and I are:

Thank you for being *there*—and for being *here*. And thank you for making this evening a *memory* I will cherish forever.

And until we meet again, God bless you, my friends.

$\mathcal{D}$uring my thirty-five years on Capitol Hill, I never saw a President who was more successful at working his will with Congress than Ronald Reagan. But one of the defining memories I have of President Reagan involved one of his few legislative defeats. In March of 1987 the President vetoed a $87.5 billion highway bill that was vastly over budget and filled to the brim with pork. As Republican leader it was my job to round up enough votes to sustain that veto, and it proved to be a very tough assignment.

*President Reagan and Senator Bob Dole, March 10, 1986.*

After surveying the situation, I told President Reagan that we were one vote short, and advised him that a proposed visit to Capitol Hill to make a final Presidential pitch would be useless, as Republican positions were locked in stone and not even his tremendous persuasiveness would change any minds. The President, however, was in a combative mood and insisted on making a personal plea, despite knowing it would not alter the final outcome.

Not long after his visit, the President's veto was indeed overridden by one vote, and pundits were quick to describe the outcome as a personal setback for him. In his seventh year in office, the so-called experts were still making the mistake of underestimating Ronald Reagan, for although he lost on the highway bill, I realized that the bigger loss would have been to do nothing. Ronald Reagan understood that there are times when confrontation is better than capitulation—and this was one of them. Like any true leader, he knew that success is never final, nor defeat fatal, as long as you have the courage to act on principle and take the heat. No doubt about it, Ronald Reagan has that courage.

ROBERT DOLE
*Republican Senator from Kansas, 1969–1996*

*F*OR DWIGHT D. EISENHOWER, June 5, 1944, was "the longest day." For over a year the Supreme Allied Commander had been preparing history's mightiest invasion force—more than 5,000 ships, almost 12,000 aircraft and 155,000 soldiers. Originally set for that day, the assault on Hitler's Atlantic Wall would have to be postponed twenty-four hours due to high winds and ominous waves in the English Channel. Then the storm broke and the most momentous decision of Eisenhower's life was made. "OK, let's go," he told the men around him. For better or for worse, tomorrow was D-Day.

Outside his tent the gray English skies began to clear. Inside he prepared for the worst. "Our landings . . . have failed," he wrote in a statement he hoped would never be used. "If any blame or fault attaches to the attempt, it is mine alone." Eisenhower, the global strategist, remained at heart a self-effacing Kansas farmboy, embodying the democratic virtues of the soldiers he led.

War is an unpredictable mix of organized confusion, improvised ingenuity and timeless courage. Eisenhower recognized this when he returned to the battlefield beside the sea in June 1964. On D-Day Plus Twenty he spoke not of planes or tanks or guns or ships, nor strategies or commanders, Allied or Axis. Instead, he thought of what might have been— of all the men buried in French soil and all their families from whom they were forever separated. He said how blessed he and Mamie felt to have had grandchildren. And he reflected with sadness on the other American couples who would be denied that blessing because their sons had fallen in the fields of northern France.

I had similar feelings in June 1984 when I visited Normandy for the fortieth anniversary of the great invasion. As I gazed out upon the endless rows of white crosses and Stars of David, his lament took a special and personal poignancy. Within sight of Omaha Beach, I singled out Private First Class Peter Zanatta, whose daughter Lisa had written to tell me of her father's extraordinary bravery. Private Zanatta had died of cancer several years before the 1984 commemoration, but he was very much in our thoughts. On that day I promised both Lisa and her father, "We will always remember. We will always be proud. We will always be prepared, so we may always be free."

Much has changed in the decade since. The Iron Curtain that rose in the tragic aftermath of the war has been consigned to the history books. Germany has united. Yet for these changes and more, our debt of gratitude remains to the boys of Pointe du Hoc and all the heroes who liberated a continent in chains.

Age has its privileges, not least among them the opportunity to distill whatever wisdom comes from a long life of experiences. My generation has lived through a cold war and a nuclear nightmare that for forty years haunted the dreams of children everywhere. During this same time we have seen the United States become, however reluctantly, a great player on the world stage. Today, fifty years after the stark contrasts of D-Day, many Americans question our role in a world less clearly divided between dictatorships and democracy. Aware of our power, we seem uncertain as to our purpose.

Some in Congress, who confuse leading with meddling and ignore the lessons of a century scarred by false utopias and maximum leaders, would have us lower our global profile. On the eve of D-Day Plus Fifty they propose the removal of 75,000 American soldiers from Europe unless Europeans pay a significantly greater share of the cost of keeping them there.

Many oppose such shortsighted policies, and for good reason. Let's be honest. Evil still stalks the planet. Its ideology may be as simple as bloodlust, its program not more complex than economic or military plunder. Call it what you will, it is evil all the same. As such, it must be recognized and countered. Acknowledging trouble is not the same as looking for it.

In the post–Cold War world it is fashionable to assert that nations must focus their energies on economic, not military factors. In the long run, it is true, no nation can remain militarily strong while economically exhausted. But it is also true that defeats on the battlefield can and do occur in the short run. Enemies driven by nationalism, religion, ethnicity or ideology are unlikely to be impressed by American automobile production or diplomatic skills, especially if the latter are divorced from military strength. Lest we forget, Kuwait's wealth did not protect it from the predatory Saddam Hussein. Moreover, can anyone truly believe that progress toward a Middle East peace has occurred in a vacuum, or that Israel's age-old enemies would consider making peace but for the disappearance of the Soviet Union as a regional military power? The question answers itself.

As long as military force remains a necessary fact of modern existence, we should employ it in the service of vital humanitarian objectives. For example, what is being done to the people of Bosnia-Herzegovina shreds every definition of human morality. "Ethnic cleansing" is a savage euphemism for an evil we've seen before in Europe. By the same token, in parts of Africa, mankind is an endangered species.

The ultimate lesson of D-Day should not be the willingness of freedom's friends to come to its defense in an hour of grave peril. It should rather be how unnecessary such sacrifice is. If statesmen do their jobs with vision and resolution, then soldiers needn't be exposed to murderous fire. Ten years ago I promised Lisa Zanatta that we would always remember. It would be tragic as well as ironic if the fiftieth anniversary of D-Day was marked only by political amnesia. Private Zanatta deserves better. So do his grandchildren.

*I*n 1960, Ronald Reagan, then President only of the Screen Actors Guild, not yet the whole United States, was about to resign and devote his time to larger issues. He'd agreed, however, to lead us through the first strike in our history. He appointed me first to the board, then to the negotiating committee responsible for winning a new contract.

*President Reagan with fellow actor and longtime friend Charlton Heston, June 15, 1981.*

Public service—pursuing a group agenda for a common goal—was a new experience for me. I soon realized that grinding the other side down in argument isn't really the best tactic. The old Marxist dialectic of the employer as the enemy is painfully out of date. What you want is the common good. For that, you have to find common ground.

Reagan was very good at that, rallying the members wonderfully, but his real skills were in the actual negotiations. He was patient, persistent, moderate and, above all, good-humored, even at three in the morning, going back into caucus to review the same ground yet again.

The dark part of the night is a naked time. Unshaven, no coat or tie, stocking feet up on a desk, keeping awake with cold coffee while you wait for the other side to come back in the room; you get a pretty clear view of a guy. I saw Ronald Reagan clear in those hours. I remember coming home past four one morning, Lydia waking as I fell into bed. "How did it go?" she asked.

"Pretty slow work," I answered. "But I do believe we've got a leader."

We did, indeed. In the end, we established pension and medical plans funded by the studios, then a new concept in union contracts, as well as fees to be paid to actors when their work was rerun on TV. In plain fact, it remains the best contract SAG ever negotiated.

Some years later President Reagan had launched and ended every one of his campaigns for office in San Diego; I was asked to take part in a rally there the day before the election—the final rally he would ever attend on his own behalf. It was hardly an exclusive invitation. In addition to the scores of thousands of real people who jammed the vast outdoor amphitheater, there were several dozen public faces appearing onstage: political eminentos, pundits and performers in various media. Milling around in the backstage crowd, I ran into Nancy Reagan, who offered me a lift to L.A. in Air Force One. I doubt that many people decline that invitation; I certainly didn't.

The program was the appropriate mix of country-western, comics, talk and fireworks. The audience response to the President was volcanic—in comparison, it made the Rolling Stones' audience sound pallid.

Air Force One that afternoon was full of very tired people, at the end of an exhausting campaign. Meese, Deaver, Baker, all looked at the end of their energies. Not President Reagan. He was in high good spirits, glowing with health; I do believe he would've undertaken another campaign the next day.

The next day was the election. I asked Jim Baker, who'd run the campaign, "Well, what does it look like for tomorrow?"

"Oh, we'll lose the District of Columbia, probably Minnesota. . . . We'll take everything else."

I was stunned. "What do you mean, 'everything else'?"

"We'll win all the rest of the United States." And so it proved. Some time later President Reagan also won the Cold War.

CHARLTON HESTON

*Actor*

*Beverly Hilton Hotel, Beverly Hills, California*
*July 29, 1994*

*G*OOD EVENING, fellow Friars Club members. I am delighted to send my warmest greetings to all those gathered at the Beverly Hilton Hotel tonight to honor an individual Nancy and I hold especially dear—Charlton Heston.

In a moment, you'll see a few scenes which will remind all of us why we've always felt safe when Charlton Heston has been around—this hero bigger than life, this actor supreme.

Chuck has breathed life into Moses and Michelangelo. He's been El Cid and a circus ringmaster presiding over the Greatest Show on Earth. He's played cowboys *and* Indians, patriots and pirates, even a President of the United States, Mr. Andrew Jackson. And, as Ben Hur, he won both a chariot race and an Oscar as best actor of the year. Chuck has fought battles on land, sea and in the air; solved mysteries, and saved millions of lives while surviving bomb scares, earthquakes, native uprisings and an entire catalog of natural and man-made disasters.

His magnificent screen performances aside, it's the way Chuck has always conducted his life that especially makes him a hero in my eyes. As a private citizen, family man and friend, I've always known him to be a singularly dedicated person of the highest moral caliber. He's never been afraid to speak his mind or stand up for what he believes in.

That's what helped make Chuck a great and dedicated leader during his six terms as president of the Screen Actors Guild, a position I also was privileged to hold during my early days in Hollywood.

And I'm certain Chuck's commitment to his fellow actors didn't escape my Friars Club compatriots when they met to select him as recipient of the Lifetime Achievement Award.

So to you, Chuck, to Lydia and the entire family, Nancy and I send our congratulations on this special evening. We are proud to call you our friends!

*D*ear Mr. President,

You wrote us that extraordinary letter, in your own hand, to let us know that you were falling victim to Alzheimer's Disease. You spoke of other families suffering with the disease. You worried about your wife. Then you chose these words to comfort the nation: "I now begin the journey that will lead me into the sunset of my life. I know that for America there will always be a bright dawn ahead."

There you go again, I thought, showing us the way.

You've always had that capacity—not just because you're a natural leader, but because of your great personal strength. My mind went back to a day when we were all picking up our papers and leaving the table after a cabinet meeting. I literally bumped into you. Now, I'm a pretty big guy, but it was like bumping into a redwood. And it struck me at the time—that's you inside and out, solid in your stance, solid in your beliefs.

Your critics always said you weren't a "detail" man. Thank you for that. What great leader is? There are plenty of people to handle the details. You knew instinctively that the President must above all lead.

I've been following your path for many years, from the day you invited me to come to Washington to be director of the National Endowment for the Humanities. I crossed my fingers, packed up and moved from North Carolina. It was a chance, I thought, to help make a difference

*President Reagan with Secretary of Education William J. Bennett aboard Air Force One, December 1, 1987.*

in the world. I never realized what a different world it would soon be.

Soviet missiles were pointed then at America and Western Europe. You rearmed the Western alliance as a moral force. And in the most daring decision of all, you announced that we would begin a defense against nuclear missiles. You dismissed the long-accepted policy of MAD, "mutually assured destruction," which depended on the threat of massive nuclear retaliation to prevent war. The Strategic Defense Initiative (SDI) met vicious opposition. But it was an act of faith in the innovative genius that freedom fosters. The Soviets simply could not compete with SDI. You knew it. Gorbachev knew it, too.

*A reflective President Reagan in the Oval Office, October 27, 1983.*

The Soviet facade began to crack, and in a desperate attempt to keep the Communist Party in control, Gorbachev began some reforms. But if he's really a reformer, you reasoned, why doesn't he dismantle the Berlin Wall? Your advisors didn't want you to include that challenge in a speech in West Berlin. They took it out in the final version. But you stood at the Brandenburg Gate, looked toward East Germany and demanded, "Mr. Gorbachev, open up this gate! Mr. Gorbachev, tear down this wall!" Then you boldly predicted that "this wall will fall." It did, taking down Soviet communism with it.

Thank you, too, for believing in us. When you came to the White House we were sinking in a sea of high taxes, high interest rates and low morale. Politicians and pundits alike told us that we had to resign ourselves to a new era of "limits." You were undaunted. With an utter faith that government was the problem, not the solution, and a firm grasp of the only economics lesson worth learning—free enterprise works—you released our creative energies and entrepreneurial spirit. You cut the highest income-tax rate from 70 percent (yes, 70!) to 33 percent, energized investment by cutting the capital gains tax and brought tax relief to every income group. Result: the longest peacetime rise in prosperity in the nation's history.

Thank you, also, for creating for us almost an ideal of the way the Presidency should be carried.

Your manner sprang from the fact that even though you were President, you were always yourself. You never had to prove anything.

Finally, Mr. President, thank you for being there when the nation needed your hope, your courage and sometimes just your reassurance. When the *Challenger* astronauts died before our very eyes in 1986, you put a comforting hand on our shoulders and spoke so simply. "I know it's hard to understand that sometimes painful things like this happen. It's all part of the process of exploration and discovery. It's all part of taking a chance and expanding man's horizons. The future doesn't belong to the fainthearted. It belongs to the brave."

In your letter to us, you reminded us again of the bonds of faith, courage and affection that unite us with you. "When the Lord calls me home . . . ," you wrote, "I will leave with the greatest love for this country of ours and eternal optimism for its future."

Thank you, Mr. President.

WILLIAM J. BENNETT
*Secretary of Education, 1985–1988*

LETTER FROM PRESIDENT RONALD REAGAN
TO THE AMERICAN PEOPLE
*November 5, 1994*

My fellow Americans,

I have recently been told that I am one of the millions of Americans who will be afflicted with Alzheimer's Disease.

Upon learning this news, Nancy and I had to decide whether as private citizens we would keep this a private matter or whether we would make this news known in a public way.

In the past Nancy suffered from breast cancer and I had my cancer surgeries. We found through our open disclosures we were able to raise public awareness. We were happy that as a result many more people underwent testing. They were treated in early stages and able to return to normal, healthy lives.

So now, we feel it is important to share it with you. In opening our hearts, we hope this might promote greater awareness of this condition. Perhaps it will encourage a clearer understanding of the individuals and families who are affected by it.

At the moment I feel just fine. I intend to live the remainder of the years God gives me on this earth doing the things I have always done. I will continue to share life's journey with my beloved Nancy and my family. I plan to enjoy the great outdoors and stay in touch with my friends and supporters.

Unfortunately, as Alzheimer's Disease progresses, the family often bears a heavy burden. I only wish there was some way I could spare Nancy from this painful experience. When the time comes I am confident that with your help she will face it with faith and courage.

In closing let me thank you, the American people, for giving me the great honor of allowing me to serve as your President. When the Lord calls me home, whenever that may be, I will leave with the greatest love for this country of ours and eternal optimism for its future.

I now begin the journey that will lead me into the sunset of my life. I know that for America there will always be a bright dawn ahead.

Thank you, my friends. May God always bless you.

Sincerely, Ronald Reagan

R O N A L D   R E A G A N

Nov. 5, 1994

My Fellow Americans,

I have recently been told that I am one
of the millions of Americans who will be
afflicted with Alzheimer's Disease.

Upon learning this news, Nancy & I had to decide
whether as private citizens we would keep this
a private matter or whether we would make this
news known in a public way.

In the past Nancy suffered from breast cancer
and I had my cancer surgeries. We found
through our open disclosures we were able to
raise public awareness. We were happy that as
a result many more people underwent testing.
They were treated in early stages and able to
return to normal, healthy lives.

So now, we feel it is important to share
it with you. In opening our hearts, we hope
this might promote greater awareness of this
condition. Perhaps it will encourage a clearer
understanding of the individuals and families
who are affected by it.

At the moment I feel just fine. I intend to live
the remainder of the years God gives me on this
earth doing the things I have always done. I will
continue to share life's journey with my beloved
Nancy and my family. I plan to enjoy the
great outdoors and stay in touch with my
friends and supporters.

Unfortunately, as Alzheimer's Disease progresses, the family often bears a heavy burden. I only wish there was some way I could spare Nancy from this painful experience. When the time comes I am confident that with your help she will face it with faith and courage.

In closing let me thank you, the American people for giving me the great honor of allowing me to serve as your President. When the Lord calls me home, ~~whenever it be~~ whenever that may be, I will leave with the greatest love for this country of ours and eternal optimism for its future.

I now begin the journey that will lead me into the sunset of my life. I know that for America there will always be a a bright dawn ahead.

Thank you my friends. May God always bless you.

                                    Sincerely,
                                    Ronald Reagan

*I*t was shortly before I took office that I sat down with President Reagan. We talked for a long time about many things that were important to us—families, our nation's future and the world. I told him how much I had enjoyed working with his White House when I was Governor, especially on the welfare reform bill he signed.

I came away that day with an even deeper appreciation of Ronald Reagan's boundless optimism about our people and our future, beyond any issues or daily debates. As President, Ronald Reagan assured the American people that nothing is impossible, and he wanted our nation to always "reach for the stars." He wanted the best for America.

President Reagan combined hope, humor and a deep love of this land and its people. Because of his humble beginnings, his sense of hope was richer, with so much more to dream about and to make real. When Ronald Reagan looked at the horizon, he never saw limits.

On leaving the Presidency, he spoke of looking out the windows of the White House, down the hall and up the stairs from the Oval Office, from the family quarters on the top floor. I often look out from those same windows, over the memorials to Washington, Jefferson and Lincoln, past the Potomac River and beyond the nation's capital. You can see a broad sweep of Americans, from families who have traveled to see the monuments, to those on their way to work. These windows are perfect for considering America's past and the people who built it, for thinking about the workers and their families who are trying to make their way in the present, and for imagining America's future.

Today, as yesterday, no amount of adversity will diminish

Ronald Reagan's dream for our nation. We all wish him the best because he has the same wish for all Americans. That generous sense of hope and optimism is his continuing gift to America.

WILLIAM J. CLINTON
*Forty-second President of the United States*

*President Reagan greeting Governor Bill Clinton at the White House, October 13, 1988.*

*T*HANK YOU. I want to thank you from the bottom of my heart for that beautiful film, and a special thanks for the people who were involved with putting it together and seeing it came on. It reminded me again of how grateful Ronnie and I are for the privilege that you and America gave us for the wonderful eight years in the White House.

It also reminded me of the life that you gave us before that, starting with the Governorship of California, a life that we never thought we'd have. It was interesting. It was challenging. It was fascinating. It was sometimes frightening. There were times when it seemed that the sun forgot to shine. But those days have dimmed in comparison to the accomplishments that now glow brightly and the remembrance of the warmth and support from so many of you across America.

Just four years ago, Ronnie stood before you and spoke for what he said might be his last speech at a Republican Convention. Sadly, his words were too prophetic. When we learned of his illness, Alzheimer's, he made the decision to write his letter to the American people, and the people responded as they always do. I can't tell you what your cards and letters have meant to both of us. The love and affection from thousands of Americans has been and continues to be a strengthening force for Ronnie and me each and every day.

We have learned, as too many other families have learned, of the terrible pain and loneliness that must be endured as each day brings another reminder of this very long goodbye.

But Ronnie's spirit, his optimism, his never-failing belief in the strength and goodness of America, is still very strong. If he were able to be here tonight, he would once again remind us of the power of each individual, urging us once again to fly as high as our wings will take us and to never give up on America.

I can tell you with certainty that he still sees the shining city on the hill, a place full of hope and promise for us all.

As you all know, I am not the speechmaker

in the family, so let me close with Ronnie's words, not mine. In that last speech four years ago, he said, "Whatever else history may say about me when I'm gone, I hope it will report that I appealed to your best hopes, not your worst fears, to your confidence rather than your doubts, and may all of you as Americans never forget your heroic origins, never fail to seek divine guidance, and never, never lose your God-given optimism."

Ronnie's optimism, like America's, still shines very brightly. May God bless him, and from both of us, God bless America.

*Mrs. Reagan congratulating her husband on receiving the Presidential Medal of Freedom, The White House, January 13, 1993.*

# Biography of Ronald Reagan

Ronald Reagan was born in Tampico, Illinois, on February 6, 1911, to Nelle and John Reagan. He attended nearby public schools and Eureka College, where he studied economics and sociology, played on the football team and performed in school plays. After working briefly as a sports announcer, Ronald Reagan moved to California, where he embarked on an acting career which would result in fifty-three major films.

In the 1950s, as a six-term president of the United Screen Actors Guild and a national television host, Ronald Reagan became a popular spokesman for conservatism. He was elected Governor of California in 1966 by a margin of one million votes and re-elected in 1970.

In 1980, as the Republican Presidential candidate who appealed to voters weary of inflation and the year-long hostage crisis in Iran, Ronald Reagan won the Presidency in a landslide victory of 489 electoral votes to President Jimmy Carter's 49.

During his first term in office Ronald Reagan inspired legislation which stimulated economic growth and strengthened national defense. By 1984, a renewal of national self-confidence helped him and Vice President George Bush win re-election with the greatest number of electoral votes ever gained by a Presidential candidate.

Throughout his Presidency, Reagan adhered to a policy of cutting taxes and government expenditures, and bolstered the military and its morale. President Reagan's foreign policy has been defined as "peace through strength." In his two terms in office, President Reagan negotiated a treaty with the Soviet Union which would eliminate intermediate-range nuclear missiles through a series of intense meetings with Mikhail Gorbachev; he declared "war" on international terrorism, sending American bombers against Libya following a terrorist attack on American soldiers; and he supported anti-Communist efforts in Central America, Asia and Africa.

Following the completion of his second term, Ronald Reagan returned to Los Angeles, where he wrote two books, traveled extensively to address government, business, civic and student groups throughout the world, and supported numerous charitable causes. On November 5, 1994, Ronald Reagan, in an open letter to the American people, announced that he had been diagnosed with Alzheimer's Disease. Since then, his primary focus has been to promote the Ronald Reagan Presidential Library & Museum and Center for Public Affairs in Simi Valley, California. President Reagan still goes into his office every day, meets regularly with friends and enjoys weekly golf.

*President Reagan overlooking Simi Valley from a balcony at his Presidential Library, July 15, 1997.*

# Researchers' Note

It is a special privilege have undertaken this project. As members of President Reagan's immediate staff, we are each in the unique position of witnessing daily his optimistic spirit, warm sense of humor and continued belief in America. This is especially appreciated given the current times in which we live. Many commentators and pundits like to speak of our country's decline. President Reagan's leadership always appealed to something greater.

America is still a country built around families and communities. This is our heritage. These are also the very institutions that have come under the most direct attack over the last two generations. This is cause for worry and, hopefully, action. The culprits are many and as varied as the theories which articulate their demise.

President Reagan has always known this and he knows that only the citizens themselves, with God's sovereign grace, can eventually find solutions to such dilemmas. He worked in the political arena for over thirty years to give people the power and the tools to do just that.

We hope, through this work and through his words, that you glean the essence of Ronald Reagan's message—that ordinary citizens, through personal initiative, hard work, great optimism and a faith in the hand of the Almighty, can turn the tide and witness the best days yet to be for our great land.

JOANNE DRAKE
EILEEN FOLIENTE
PEGGY GRANDE

251